SNOWFLAKES AND SNOWDRIFTS

Individualism and Sexuality in America

David Bertelson

UNIVERSITY
PRESS OF
AMERICA

LANHAM • NEW YORK • LONDON

Copyright © 1986 by

University Press of America,® Inc.

4720 Boston Way
Lanham, MD 20706

3 Henrietta Street
London WC2E 8LU England

Library of Congress Cataloging in Publication Data

Bertelson, David.
  Snowflakes and snowdrifts.
  Bibliography: p.
  Includes index.
    1. Sex role—United States.   2. Individualism.
3. Sex customs—United States.   I. Title.
HQ1075.5.U6B47   1986   305.3'0973   86-15837
ISBN 0-8191-5578-0 (alk. paper)
ISBN 0-8191-5579-9 (pbk. : alk. paper)

All University Press of America books are produced on acid-free
paper which exceeds the minimum standards set by the National
Historical Publications and Records Commission.

For Kimo

ACKNOWLEDGMENTS

Anne Houdek, Haunani-Kay Trask and Judith Hughes have read and criticized earlier versions of the manuscript in most helpful ways. Professor Hughes has been particularly supportive over a long period of time, and I would like to thank her for this. I have tried out my ideas in several of my courses, and my students at the University of Hawaii over the years have helped me to expand and to clarify my thinking in many important respects. Reviewers from various presses offered useful suggestions. The most useful, however, came from the reviewer for the University Press of America. James E. Lyons and Helen Hudson of the staff there have been very efficient in getting the manuscript finally into print. Sandra Enoki and Linda Cristobal of the American Studies Department secretarial staff have been most kind in helping me learn to use a word processor effectively and handling matters of manuscript preparation. The dedication acknowledges a debt for many years of understanding and support for which I will always be grateful.

TABLE OF CONTENTS

PREFACE

My purpose in writing this book has been to examine sexuality in a particular cultural context. Human sexuality is universal--something we share with men and women everywhere. How it is expressed is shaped by the dominant assumptions and practices--the symbols--that make the world meaningful to specific groups of people. This work has a personal dimension as well, for it is my effort to understand and to come to terms with aspects of the world in which I live. From understanding come perspective and hopefully freedom based on greater awareness. But one must begin by acknowledging the impact of realities over which one has had little or no control and further that the tools of understanding one draws upon are limited because they are uniquely one's own.

Two experiences particularly have shaped the basic elements of this study. The last twenty-five years have seen enormous change in the area of sexuality in American life. For one who was never entirely comfortable with many of the conventions that were virtually unquestioned when I was growing up, these have been exciting times in which to live and to try to absorb the meaning of what has been taking place. A second very powerful experience has come from living in Hawaii for the past fifteen years. Dealing with people from various cultures and cultural backgrounds has greatly increased my awareness of how very different people's basic assumptions can be and thus how complicated are the processses of interaction that attempt to acknowledge rather than to ignore the reality of these differences.

The topic of this study came to me slowly, and in many respects it grew almost of its own accord over several revisions of the manuscript. Everything has seemed to fit together in my own mind, but how to put it down in ways that others might find equally compelling has proved to be a very challenging task. I remain convinced that my topic has real potential, but my ability to do it justice has proved to be more limited than I would wish. As someone who is both a part of and outside the reality he attempts to analyze, I often see things in different ways from those with whom nevertheless I would like very much to communicate.

SNOWFLAKES AND SNOWDRIFTS:

INDIVIDUALISM AND SEXUALITY IN AMERICA

INTRODUCTION

Since the time of Alexis de Tocqueville assumptions about the primacy of the individual as a special characteristic of our way of life have remained commonplace. How these assumptions have affected the cultural and social meaning of sexuality in America is the subject of this inquiry.

Sexuality has several interrelated dimensions. On a cultural level it is intimately linked with a cluster of symbols which make it collectively and individually meaningful within an American context. On a level of social institutions it is expressed in a variety of structured behaviors and contexts. On a personal level the socialization process instills in males and females the attitudes and role behaviors that are culturally expected of them. Under ideal fixed conditions sex-related cultural values would be clearly understood and accepted by everyone, whose aspirations and behaviors would mesh simply and easily with these values and related social institutions. Probably no society has ever totally conformed to such a static ideal, and America is far too complex and dynamic to do so.

As Clifford Geertz points out, culture and social structure are independent though not self-sufficient. Social change arises from a lack of congruence between cultural patterns and forms of social organization. To assume that either simply mirrors the other inhibits any real understanding of the processes of change.[1] While cultural and social factors are dynamically interrelated, they do not function independently of individuals but through them. Collectively as well as individually people strive to understand their world and function effectively within it, formulate models of change and implement these models, participate in new social relationships and reconcile these with established expectations. I shall therefore be dealing with sex-related cultural assumptions and social behavior as these have been presented in a variety of writings over the years.

I will be concerned with four specific ways in which the relationship between individualism and sexuality has been important. The first is treated in Part I and deals with conventional sex roles. The truly masculine male is seen as markedly individualistic, and the individualist is almost always assumed to be a male. Femininity, by contrast, is conceived as essentially the opposite of what individualism implies though women are permitted and even encouraged to be individualistic in some ways. The second focuses upon certain departures from the norm, specifically homosexuality and variant expressions of masculinity. These are examined in Part II. The third is concerned with how Americans conceptualize and deal with sex-related differences. Biological sex is assumed to differentiate people in fundamental respects and is doubtless seen by the majority of Americans as

1

the most important distinction in our society. In the twentieth century the homosexual/heterosexual dichotomy has acquired almost as much significance. This theme runs throughout the book, which in a larger sense is a case study of how our culture defines and our society manages what are deemed crucial differences among its members. Finally, I will analyze in Part III how sex-role definitions and sex-related differences have been challenged and altered in recent years.

My examination will focus essentially upon mainstream assumptions that have their origins in the English Protestant culture that formed the basis of the later American culture. Individualism and the sexual attitudes and values associated with it have long been basic characteristics of middle-class American life. At the same time, they represent general cultural expectations and so affect everyone even if they do not apply equally to all. Much of what seems to me special about mainstream America can be highlighted by contrasting it with traditional cultures. Such a distinction has been recognized at least since Tocqueville contrasted aristocratic nations with democratic ones, and it has recently been analyzed with special reference to America by Richard D. Brown. An emphasis upon self-determination and personal independence has very different implications as far as sexuality is concerned from an emphasis upon tradition, hierarchy and formalized social authority. The break with the past which individualism in America represents was never complete here and has occurred in all other modern societies as well. Still, because the break was sharper here, it has permitted a much freer play of individualistic assumptions than has been the case elsewhere. At the same time it is useful to keep in mind Brown's suggestion that movement in the direction of modernization has been neither unidirectional nor uniform throughout all elements of the American social structure; "indeed, in different spheres, movement in contrary directions may actually occur simultaneously."[2]

At its deepest level individualism represents the sense that each individual has a validity apart from the social context. Because the expression of sexuality is part of that context, there is a tension between individuality and sex-related expectations that American culture has never fully resolved. Individualism has fostered a tendency to fix upon abstract sexual categories (male-masculine/female-feminine, heterosexual/homosexual) and to assume a fundamental alikeness among everyone within each category. At the same time it encourages people not simply to express their individuality in terms of these categories but also to question them precisely because they pose arbitrary limits upon personal freedom and self-determination. While the idea that everyone is unique as each snowflake is unique is a characteristic product of the individualistic value system, so is the disposition to think in terms of sexual cate-

2

gories--to see people as joined together into larger wholes even as the snowflakes within a snowdrift are merged into a larger whole. Sexually speaking, it has generally seemed very important for everyone to be clearly male as well as masculine or female as well as feminine, and in the twentieth century heterosexual as opposed to homosexual. Nevertheless, the supposition remains that these categories cannot adequately comprehend either the uniqueness of each individual or the fundamental alikeness of all human beings that we also claim to accept.

Because sexuality touches us all so deeply and personally, the range of expression on the subject--particularly in our own day--is enormous. One is naturally inclined toward judgments about quality of insight and accuracy of perception. However, in terms of cultural analysis it is impossible to make easy distinctions between, say, serious and credible studies and so-called popular works because all are informed by deeply held values and ways of seeing the world. Often there is a marked tension between an effort to be logical, objective and even enlightened and less conscious feelings and responses that lie beneath the surface. I have therefore tried to approach my sources from a perspective that recognizes that all attempts to interpret sexuality are valid cultural expressions. To examine the attitudes and viewpoints that underlie each person's perspective rather than to concentrate on the "objective" accuracy or utility of what is said seems to me a more fruitful way to get at the meanings and implications of shared assumptions.

Such assumptions change over time and have not been interpreted identically by everyone. Nevertheless, patterns can be identified, and these are what link the interpretations I have chosen together. At the same time each writer brings a unique perspective to his or her materials, and I have tried to recognize each person's individuality by being sensitive to each perspective. This means that the contours of any chapter or section of what follows would be altered by further inclusions or omissions although the overall thrust of my argument does not depend on the presence or absence of any particular work. The writers I draw on include novelists, playwrights, scholars, public figures, polemicists and cultural commentators. The works dealt with fall essentially into three categories--general treatments of American culture usually with special reference to individualism, creative writings particularly novels, and works dealing with elements of sexuality. They provide us with important insights into certain fundamental aspects of our culture and the ways in which various individuals have sought within this context to understand human sexuality.

3

PART I
AT THE CENTER

CHAPTER ONE

A SOCIETY OF INDIVIDUALS

By the mid-nineteenth century a word which reflected their attachment to the primacy of the individual had become part of the vocabulary of most Americans. That word was individualism. Before taking up the subject of sexuality directly, it is necessary to say something about individualism in general terms. The primacy of the individual has been thought of in different ways and evaluated differently over the years, and so individualism has acquired many interrelated meanings. Thus it will be helpful to begin with a brief historical overview and then to look more closely at these meanings and their implications.

Changing Views of Individualism--

In the second volume of Democracy in America, published in 1840, Alexis de Tocqueville defined individualism as "a calm and considered feeling which disposes each citizen to isolate himself from the mass of his fellows and withdraw into the circle of family and friends."[1] In complete contrast, Tocqueville saw the aristocratic societies of pre-modern Europe as having been characterized by an extensive involvement of people in public life. An elaborate structure of traditions, customs, prescribed duties and reciprocal responsibilities linked people hierarchically and largely insured the role behavior appropriate to each person's station in life. The collapse of this structure, he believed, left the populace of modern egalitarian societies socially unconnected and thus created the conditions for individualism to flourish.

Tocqueville was convinced that human beings require established institutions and prescribed rules of conduct to insure the viability of society. The deference of the peasant to his lord or the son to his father must be taught and socially reinforced. In the absence of social pressure such behavior would not "naturally" occur. Thus the interactions that custom dictates create the "feelings and ideas" necessary to enlarge the "heart" and develop the "understanding." Because such influences do not exist in democratic societies, Tocqueville believed that they must be "artificially created" by a social policy designed to promote the growth of associations. Fortunately, he observed, free associations of all sorts seemed to thrive among Americans, who were drawn into social and political life despite contradictory individualistic pressures. Tocqueville felt that one of the differences between aristocratic and democratic societies is that in the latter "the substance of behavior comes to count for more than the form."[2] It is not surprising that he, with his aristocratic sympathies, continued to place the greater premium upon form. One is reminded of the debate in Reformation times between Catholics and Protestants over much the same issue of an outward focus on forms versus an inward focus on attitudes and intentions.

If one were therefore to look at America in Tocqueville's day from a strictly Protestant perspective, a different and less ominous sense of what he was talking about emerges. In democratic times, he felt, "the duties of each to all are much clearer but devoted service to any individual much rarer." Thus "the bonds of human affection are wider but more relaxed." Moreover, "democracy loosens social ties, but it tightens natural ones."[3] Devotion to individualism thus causes people to focus on a personal world of friends and family as well as upon society in general. At the same time Americans form all sorts of voluntary associations. Because social interaction is based on freedom and voluntary commitment, people's involvements are essentially the uncoerced consequences of inner desires and personal goals rather than the result of bowing to the dictates of custom. Social unity, it would follow, stems from shared beliefs individually held rather than from institutions and traditions which endure over time. Such a conception is at once more personal and more general than Tocqueville could approve, for it reflects the privatization of the medieval public world.

Evidences of individualism can be found in colonial times and in the Protestant world view that informed the social expectations of the early settlers. Particularly among the Puritans the Catholic emphasis upon the Church as a vehicle of salvation was replaced by a belief that in matters of salvation each man must deal individually with God. Organized churches were seen as embodiments of the faith of their members rather than as structures which helped to create it. In civil life too the focus on the primacy of the individual was evidenced in compacts and other forms of voluntary agreement. Initially there was absolutely no disposition to reject a basically medieval and hierarchical organization of society. As Elizabeth and Joseph Pleck point out, "the ideal of a stable social hierarchy ruled by natural male leaders was accepted not only as family practice but as political doctrine that placed masters over servants, older ahead of younger, and wealthier above poorer."[4] Nevertheless, there was an important shift in emphasis. Customary social distinctions were to reflect each person's inward assent to the divine will rather than acquiescence in conventions external to the self.

Men were not granted any substantial freedom to determine what form their assent would take. Nowhere is this clearer than in the Puritan conception of the "Christian calling." A person's occupation, it was assumed, was determined not by custom but by God. Thus each man was under no traditional obligation to follow in the ways of his father, but he was obliged to ascertain God's intentions in endowing him with special talents and interests and then to pursue his life's calling with faith and steadfastness. This early formulation of individualism in America was essentially a reinterpretation of traditional concepts of society. As John Cawelti has shown, many of the devotees of the cult of success in America continued well past the middle of the nineteenth century to seek "the perpetuation in the new world of traditional religious and social patterns" by "encouraging young Americans to follow in the secure and respectable paths of the established social and religious tradition."[5]

From the first, however, the focus on the individual tended to undercut the authority of established traditions and graded social arrangements, as the early Puritan impatience with religious hierarchies evidenced. To some degree the individual became socially though not culturally independent, and thus in time was assumed to be relatively free to determine his place in an increasingly dynamic and secular world. Benjamin Franklin's career well illustrates the breakdown of the attempt to link personal freedom and responsibility to an essentially traditional conception of the social order. As Cawelti notes, "men were beginning to think of themselves not as members of a traditionally defined group with an established social role but as individuals with the capacity to choose between social roles, or to create new ones."[6] While this next stage in the development of individualism in American life reflected the assumption that the individual had a responsibility for the well being of society, the connection was looser and the subordination of social structures to individual goals and aspirations went much further.

Richard D. Brown contends that the modern personality, which "exhibits a significant drive for individual autonomy and initiative," was "operating widely, though not everywhere, in social, political, and economic life in the first third of the nineteenth century."[7] David Hackett Fischer sees the period from 1770 to 1820 as a time of fundamental social revolution. Though his emphasis is upon age relations, his analysis suggests the general transformation of attitudes that Tocqueville associated with the triumph of individualism. Fischer stresses the radical expansion of the ideas of equality, which "destroyed the hierarchy of age, just as it destroyed the hierarchy of social orders," and of liberty, which "snapped the ties of obligation between generations as well as between classes." These tendencies had long been inherent within Protestantism but had been held in check by contrary traditional tendencies that had initially been strengthened in the New World by isolation, physical dangers and military insecurity.[8]

The word "individualism" originated in Europe in Tocqueville's day as part of the counterrevolutionary critique of the Enlightenment.[9] There, in Yehoshua Arieli's words, the term "was almost synonymous with selfishness, social anarchy, and individual self-assertion." As it was picked up by Americans, its "value content changed completely," for here it came to connote "self-determination, moral freedom, the rule of liberty, and the dignity of man." Clearly Americans shared none of Tocqueville's skepticism about the primacy of the individual and the viability of a society based on liberty and equality. In the following years the word became increasingly popular by supplying "the nation with a rationalization of its characteristic attitudes, behavior patterns, and aspirations." Thus James Bryce observed in 1888 that everything about the American experience "went to intensify individualism, the love of enterprise, the pride in personal freedom."[10]

During the course of the nineteenth century the links between the individual and society became steadily more tenuous, and individualism was increasingly associated with making one's own way economically in the world. As Cawelti observes, "the concept of the republican community gave way to the image of a loose association of individuals, each making his own way in the world." There was new emphasis upon competitiveness to go along with "a conception of a dynamic, changing society in which individuals competed with one another for a limited number of prizes."[11] In such a world most relationships with other people were impersonal ones. To William Graham Sumner this was the glory of modern society. In his opinion only impersonal contractual relationships permitted "a society of free and independent men" with "the utmost room and chance for individual development.[12] Sentimental relationships--which, he argued, characterized all ties in feudal times--persisted in the modern world only with regard to dependents, specifically wives, children and paupers. The independent, self-sufficient man--the person who asks no one to assume his responsibilities in life--alone deserves to be considered an individual. He has duties and obligations to society, but these are impersonal and relate only to his carrying his fair share of the load. Individuality for Sumner, therefore, was a matter of independence and self-reliance, not of eccentricity or anti-social self-assertion.

In the West too individualism meant self-reliance and independence in a context which came increasingly to include a good many impersonal relationships. Even the cowboy became tied to a complex economic system that was a prerequisite for profitable ranching. The historian Frederick Jackson Turner was both proud of the emphasis upon independence and self-determination that America's frontier experience had fostered and concerned that individualism implied too much selfishness and too little regard for the larger good of society. In his famous 1893 address on the influence of the frontier he described "democracy born of free land" as "strong in selfishness and individualism, intolerant of administrative experience and education, and pressing individual liberty beyond its proper bounds."13

"Throughout most of the nineteenth century," Moses Rischin has observed, "the success ideology was trumpeted in hyper-individualistic terms and with an innocence and simplicity that did little to prepare Americans for the world of industry and organization which they soon faced."14 A good many liberals as well as conservatives came to the conclusion that modern realities had simply put an end to individualism. It was no accident that this conclusion coincided with the closing of the frontier. John D. Rockefeller declared that individualism was dead. Cooperation was what large-scale forms of business organization required. In practice many people assumed that the bureaucratization of business and government and the greater involvement of each with the other could not be based upon the rugged individualism of the past. For different reasons liberals agreed that the celebration of individualism--understood as the pursuit of economic self-interest in a context of minimal government interference--must be replaced by positive governmental policies designed to promote social justice and the development of a genuinely social ethic. One critic in the 1930's was concerned that "the individualism, localism, and the laissez faire suitable to that bygone day" would seriously cripple American society's capacity to deal with contemporary problems.15

Despite the widespread conclusion that individualism seemed to have no place in the twentieth-century world, it continued to be affirmed. To some social critics nineteenth-century America stood as a reproach to the collectivism of an age in which "the individual was approaching anonymity, squeezed between the closing frontier and the expanding powers of the political state and a machine society."16 Out of such a sense of profound disenchantment there emerged an emphasis upon individualism as an assertion of the self against the endless array of forces in society aimed at controlling the individual. This interpretation still has considerable currency and rests on a view of nineteenth-century America as a time when the individual was especially free to make something of his own life. If the settled parts of the country seemed too restrictive, the West promised unlimited chances for a man to become the architect of his own destiny. Such assumptions explain the special appeal which figures like the pioneer, the cowboy and the self-made businessman still exercise over our collective imagination. Many who espouse this approach to individualism are fairly hopeful about reasserting its importance in the lives of modern Americans. Some see it as a meaningful form of personal self-affirmation. Libertarians and neo-conservatives see broader applications if only the extensive apparatus of institutional limitations upon individual freedom can be, if not dismantled, then at least reduced in scope and importance.

11

In the 1950's a group of scholars and intellectuals held a symposium dealing with "the problem of man's freedom in the face of modern society's seemingly irresistible urge to socialize and regiment the thought and action of the individual."[17] The belief that conformity is a violation of individualism is a legacy particularly of this period. More generally, David M. Potter argues, the contemporary importance attached to the principle of non-conformity or dissent reflects a shift in the meaning of individualism from the nineteenth-century emphasis upon self-reliance to the modern emphasis upon "intellectual independence and personal self-expression."[18]

The primacy of the individual has always meant that one ought to be free to do what one chooses to do. In the seventeenth century there was no sense that each person should have the power to determine what to choose in the first place, and since the late eighteenth century the concern has been mostly with such external limitations to freedom of action as class barriers and special privileges. What has been of greatest importance all along has been the psychological sense that one is in control of one's life. Americans do not feel that their individuality is violated even if they choose to do what everyone around them is doing. An insistence upon the right of dissent now seems to many an essential element of individualism, but it has never attained the importance of the freedom to act upon one's own choices. Today those who prize non-conformity think of themselves as individualists, but individualism cannot be simply equated with non-conformity.

Still other people in the twentieth century who have sought to assert the primacy of the individual have been critics of nineteenth-century-style "rugged individualism." Even in that earlier period there were efforts to try to distinguish the positive elements of individualism from the negative excesses associated with laissez-faire economics. Proponents of the Social Gospel, for instance, endeavored, in Arieli's words, "to separate the ethical and religious values of individualism, which they wished to maintain, from its economic and social theories, which they wished to discard."[19] The distinction that they were seeking to make closely parallels the effort of many French thinkers of the time to distinguish between "individualisme (implying anarchy and social atomization) and individualité (implying personal liberty and self-development)."[20]

In Individualism Old and New (1930) John Dewey argued that while America's material culture was becoming increasingly "collective and corporate," its moral culture--along with its ideology--was saturated with the values "of an individualism derived from the prescientific, pretechnological age." Thus "there is a perversion of the whole ideal of individualism to conform to the practices of a pecuniary culture." Only with the elimination of

12

this older economic and political individualism could "equal opportunity and free association and intercommunication" become a reality. Then "the balance of the individual and the social will be organic." Dewey's conception of a "new individualism" stressed the assumption that self and society can be harmonized when individuals voluntarily commit themselves to social ends. He felt that the freedom to be self-determining had been lost in a society which was unwilling both collectively and individually to assume responsibility for the complex structures of modern life. For Americans to control their world rather than to be controlled by it would take effort rather than "acquiescence, in the sense of drifting." Where society "is accepted as something already fixed in institutions," Dewey insisted, individuality is inevitably undercut.[21]

In 1951 in an essay entitled "Individualism Reconsidered" David Riesman noted that it had proved possible in the past "to carry individualism to its limits of usefulness--and, in some cases, far beyond these limits--because a fair amount of social cohesiveness was taken for granted." Still, "to the degree that capitalist individualism has fostered an ethic of callousness," he maintained, "the result has been to undermine all forms of individualism, good and bad." At the same time that Riesman, like Dewey, was opposed to the claims of an outworn economic individualism, he was highly skeptical about "the demands for greater social participation and belongingness among the group-minded." "No ideology, however noble," he concluded, "can justify the sacrifice of an individual to the needs of the group."[22]

Some two decades later in The New Industrial State John Kenneth Galbraith criticized economic individualism as a pernicious myth because it obscures the economic dominance of large corporations and prevents effective regulation. Thus "a doctrine that celebrates individuality provides the cloak for organization." While Galbraith found value in the sensitivity to others and interdependence which modern business emphasizes, he placed his greatest faith in the members of the educational and scientific communities. Unlike those who belong to the corporate "technostructure," they can act responsibly as free individuals because they are "not handicapped in political action by being accustomed to function only as part of an organization." One could therefore expect the kind of critical understanding and political initiatives required to put the industrial system in its place as a necessary but subordinate part of American life.[23]

It might seem as though Americans in the twentieth century have been faced with a choice between a dominant collectivism fostered largely by big business and the liberal state and a minority protest in the name of individualism. This puts things much too neatly and suggests a far greater eclipse in allegiance to individualism than has actually been the case. As Cawelti points out, a leading theme of twentieth-century American politics has been "expanding equality of opportunity through social and political reform."[24] The means employed--the power of the state--might seem a violation of individualism to men like Sumner, but the aim--though not necessarily the result--has been to free individuals in one way or another from forces that limit their chances in life.

Similarly the world of business and industry cannot be accurately portrayed as antagonistic to any expression of individualism. It is true that as more and more people have become employees of larger and larger organizations, they must deal with and get along with many more persons than was true a century ago. Competition for advancement within organizations is usually keen, and the need to work well with others must be balanced by reserve and caution as each person seeks to maximize his own advantages. As Peter Stearns has suggested, "the jungle is still there, though its tensions may have become more subtle as a result of the friendlier, personal style that has infused bureaucratic contacts and service jobs."[25] The pursuit of opportunity can rarely be carried far without involvements of many sorts with other people. This is an obvious lesson of Benjamin Franklin's Autobiography. It cannot have become irrelevant to success in the nineteenth century, and of course it is not today. The commonly offered contrast between the world of a century ago and that of the present exaggerates the independence of men in the past as much as it fails to consider the disposition of contemporary Americans to see work situations mainly in terms of personal advantage. Within limits which vary as one moves up or down the socio-economic scale, they think nothing of changing jobs when they believe better opportunities can be found elsewhere.

A related concern has been whether organizational structures are sufficiently flexible to allow for individual initiative. In the period before the exaggerated conformity of the 1950's, the president of Sears insisted that "while systems are important, our main reliance must always be put on men rather than on systems." A 1950 study of the company emphasized that "basic to the principle of decentralized management is a tendency to rely on individual initiative."[26] This philosophy seems to have outlived the ideal of the "organization man" and to be regarded today as still a sound business practice. Concern for initiative and individual input appears to be particularly characteristic of newer and more innovative companies. By the late 1950's The Harvard Business Review observed that the need for increased individual freedom within the organization was gaining serious attention.[27] With regard to successful higher executives at about this same time, W. Lloyd Warner felt that "their most dominant psychic characteristic is a feeling that they are

14

on their own and capable of independent action."[28] Thus Americans continue to think of themselves in generally individualistic ways and to judge business structures and involvements in terms of how much personal initiative and freedom they permit.

An important aspect of individual freedom in America has long been the ideal of mobility. In 1964 John W. Gardner insisted that this is crucial not only to organizations but to society as a whole. The free movement of people within organizations promotes individual versatility and organizational fluidity, and "both society and the individual profit by the free movement of people from one organization to another, and from one segment of society to another." Gardner especially praised the variety of organizational forms in America--a variety "increased by our national habit of forming voluntary associations to accomplish almost every conceivable shared purpose."[29]

Implications of Individualism--

Individualism is a term that, in the words of Steven Lukes, ranges "over a wide variety of attitudes, doctrines, and theories." None of the component ideas of individualism which he enumerates originated in America and many long antedated its founding. Still, the United States can be seen as a special though by no means the only example of a modern culture which places a very high premium upon this cluster of values. The idea of "the supreme and intrinsic value of the individual human being" is part of the Judeo-Christian heritage, and since the Renaissance "has come to pervade modern ethical and social theory in the West."[30] As a complex cultural symbol individualism has important implications on a personal as well as a societal level.

Individuals are assumed to be the building blocks of modern society, which rests, in the words of John Stuart Mill, on "the freedom of action of the individual--the liberty of each to govern his conduct by his own feelings of duty, and by such laws and social restraints as his own conscience can subscribe to."[31] This means that society is held together by the shared values, feelings, concerns and goals of its members--not by externally imposed customs and traditions nor by formal social, economic and political institutions, which are merely embodiments of shared values. In contrast to traditional times social roles have a secondary importance because they are viewed as the consequences of the choices individuals make about their involvements with other people rather than as the essence of such involvements. Americans do not believe that their lives should be "determined" by larger structures of which they are a part or by roles they play within these structures. They assume that the individual is ultimately responsible for himself, and so he must be free to choose the course of his own life. The geographical and social mobility so long prized by Americans reflects the belief that an individual's choices should not be limited by outward circumstances. Similarly the impatience with tradition and the weight of the past evidences a belief that the individual should be free of the limitations of time as well.

The American conception of individualism does not assume that a person's control over his own life can or should be total. There is general agreement that actions which limit others' freedom are not appropriate exercises of one's own individuality. Constant change has long been considered a basic fact of American life. Hence each person must be free to exercise his ingenuity if he is to deal effectively with unpredictable situations. The practice of individualism seeks more to avoid being controlled by rather than to control the changing milieu around one. One's real aim is the freedom to direct the course of one's own life, not the power to control others or the world outside the self.

From an American--rather than a conservative European-- perspective individualism represents the attempt to harmonize individual freedom and self-determination with larger social claims, not the rejection of those claims. As David Potter points out, "the freedom of the individual, in relation to his society, cannot be absolute, basically because the individual and the society are not really separate." Individualism in America has always been justified in social terms. Moreover, "society itself is, in the last analysis, a multiplicity of individuals."[32] Individualism, therefore, is a non-collectivist, non-organic, non-traditional way of viewing society and each person's relationship to it. Most approaches to individualism throughout American history have assumed that voluntary agreement is the key to reconciling self and society. Two different though intermingling traditions in American thought can be distinguished in terms of basic assumptions as to just how this is possible.

The dominant tradition can be traced back to Calvinistic and especially Lockeian assumptions of social contract. Though in reality the individual is always a part of society, from this perspective in some absolute sense he exists separately from it and only consents to live with others because he finds it in his interest to do so. Mutual self-interest enables men to interact without having to sacrifice their individuality any more than is absolutely necessary, but the tension between self and society cannot be entirely eliminated. While "the only untrammeled individualist," Felix Morley asserts, is "man in the state of nature," practically speaking individualism means "the latitude of a person to choose for himself among the many fruits of a civilization in which he is an active participant." Because the kind of man Morley is talking about makes choices in accordance with his own basic interests, a social system which facilitates such choices is clearly the most desirable. That men are equal in terms of rights but not in terms of abilities has always seemed quite obvious to those within this tradition. Equality is really a matter of equality of opportunity. As Morley points out, "to say that men deserve equal opportunity is tacitly to admit that with this opportunity they will become unequal."[33]

Hence the close connection between success and this interpretation of individualism. In practice the pursuit of success limits individual freedom and self-determination in many ways. Moreover, David Hackett Fischer distinguishes the emphasis upon equality and liberty that lay behind the modernization of American society in the late eighteenth century from the inequality of wealth distribution that also began to grow in the years after 1760.[34] Since that time, however, it has been extremely difficult to value the individual without valuing his worldly success as well. Studies have indicated that American society has never approached the ideal of true equality of opportunity, but as Cawelti has pointed out, "mobility through individual economic achievement remains the primary career pattern for which young Americans are educated."[35]

A more idealistic and less dominant line of thinking in America minimizes the emphasis upon success as well as the inherent tension between self and society. For those within this tradition self-determination is intimately linked with voluntary relationships with and concern for other people. It is possible to trace this conception of social unity back to much earlier religious views. Rather than any formal institutional structures, Protestant ministers felt, what really held the faithful together was their spontaneous love for and concern about one another as participants in the priesthood of all believers. A similar secularized view of social unity was applied to American society by the more fervent clerical supporters of the American Revolution.[36]

Thomas Jefferson held remarkably similar views, which came by way of the moral sense philosophy of the Scottish Enlightenment. As Garry Wills has pointed out, Jefferson considered man as destined for society. In contrast to Locke's system of government based on the individual's autonomy, that of Francis Hutcheson, one of the leading Scottish philosophers whom Jefferson greatly admired, began with social drives and interdependence. "Men," Wills elaborates, "are already associated in families, and in the exchange of goods and ideas, before it becomes necessary for them to form civil government. We begin in society, which is our state of nature."[37] Because social unity ought to rest on uncoerced mutual agreement, Jefferson could without contradiction affirm both man's social nature and express a profound uneasiness about formal governmental and social struc-

17

tures. Though he did not as a practical matter reject them, he did try to insure that their hold over Americans' lives would be kept to a minimum. Similarly in 1958 Richard M. Weaver observed "that the individual is indebted to society for many things which allow him to be an individual." Indeed, "its institutions, its customs, usages, its settled preferences, and its means of communication" permit a person "to express himself in his own way." This led Weaver to conclude that "it is silly to think of being an individual alone in the big woods or at the North Pole."[38]

One tradition thus emphasizes self-interest and success and remains vaguely uneasy about social involvements, which are inevitable and necessary and yet threaten to undercut self-determination. The other assumes a greater degree of mutually accepted sociability on the parts of men who probably are less cautious because they are less concerned with the pursuit of opportunity. The former tradition stresses impersonal commitments while the latter puts more emphasis on the personal aspects of human interaction and a generalized supportiveness of others as fellow human beings. Both approaches stress the importance of basic agreement as the glue holding society together. This emphasis upon likeness of mind among individuals is an important element of commonality and suggests that the two traditions cannot be totally distinguished from one another. Both, moreover, share a skepticism about larger social structures and prefer voluntary ties which do not subordinate the individual and so leave him free to direct the course of his own life. While the ideal of uncoerced unity is not easily institutionalized, it does comprehend the possibility of many forms of social interaction as long as these are freely and willingly entered into.

Individualism, finally, is not an inherent quality but rather implies a self-affirming posture or way of living one's life. It involves assertion and can be forfeited, for one's claims to individuality depend on one's being responsible for one's life and believing that individuals matter more than larger social structures. According to John Dewey, "freedom or individuality . . . is not an original possession or gift. It is something to be achieved, to be wrought out."[39] Because it has been seen as so central to the American way, those who do lay claim to it can be defined as insiders. They are first and foremost males--in theory all American males, in reality those males whose lives fulfill a set of expectations which distinguish them from outsiders of various sorts.

Diversity in American Society--

As a cluster of shared values in our culture, individualism is closely related to the conception of an American identi-

18

ty. Philip Gleason has emphasized the universalist ideological quality of American national identity as it was formulated in the age of the American Revolution. To be or to become an American was not a question of a person's background, but of his individual willingness to commit himself to a political ideology based on certain abstract ideals. Gleason sees American nationality as an open conception oriented toward the future rather than as "'WASP ethnicity' writ large," though clearly it rested on cultural traditions brought over from England.[40] American identity was therefore comprised of a set of individually held and freely adopted values. It was not imposed by higher authority or accident of birth. Crevecoeur's famous discussion of what it means to be an American focuses also on a set of values to which the individual comes to adhere, but these are more specifically opportunistic. "The American is a new man," Crevecoeur insisted, "who acts upon new principles; he must therefore entertain new ideas and form new opinions." These point toward a comfortable life, but "it is not every emigrant who succeeds; no, it is only the sober, the honest, and industrious."[41] It is clear from Crevecoeur's treatment of American life that New Englanders fitted most perfectly his definition of Americanness. Yet basically he was concerned with values and how they contributed to any person's success and hence his Americanness. One could become an American if one chose to.

While American identity is not a concept which has ever been fully fixed or clearly agreed upon, it remains true that it focuses upon individuals who are united one by one in their allegiance to a set of general values and their commitment to the basic principles of individualism. Here it is worth reemphasizing that individualism represents a cluster of values and a way of living one's life in accordance with these values. It does not dictate the substance or content of a person's life so much as how he lives it. At the same time because individualism is central to the concept of an American identity, there are direct consequences as far as diversity within American society is concerned. As Yehoshua Arieli points out: "In societies in which the principle of unity is a natural or a given datum, a variety of ideologies may compete with each other. But in a nation in which social and national cohesion is based on an ideological proposition, diversity can develop only within the framework of its ideological premises."[42]

Either directly or indirectly all collectively meaningful differences among human beings are cultural in nature. Even biological factors are affected by social conditions, and more importantly culture determines the significance attached to them. If it were possible to assemble a number of people living by themselves in some kind of Lockeian state of nature, many familiar distinguishing characteristics would have little importance for them. It is the symbolism that is attached to skin

color, weight or size that really gives these differences importance in our eyes. Other differences which are more directly
the products of social intercourse would obviously not exist.
Moreover, we depend on cultural symbols to interpret these kinds
of diversity as well. Thus human variety is essentially the
consequence of social involvements as is the meaning it has for
people.

Individualism almost by definition includes an acknowledgement of the fact that each person is in some absolute sense
unique. Because it is also assumed that one's individuality is
often expressed through associations with like-minded others,
collective differences that are reflections of individual differences in tastes, values and interests are inevitable in a
free society. At the same time their range is limited by the
emphasis in America upon unity as a consequence of basic agreement or general likeness of mind. Values, attitudes or beliefs
--and actions based upon them--which lie outside the area of
fundamental agreement pose definite problems. They are likely
to create considerable anxiety, for such differences cannot
easily be accepted when by definition they strike at the very
foundations of the social order.

There is another class of differences which cannot be seen
as flowing from freedom of choice. Rather the operation of
forces beyond the control of the individual--aging, ethnicity,
race and sex, for instance--set some Americans off from others
in special sorts of ways. Individualism does not comfortably
take account of these differentiating factors, for it rests on
the affirmation of a common humanity. One goes beyond--or at
least aspires to go beyond--the accidents of birth, time and
place that stamp each person in special ways. Thomas Jefferson's emphasis upon likeness of mind led him to reject the possibility of including several groups of people within Virginia
society. He was opposed to wholesale immigration to the state
on the grounds, according to Wills, that it "would loosen the
social bonds by destroying the common ethos and republican character of Virginia society." Belief in a shared ethos made him
doubt also that blacks could ever be incorporated into the society. Too much mutual suspicion and ill will existed between
whites and blacks ever to permit the shared affection necessary
to insure adequate social cohesion. For different reasons he
felt Native Americans had no place in Virginia society. They
were so clearly "one people" and thus different from whites that
they must be recognized as self-governing separate nations.[43]

The anxiety over perceived differences stems from two as-
sumptions--that the social good always depends on the attainment of fundamental agreement and consequently that there is no
easy way significant differences can be positively incorporated
into the social process. The contrast with traditional socie-

ties, particularly the aristocracies Tocqueville used as coun-
terpoints to American society, is quite dramatic. There culturally affirmed differences are the key to social integration.
Social structure and tradition support a variety of important
distinctions among people which are played out through dissimilar social roles. Differences in status, power and authority
link them together in terms of complementary duties and obligations. A common assumption is that if there were no social hierarchy based on such distinctions, human beings would have no
need of one another and society would disintegrate. At the same
time people of very different cultures may live for long periods
of time in reasonably close proximity, even under the same political system, and yet remain culturally separate. Neither of
these responses places a premium on the achievement of fundamental likeness of mind, and thus neither betrays the kind of anxiety Jefferson manifested.

The individualistic assumptions of American culture suggest a variety of strategies which seek to vindicate the premium
placed on like-mindedness. Where significant differences seem
within the range of individual choice, efforts are generally
made to change people's attitudes and actions so as to bring
about a greater degree of cultural and social unity. Those who
persist in being different when presumably they do not have to
be have often been the objects of considerable annoyance and
even outright hostility. On the other hand, differences that
are not considered contradictory to the fundamental values of
the culture can be accepted with relative ease. In either case
the validity of differences is minimized, and so the importance
of unity based on willing assent remains unchallenged.

Another strategy for dealing with differences is a consequence of the fact that the emphasis upon agreement among individuals means that only those within the circle of agreement really matter. Those outside in a sense become invisible. If
likeness of mind and consequently of actions is not possible or
forthcoming, those who remain beyond the circle of shared values
have no meaningful existence as far as those within the circle
are concerned. The consequences of invisibility may be benign
or quite the opposite. Where freedom of choice is involved,
what invisibility means is that for certain purposes the circle
of agreement in which one functions does not include people who
do not choose to be there. A greater or lesser part of a person's life may be involved, and circles of agreement may expand
or contract as people's desires and circumstances change. Invisibility is less benign when no choice is exercised. Usually
what this means is that whole categories of people are deemed
outsiders solely on the basis of perceived differences. They
exist as stereotypes and disappear as individuals. Invisibility
lessens the need on the part of the majority to confront differences, and so an appearance of unanimity is maintained.

21

Each person's psychological sense of the extent of society consequently is much smaller than the mechanical extent. The invisible are not excluded from many forms of participation in the larger society. Yet because individualism places no premium on involvements where there is thought to be little likeness of mind, there may often be scant awareness, sympathy or sense of relatedness on the part of the majority. It has in many respects sought to ignore wherever possible the existence of those considered very different rather than to subordinate them to an explicitly defined inferior status. Even segregation has functioned mainly to promote as much invisibility as conditions allow. The contrast with South Africa is instructive. According to George Fredrickson, apartheid is consciously "intended to preserve and accentuate cultural differences of a fundamental sort." Such differences are the key to the functioning of South African society in its present form. As workers blacks play a crucial role in the economy, but only as socially subordinated workers are they "meant to have a place in the common life of the South African nation." Southern blacks and whites in the days of Jim Crow, on the other hand, "were involved in the same culture, society, economy, and legal system." Jim Crow, Fredrickson points out, was "a much more nakedly and overtly racial form of domination." Subcultural differences were not recognized "but were generally attributed to genetically determined characteristics and capacities."[44]

This brings us to the most important strategy for dealing with differences: the elaboration of cultural symbols that account for differences without contradicting the basic tenets of modernism. Ascribed roles and other socially mandated traditional differences have long been considered unacceptable in America, but "natural" ones are altogether different. Power and privilege allotted solely on the basis of one's birth into a particular social class seem to most Americans arbitrary and unfair. Yet power and privilege as reflections of innate talents --Jefferson's natural aristocracy is one example--seem fairly bestowed. Closely related to this line of thinking is a concern with biological differences. If nature established distinctions of race or sex, for example, these must be accepted because they are, if not divinely sanctioned, then at least immutable. Cultural categories supposedly ordained by nature stereotype everyone who is included in them; all are assumed to be alike because nature made them so. Fredrickson's analysis points up the fact that it is Americans who are inclined to think in explicitly racist terms, not South Africans. There distinctions are perceived in self-consciously cultural terms, and tribal differences among blacks are clearly recognized and even endorsed. Because basic differences have such negative implications for Americans, they do not regard them as simply cultural givens. Something deeper and less subject to change must be involved.

22

Perceiving people in terms of categories is a way of distinguishing insiders from outsiders. The qualities that define outsiders in usually negative ways also define insiders in opposite and usually positive ways. Unlike culturally prescribed differences in a traditional society, categorization is not a way of directly facilitating interaction among various sorts of people. It is rather a way of symbolically accounting for distinctions that are considered too important to ignore. Beyond this categories function as blueprints for social groupings and for the social structures and practices which define in large measure how the categorized lead their lives and also how they perceive themselves. Categorization affirms individualistic assumptions by emphasizing inner as well as outer alikeness as the basis of group unity. It is precisely because they all seem fundamentally alike that members of social groupings can be considered and treated as if differences among them are of no consequence. Nevertheless, determining the precise social meaning of categorical differences involves many competing interpretations, and the customs and policies that evolve over time represent the interplay of a diversity of attitudes and interests.

The labeling process is not really one-sided. It rests on perceived differences that are likely to be acknowledged and even embraced by those who are labeled in special ways. Categorization fosters social groupings by encouraging a sense of collective identity among people who may wish to see themselves as distinctive in a culture that rejects traditional distinctions. The result is not an explicitly affirmed pluralism in which American society is functionally divided into groups whose collective uniqueness is acknowledged and even guaranteed. Instead the desire for social unity based on likeness of mind—when it comes up against human differences that are deemed too significant to pass unnoticed—results in a symbolic elaboration of these differences in categorical terms. Thus a person's awareness is focused on like-minded others, and those who do not belong within the circle of agreement are "written off" insofar as their distinctiveness is emphasized.

Categories may have greater or lesser relevance to people's lives, and fundamental kinds of agreement usually transcend categories and unite Americans in many important ways. Ideally members of all categorically defined social groupings are separate but equal and thus are free to pursue their own aims and live their own lives in accordance with the identities that applicable categorizations presumably reflect. In fact categorization results in many social limitations—often blatant limitations—on the expression of freedom and individuality. Nevertheless, if categories are accepted as legitimate symbols of what cannot really be changed, they incorporate everyone within the individualistic value system though not necessarily to the same degree or always in the same ways. Categories are

23

not equivalent to caste distinctions, and they do not forbid interactions across categorical lines on the basis of likemindedness even if in many obvious ways they do not facilitate it. The importance of basic agreement may be affirmed by invisibility, or it may be justified by the feeling that despite certain significant differences among groupings of people in America, as individuals we can come together in limited ways.

No human difference has seemed so important to Americans as the distinction between men and women. Sexual differentiation thus easily lends itself to categorization, and it is very "natural" to assume that all men can be labeled as fundamentally alike, just as all women can be. Egalitarianism within sexual categories rests on the assumption of shared innate qualities, and this assumption also accounts for another important contemporary cultural distinction, that between heterosexuals and homosexuals. It is only within the framework of sex-related categories that sex or gender roles have any meaning. For Americans they are not so much sexually based modes of behavior which facilitate human interaction as they are reflections of fundamental differences--differences which individualistic assumptions both magnify and at the same time challenge.

Overview--

Individualism represents a non-collectivist, non-organic, non-traditional approach toward society. It is intimately linked with the processes of modernization in the West, a fact which has long prompted many European critics to equate it with selfishness and social irresponsibility. While an anti-social interpretation has been advanced in America as well, most Americans have seen the emphasis on the primacy of the individual as a positive aspect of our culture. From this perspective individualism does not signify the rejection of social commitment; instead it represents an effort to harmonize individual rights and freedoms with larger social claims. Each person should be free to control his own life, but he is not granted the power to control the lives of others. Individuals are seen as the building blocks of society. They are linked together by a variety of voluntary ties. One school of thought emphasizes self-interest as the cement holding individuals together. Though they find it in their interest to cooperate with others, they remain suspicious of social authority and institutions as potential threats to individual freedom. Equality of opportunity is strongly emphasized, and this is assumed to result in inequalities of status and wealth. A second school of thought sees people as naturally social and cooperative, less success-oriented and more fundamentally egalitarian in their attitudes toward one another.

Both schools stress likeness of mind as the factor which permits unity without sacrificing individuality. This viewpoint applies equally to the concept of American identity. Any individual who subscribes to the basic values of the nation can presumably be an American. The emphasis upon likeness of mind leads also to anxiety about significant differences among people, for these strike at the very essence of social unity. There are several strategies for achieving likeness of mind. The significance of differences can be minimized. Where possible people can be persuaded to give up whatever sets them apart. Those who are different can in effect be rendered socially invisible. Finally, people can be conceptualized in terms of cultural categories which symbolically account for collective differences as "natural" and therefore immutable. From the mainstream point of view such distinctions, including biological sex and sexual object choice, do not violate individualistic assumptions, for individuals are assumed to identify themselves willingly with others most like themselves. Members of different social groupings may remain isolated in many respects from the larger society, but they are still in theory equal as well as separate and free to fulfill themselves as individuals in accordance with their "natural" predispositions.

CHAPTER TWO

MASCULINITY AND THE MAIN CHANCE

Though we live in a period in which conventional values are in flux, a generally recognized masculine code still exists. Change--both on a cultural and a social level--is of course taking place, but in partial ways and at different rates. Masculinity is comprised of the values that the socialization process instills in males. While individualism figures prominently in this process in American society, masculinity and individualism do not coincide in all respects. The art of manliness for middle-class American males, therefore, consists in balancing the elements of individualism against potentially conflicting values that have long been associated with masculinity. How successfully the conflicts are resolved reflects the quality of their individualistic loyalties and the adequacy of their masculinity.

Basic Components--

Many of the commonly listed components of masculinity in America are virtually synonymous with the essential elements of individualism. In the words of one study: "One of the most basic routes to manhood in our society is to be a success: to command respect and be looked up to for what one can do or has achieved."[1] Everything that success in this context is presumed to include--money, prestige, influence, social position--relates specifically to a man's individual achievements. Inherited wealth, family status and influence based on that status would not strike most Americans as substantial evidence of manliness. This aspect of masculinity remains essentially middle-class in its emphasis on striving and achievement. Upper-class status may militate against masculinity by undercutting incentives to succeed. Lower-class status may involve serious liabilities that impede a person's chances to advance. Anyone who sees himself as unable to overcome such impediments in effect admits that he is subject to forces beyond his control. This is one reason why poverty and unemployment are so often viewed as threats to a person's manhood. Thus a man must be individualistic by choice and by circumstance if he is to be considered really masculine in this regard.

A closely related masculine attribute is a strong commitment to personal independence: "a man should always be 'his own man,' should think for himself."[2] Moreover, he should be willing and able in every respect to take care of himself. Depending too much on others betrays a lack of self-reliance. William Dean Howells' Silas Lapham strongly disapproves of the fact that Tom Corey is supported by his father. "I like to see a man _act_ like a man," Lapham remarks. When Tom confesses to his father

27

that he is ashamed of his dependent status, the older man responds that America will never have "a real aristocracy" as long as young men are reluctant "to live upon a parent or a wife."[3] Thomas Bailey Aldrich's young man in The Story of a Bad Boy tells how he had become "more manly and self-reliant" by learning that the world was not created solely for him.[4] Masculinity, like individualism, implies overcoming whatever stands in the way of one's freedom to be oneself. Self-reliance enhances a male's ability to deal with a world that he has no expectation of fully controlling.

Teenage males especially face the challenge of coping effectively with forces they cannot readily control. In the novel James at 15 the young protagonist considers himself a prisoner of his parents' decision to move from Oregon to Boston to further the father's career. As a dependent James is subject to such limitations, yet as a person emerging into manhood he must be independent, self-reliant and successful. He decides to run away to "escape the forces that held him." Initially he seeks his masculinity in a fantasy of life on the northern Canadian frontier, "where men were forced to make their own lives." He resolves, however, to return to his new home when he meets a woman who encourages his masculinity by insisting that, while she can give him advice, she cannot tell him what to do: "Nobody can. You've got to figure it out for yourself." Back at school James decides to try out for the swimming team. No one may care whether he makes it or not, but he does and that is enough. He sets an unofficial record and this immediately wins him friends and acceptance. His schoolmates "saw him as he really was-- James Hunter, a winner."[5] He may have wanted solely to prove something to himself, but he does not become a "winner" until he is publicly measured against others' efforts.

Like individualism, masculinity must be constantly and actively proved. Males are not merely assumed to be masculine and therefore treated as if the privileges and responsibilities of masculinity were theirs as a birthright. A man's having to prove himself is often justified in biological (and hence irrefutably categorical) terms. Because women can bear children, it is argued, their femaleness and hence their essential femininity cannot be doubted either by others or themselves. Lacking such an absolute assurance of their maleness, men must constantly prove their masculinity--for categorization inextricably links the two. If, however, American culture assumes women need not prove their femininity, it is because femininity is not associated with self-assertion rather than because biology does not require it. As Jeffrey Hantover points out, "a woman receives sex-role reassurance from her body because her body has been taken as the central defining element of her sex role." By contrast a man's "body is not an end but a means for the performance of culturally prescribed behaviors."[6]

The individualistic emphasis on personal achievements and proving oneself means that purely physical factors are suspect as reliable criteria of masculinity. Here to a large extent one is at the mercy of one's natural endowments--a reality which women are taught to improve upon and men to ignore. Physique, which would seem mostly within the range of a man's control, has a certain acceptability as a criterion of masculinity. It takes work and self-discipline to develop one's body, and successful results are an indication that a man is likely to be able to take care of himself in any situation requiring physical prowess. If men appear to be objects of aesthetic contemplation rather than active doers, however, their masculinity is possibly suspect. Muscle builders often cause uneasy amusement though Arnold Schwarzenegger's entrepreneurial successes provide in his case an adequate measure of reassurance.

Physical good looks are probably the least reliable indication of masculinity from an individualistic point of view. Indeed to be too good-looking may take away from a man's masculinity whereas minor flaws thought to heighten it refer not to aesthetics but to character. Women may appreciate good looks in a man, but they are taught to judge the opposite sex by measures which men understand place them far less at the mercy of circumstance. More is made of the physical aspects of masculinity in the case of many film stars, and this is probably due to the fact that they are highly dependent on the acceptance and approval of others. This detracts from individuality and thus contributes to the greater premium on such passive characteristics as good looks and physical endowments.

To be an accomplished ladies man does not signify unqualified masculinity in America. Robert Sklar suggests that as a great screen lover whom women found very attractive Rudolph Valentino made many American males in the 1920's uneasy: "For a man to make himself appealing to women they considered a certain sign of effeminacy."[7] Too active an interest in women means that one's life revolves around femininity to a degree that undercuts its categorical opposite, masculinity. Being successful with women is not to be scorned as a masculine achievement, particularly on a simple level like "scoring." On more complex levels a man is likely to enter a dangerous realm, where his masculinity cannot be so simply validated as in areas where individualism comes more fully into play. There is a dependence on a woman's responsiveness that makes a man quite vulnerable, especially if his failings ever become public knowledge. Most men feel a certain peer-group pressure to be seen as successful with women, but very often they content themselves with boasting of conquests--and other males carefully refrain from attempts at verification.

A basic ingredient of individualism is freedom from arbitrary social constraints. To the degree to which assumptions concerning masculinity and individualism coincide, there is no basis for seeing masculine expectations as arbitrary impositions. Because Americans paradoxically see masculinity as acting according to imperatives that are rooted in one's nature as a male and as asserting one's freedom from restrictive social forms, individualistic assumptions operate on two levels. A categorical level stresses willing assent to natural necessity. The first lesson in sexual categorization that every "normal" child learns is sexual identity--recognizing oneself as a being defined in large measure in terms of sex. American males are socialized to want to be what all men in their society must be if they are to fulfill themselves as males. Each one thus willingly includes himself in a social grouping comprised of all members of his sex and acts out the sex-role expectations associated with it.

It is commonly observed that such expectations in America are primarily negative. As Hantover puts it, "there is more discouragement of inappropriate sex-role behavior than rewards for appropriate behavior." A little girl is taught to see her mother as a concrete role model, but a boy has to differentiate himself from the "feminine matrix" of his early childhood and identify himself with "an abstract cultural ideal" transmitted by his mother.[8] This ideal is seen as part of his very being, not simply as a form of outward conformity to specific role expectations. Inappropriate actions are violations of a male's identity to a degree that is not true for females. Masculinity is not, therefore, essentially an ascribed but rather an earned quality the significance of which lies in the symbolism attached to expected behavior. While role expectations are themselves ascribed on the basis of sex, what a person does is important mainly for what it says about his identity as a sexual being. Thus each male has little sense of acting out a prescribed sex or gender role, for outward behavioral expectations are incorporated into a much larger cultural category which includes all aspects of gender. Each male thus simply expresses his masculine identity, and so the cultural basis of masculinity is obscured and its "naturalness" highlighted.

On a second level the cultural basis of masculinity is also ignored. The assumption is made that the individual must control his own life rather than be controlled by social forms and structures. On this level mainstream masculinity, psychologically considered, does not mean taking upon oneself the role behaviors that American culture assigns on the basis of sex--but rather quite the opposite. This requires that masculinity remain vague and general, involving a range of possibilities that allow each male to feel that he is fairly free to be what he wants to be. Because self-assertion is so commonly linked with striving and success, a generalized definition of masculinity greatly enhances a man's ability to function effectively in different milieus. At the same time the very fact that the criteria of masculinity, as of individualism, are vague and general means that a person cannot be entirely certain how well he fulfills them, and this only enhances the necessity of proving his manhood.

In traditional cultures, where ascribed sex roles are seen as inevitable, the notion of proof is, practically speaking, less important. Of course men must demonstrate their competence in hunting and warfare, for instance, but the emphasis is upon outward role conformity rather than inward assent. All that is required is that a person master the details of prescribed behavior. He is not asked to scrutinize his conduct for subtle evidences of an imperfect commitment to masculinity. Moreover, the social inevitability of men's roles means that the whole social structure is mobilized to aid the person in passing the tests of manhood. The situation for a young man in American society is very different, Mark Gerzon maintains: "Without a rite of passage, he can only prove what he is not."[9] Masculinity and maleness are intricately linked symbols that function in largely negative ways to define and insure the essential distinctiveness of American males. The first gender role lesson boys learn, James A. Doyle argues, is "to avoid anything that even vaguely smacks of femininity."[10]

If masculinity is precisely defined in traditional contexts, it is also closely linked to equally well defined roles of class, status and occupation. In America, by contrast, masculinity is most closely tied to a system of values which rejects fixed definitions of the individual's place in society. The connection with individualism, furthermore, enhances the assumption that masculinity is bound up with self-assertion. In traditional societies a deviant male asserts his rejection of his assigned masculine role. In America all males must assert their acceptance, for the absence of masculine self-assertion is itself strong evidence that one's claims to manhood may well be dubious.

The fact that masculinity implies an affirmation of individualistic loyalties apart from the social milieu may explain the observation that "to be seen as a 'real man' . . . there should be at least a hint of untamed, primitive force beneath a civilized exterior."[11] Even for the mainstream male, who is fully immersed in the affairs of the community around him, the assumption persists that in some sense as a man he stands apart from the processes of civilization and that to project this apartness is inherently masculine. Burt Avedon suggests that many, if not all, men feel "a yearning born of the energy they feel as men, countered by a diametrically opposed energy telling them to settle down, to conform to the social norm."[12]

31

A Single Standard--

The levelling effects of democracy in early nineteenth-century America materially enhanced sexual distinctions, just as they did racial distinctions, by encouraging people to view them in categorical terms. G. J. Barker-Benfield argues that this resulted in a greater degree of sexual solidarity in America than in Europe, where ties of class, rank and religion were often more important than ties of sex.[13] Since then generalized masculine expectations have been assumed to apply to all men, for no distinctions of status or background are acknowledged to override their categorically based alikeness. Quite possibly, therefore, the specifics of a man's behavior may be at variance with the general standard. At best conformity will always be imperfect, and so each male is likely to harbor some sense of deficiency. How strong this sense will be depends on many factors, such as the impact of mainstream expectations and more immediate social supports for or pressures against departures from these expectations.

As a young man Saul Bellow's Tommy Wilhelm in Seize the Day had tried and failed to parlay his charm and good looks into a successful movie career. Now as a salesman down on his luck what he most wants is help and encouragement from his father, an affluent retired doctor. The latter clearly exemplifies the individualistic and assertive values his son has in practice rejected. He has little patience with Tommy's feelings of helplessness and hopelessness and advises him to "carry nobody on your back." The son by contrast no longer thinks of free choice in his own life, sees his father as selfish for not picking up his hotel tab on occasion and regards himself as a victim of his mistaken selection of a wife. He consistently exhibits behavior that is unacceptable in a conventional male; "from his mother he had gotten sensitive feelings, a soft heart, a brooding nature, a tendency to be confused under pressure."[14] Unfortunately Tommy feels himself judged and found wanting by a code of masculinity exemplified by his father to which he does not truly adhere and yet which he cannot fully repudiate.

The emphasis upon a single standard of masculinity makes no provision for significant individual or collective deviations. Because masculinity is thought of in categorical terms, American males find it difficult to understand masculine behaviors different from those they have been taught to honor. Traditional societies, which have more fixed notions of masculinity, tend also to be more flexible than ours in permitting alternatives--special roles for shammans or priests or hermits-- for those who are misfits in some way. If masculinity, however, is not seen as culturally prescribed behavior--which may differ from context to context--but as an expression of all men's basic nature, there cannot be much scope for variation.

Nevertheless, in many ways American males are aware of and have to deal with behaviors which cannot be labeled necessarily unmasculine but which do not fully accord with mainstream individualstic assumptions. The result is some degree of uneasiness, avoidance or rejection. One of the most obvious traits of behavior has to do with the expression of emotion. Conventional masculinity has generally been associated with emotional self-control, which Deborah David and Robert Brannon see as extending to all aspects of a man's life; "inexpressiveness becomes a way of behaving in intimate relationships as well as in more impersonal ones."[15] In many societies, as well as in their American subsocietal counterparts, such constraints are not required of males. However, categorical assumptions do not permit such a difference to be readily acknowledged. Minority-group males may be subjected to conflicting pressures when subcultural values allow behavior which is unmasculine when judged in terms of individualistic expectations. Critics of emotional restraint have called on men to be more expressive, and there is a certain marginal acceptance of a man's right to be open and to cry. Still, most people remain uneasy about such behavior precisely because it suggests an unmasculine lack of self-control.

Not surprisingly, emotional restraint is especially called for toward other men, whose individuality most deserves the respect of equals. James Hunter's last encounter with his closest friend before leaving Oregon includes calling each other names, punching each other on the arm, wrestling and then separating as the friend says casually "see ya around" and walks away.[16] There is clearly real affection between the two young men, but it must be screened through a number of rituals that establish an appropriate emotional distance between them. Involvement is thus limited and the independence and individuality of each is not undercut. Burt Avedon feels that "men still suffer great discomfort and embarrassment if another man tries to get close, tries to confide." Significantly, they "are suspicious of the man who makes an overture and of themselves if they are receptive to it."[17]

Mainstream males would logically be expected to value especially those friendships with other men which do not violate their freedom, independence and loyalty to individualism. Sinclair Lewis's Babbitt considers Paul Riesling his very best friend and admires him "with a proud and credulous love passing the love of women." Once when they are open about how much they are enjoying each other's company, "the shame of emotion overpowered them; they cursed a little, to prove they were good rough fellows."[18] His friendship with Paul appeals to Babbitt precisely because it does not put constraints on him as the love of a woman does. This makes it more valuable and hence more "real" than the relationship with his wife.

33

Of all manifestations of possible closeness among males touching in other than aggressive or highly formalized ways is the most suspect and indeed the most forbidden. It violates a person's "space" without any compensating distancing. Team sports provide one of the few contexts in which spontaneously affectionate touching is regularly permitted. Because the general situation is routinely a highly competitive one and there is much striving among team members for stardom, audiences perhaps are more willing to pass over the fact that effective teamwork requires subordination of individual interests to the larger whole. This tends to downplay competitive individualism and thus to lower the barriers against affectionate touching. This seems to occur, however, only under special conditions when players are most caught up in the excitement of the game. While athletics seems the most masculine of endeavors, the sports world is also the subject of a good deal of anxious scrutiny and rumor.

Military organizations are also likely to elicit mixed reactions from most Americans--again partly because the masculine images projected do not wholly mesh with the requirements of individualism. Americans have frequently welcomed war as an opportunity for masculine assertiveness. Nevertheless, military discipline, obedience and loyalty to the group are not obviously individualistic virtues. There has never been much admiration bestowed upon military men as members of organizations, nor have the military virtues stressed in many countries seemed especially masculine to us. We prefer instead to admire individualists like the Green Berets, leaders like Patton and heroes who are seen as having acted mostly on their own. A veteran of the North Africa campaign during World War II described "a real soldier" as "a guy that can take care of himself."[19] Military service often fosters very close male ties. Speaking specifically about World War I, Mark Gerzon observes that "tenderness, camaraderie, affection--all the emotions normally taboo between men were permitted, even respected, on the battlefield."[20] Close ties even off the battlefield are generally accepted in context despite much official anxiety about possible "perverted" consequences which they might have. Although such consequences are probably rare, it is significant that close ties are not easily transferred to the more individualistic ethos of civilian life.

The Pursuit of Success and Power--

Because of the pressures to be successful in American society, Clyde W. Franklin argues, most males continue to make use of the competitive strategies learned early in life despite the fact that "the arena of competition changes from one requiring physical strength to one requiring intellectual and interpersonal skills."[21] In the pursuit of opportunity other people are important, for a man cannot succeed solely on the basis of his

34

own isolated efforts. Success requires the ability to establish effective connections with people who have something to offer, to coordinate their efforts and forge links based on ties of interest or loyalty. This is as true for an "independent operator" as it is for someone deeply involved in the workings of a large-scale organization. The problem is that this involvement is not always compatible with independence and self-determination. In John Knowles' novel Indian Summer, a successful businessman scorns the ideal of independence upheld by a younger character. Nobody is independent, he insists.[22]

Success is closely linked with power, which both stems from it in American society and is necessary to consolidate and perpetuate it. Certainly an emphasis upon success encourages men to exercise power based on their own initiative and enterprise. C. Wright Mills defines the truly powerful as "those who are able to realize their will, even if others resist it."[23] In more general terms power in interpersonal relations represents "the ability to get another person to think, feel or do something he or she would not have ordinarily done spontaneously."[24] Power therefore represents a person's potential to get others to do what he wants them to do and to prevent others from forcing him to do what he does not wish to do . An individualistic stance may seem to depend upon power, for some measure of it would appear necessary in order to insure control over one's own life. Nevertheless, as John Stuart Mill long ago argued, "the love of power and the love of liberty are in eternal antagonism."[25] If individualistic values are strictly adhered to, men's loyalty to freedom prevents them from seeking power over others and takes away the necessity of using it for self-protection. All forms of compulsion contradict the freedom of choice which the individualist cherishes. While power remains important in American society, individualistic assumptions limit both its implementation and even more its legitimacy.

Only in very limited ways is power really personal. For the most part it is rooted in institutions and in extensive and often not necessarily voluntary relationships with other people. Thus it implies dependence on others and usually upon institutional structures as well. Then too one depends in a sense on others as objects of power, for without them it cannot be exercised. All of these kinds of dependence entail limits on the practice of individualism. If real power means the capacity to control others, individualism demands that one be in control of one's own life. The essential challenge for the American male is that masculinity requires an allegiance to both power and individualism as well as to success, which tenuously joins the other two. Because power is intimately linked with dominance and submission relationships among males, it is a traditional attribute of masculinity which long antedates the ascendancy of individualism and still retains an influence over men's ac-

tions. It is also integrally a part of an evolving modern order
in which ambitious men are encouraged to acquire power over some
men and exercise countervailing power against others. Thus the
pursuit of power in America links traditional hierarchical assumptions with competitive, success-oriented ones in a way which
neither wholly denies nor fully accepts the logic of individualism.

Though in fact the exercise of power may involve much more
than persuasion or voluntary agreement, this is the only tactic
which is fully consistent with a dedication to individualism.
This of course undercuts power by conceding to others the right
to do what they want despite one's best efforts to bend them to
one's will. Nevertheless, those who desire the most harmonious
balance between power and individualism have to be able to persuade people rather than to coerce them.   Masculinity dictates
forcefulness and determination, but it also suggests in America
more the art of charismatic leadership than of command or coercion.

While Horatio Alger's heroes may seem remote from contemporary reality, they demonstrate what still remain several crucial ingredients in the formula for attaining success and some
measure of power and thereby proving one's masculinity.   The
process must begin with an affirmation of the importance of the
individual and a commitment to self-reliance.   A typical young
man is "sharp and shrewd, and accustomed to depend upon his own
exertions."[26] If independence and self-reliance are accepted,
then the fact that economic mobility leads to hierarchies of
power and influence poses no problem.   It is understood that
these are fluid and shifting, accessible at least in theory to
all people of enterprise and determination.   The widespread assumption that America is an open society has always helped to
reconcile, though tenuously, success, power and individualism.
Men must be willing to work with others and thus to be objects
of power as much as wielders of it.

Alger's tales are filled with examples of how ambitious
young men can gain the willing support of powerful people whose
help and influence become important ingredients in their rise in
the world.   Strictly speaking, his heroes do not succeed on
their own. They must have the ingenuity to cultivate those who
are well placed enough to help them out. Evan Connell's Mr.
Bridge encourages his son to join a fraternity because the contacts will be very valuable to him later on when his fraternity
brothers will have become successful business and professional
men: "It will pay you to know them." Regarding his own fraternity experience he notes: "The men I became acquainted with as a
result have been extremely useful to me on a number of occasions."[27] An ambitious man cannot be entirely independent, but
he freely accepts certain kinds of conformity as the price nec-

essary for success and influence. Successful scientists, F. Rief argues, are highly dependent on the good opinion of important other scientists. Without this, professional mobility is seriously impeded. This often causes them to work along familiar lines which will assure them a steady stream of publications.[28] Someone without funds, influence and mobility would not really appear to the success-oriented masculine individualist more free to determine the course of his own life.

To be successful mainstream males must develop a great deal of skill in understanding the compromises that are required and those which are not to preserve their independence and self-determination and still be able to deal effectively with other people and the world around them. One might assume that the more power and success a man has the more free he is to do what he wishes, but this is a fantasy of powerlessness. In America power, status and influence will always be insecure and limited. To understand this puts a man in the best position to succeed in gaining as much as is compatible with his allegiance to individualism. Too much concern for independence and self-reliance and the separateness of the self militates against both success and power. At the same time the successful and powerful may surrender too much of their independence and self-determination.

The particular challenges I am dealing with are relevant in varying degrees to the lives of all middle-class males from the modestly competent to the fairly affluent. While many lower-class males may not fully accept or evidence these middle-class concerns in their lives, they are not immune to them. As Moses Rischin has observed, "to be middle class in the United States has been a state of mind, a novel presumption, a birthright of all."[29] The balance I have emphasized is probably especially middle-class, for it stresses a position between the relative powerlessness of the poor and the class consciousness of the rich. Mainstream masculinity calls for willingly conforming to categorically based expectations which assume that all men are alike in terms of their general goals, the way they pursue them, and how their successes are to be judged. By contrast the very rich are more likely to think and act as a class, or at least to be constrained in ways that safeguard their power and wealth. Individualism most likely means less to them and power more.

Formal Social Structures--

The premium placed upon individually held feelings and values as the basis of social cohesion has over the years fostered varying degrees of uneasiness because it seems too formless and general. This suggests the utility of institutional structures to guarantee unity and continuity without relying exclusively on personal feelings of self-interest or mutual concern. Such structures have been championed by some and accepted by most without really calling into question the premium placed on individualism. As Robert Wiebe has shown, progressive reform at the beginning of this century envisaged "a society of ceaselessly interacting voluntary groups assisted in their course by a powerful, responsive government." Nevertheless, he argues, "bureaucratic management lent itself equally to social control and to social release."[30] These two tendencies have remained inherent in all aspects of the bureaucratization of modern American society.

The fact that twentieth-century Americans have been more dependent on larger structures as a matter of social practice than cultural assumptions endorse has caused many misgivings. Writing in 1909, Charles Horton Cooley defined the social mind as made up of "cooperating individualities" much like the music of an orchestra. Modern communications, he felt, make it possible for society to be organized increasingly in terms of "the higher faculties of man," which he called "intelligence and sympathy," as opposed to "authority, caste and routine." He saw democracy simply as the large-scale application of small-group principles of "free cooperation." Cooley was suspicious of institutions because they only deal with parts of individuals. While institutions depend for their vigor and adaptability on individuality "provided it be in harness," nevertheless they also have "a sober and tried goodness of the ages." Cooley was concerned about what he called too much "mechanism" in society, meaning such things as "institutionalism, formalism, traditionalism, conventionalism, ritualism, bureaucracy" though he admitted it is difficult to determine just what is too much. In the final analysis the test is whether individuality is suppressed or furthered.[31]

Because individualism makes men cautious about the formal institutional structures which have increasingly come to play important roles in their lives, American males must maintain their freedom and independence in the course of such involvements or run the risk of losing their masculine credentials. The loyalty of Mormon men to individualism is explicit, and each is encouraged throughout his life to place a high premium upon the manhood which is recognized as the basis of special privileges and responsibilities. To many Americans Mormons remain an oddity despite the fact that dedication to the basic values of our culture has resulted in a steady and successful movement into the American mainstream in this century. Mormon males, therefore, are an interesting case study in the interplay between individualism and a strong emphasis upon group solidarity and institutional authority.

Mormons constantly stress the importance of man's "free

agency," and they reject any idea of original sin because it seems to them to shift responsibility from the individual onto forces beyond his control. God's grace is given solely on the basis of merit, and Mormons are taught to aim for the highest place in a heavenly hierarchy which reflects personal attainment. Their commitment to equality of opportunity, hard work, success and self-help impels them to view this world and the next in terms of social gradations which attest to the fact that some people strive harder and achieve more than others. The Church has no professional ministry and is governed by lay priesthood members. All males over the age of twelve may enter the lay priesthood and according to merit are eligible to occupy a wide variety of hierarchically arranged administrative positions. As in the business world, a person is invited to assume positions of authority by those who have the recognized right to make the offer. Also like most business hierarchies, the Mormon Church does not function as a democracy. Nevertheless, Mormons regard it essentially as a vehicle of personal salvation and the Mormon community as an opportunity for mutual support and free association.

Since no male's status is fixed, everyone is accustomed both to lead and to follow. Thus Mormon males support the emphasis on equality of opportunity which leads to a fluid differentiation in terms of power and influence. They are part of the Church's power structure, which they experience not as some distant force controlling their lives, but as a joint endeavor in which some have temporarily more authority than others. Because the commitment of each member to the Church is a voluntary one, because each plays a part in accordance with his recognized qualifications, and because the proximate and ultimate rewards each seeks are essentially personal ones, neither individualism nor masculinity is felt to be violated. While the business analogy should not be overstated, the parallels I have drawn suggest how individualistic males are able to relate to powerful organizations which they see as means for realizing their own personal goals.

The particular challenge for Americans engaged in military service is to maintain a similar balance between individualism and institutional authority in the face of much stronger anti-individualistic pressures. These are compounded in many people's opinion by all the forces in modern life which undercut the autonomy of the individual and hence his masculinity. Shortly after the end of World War II, Roy R. Grinker and John P. Spiegel published a study of combat stress which attempted to determine why some men were less able than others to cope with military life. American society accepts as its ideal of manhood, they argued, someone who "is a lover of liberty and independence" and who believes "it is possible to be aggressive, independent, to look out for his own interest, in short, to be a man, without exploiting, enslaving or doing violence to another man or group of men." He must rely on others for material and emotional support, and his "dependence upon the community or group is in a nice balance with his independence." During the war American servicemen found themselves in "situations of un- dreamed of insecurity and threat" which called for reliance on the group. Most of them were motivated by a love of their fel- low Americans which enabled them to accept such dependence as a temporary necessity. The American has the "ability to throw himself into large organizations or teams on a voluntary basis, rather than by force."[32]

Grinker and Spiegel distinguished two different kinds of groups. "The first is intended to fix the individual in a de- pendent position, requiring of him absolute submission to au- thority," as in the case of "the fascist dictatorship." Volun- tary groups are totally different and harmonize with American values because they are "dedicated to furthering the indepen- dence and strength of the individual." Unfortunately many Amer- ican males were unable to resist, the authors felt, the pres- sures inherent in the military scheme of things which are con- ducive to the first kind of group association. The basic prob- lem for American civilization in the postwar period, they con- cluded, was the conflict between "the strong dependent needs of the boy," fostered in part by "the increasing feminine dominance of family life," and the "forces pushing toward aggressive, in- dependent, masculine and competitive existence."[33]

Concern about "momism" was particularly acute in the peri- od before and after World War II, and it reflects an anxiety about the viability of individualism in modern American life. The subordination of the individual to the group that was em- phasized in Nazi Germany obviously did not imply the "feminiza- tion" of German males. Nazism was a celebration of traditional masculine power and dominance, and wherever these values are strongly emphasized some men will be subordinated to others. Power and fixed hierarchical social arrangements inevitably com- plement one another and will not be seen as threats to masculin- ity as long as individualistic concerns have little or no rele- vance to how manhood is defined.

Joseph Pleck argues that the Male Sex Role Identity para- digm, the dominant conception of the male role in America for the past fifty years, emerged in part as a product of concerns about masculinity in the late nineteenth and early twentieth centuries. These stemmed from "the decline of the social insti- tutions formerly externally controlling men's and women's behav- ior," and it "stimulated the emergence of more internalized, psychologically based mechanisms." Traditional sex roles, he maintains, "have been supported--indeed defined--by a rigid seg- regation of the social spheres of women and men, particularly in employment and the family."34 Pleck's argument would suggest that within the Mormon community, as well as within many areas of the business community, there is a stronger emphasis upon external institutional controls and thus a somewhat more traditional emphasis than is the case in more purely voluntaristic settings. This would account for the greater acceptance of authority and dominance-submission relationships that are characteristic of all hierarchical structures. Mormonism blends these traditional elements with an accent on the individual which to a degree blurs the distinction between the two types of groups that Grinker and Spiegel describe.

For Americans in general in the twentieth century, institutional structures have become potentially awesome threats to masculinity because it has seemed increasingly difficult to deal with them in voluntary terms. It is possible, however, that the threat is less for those who are drawn more to power and guided more by ambition than it is for those who are concerned more with individualistic self-determination. As among Mormon males, dominance and submission would be less likely to seem a contradiction of masculinity. Power always involves both; only God is omnipotent.

In contrast to Pleck, moreover, my own belief is that internalized mechanisms of social control with respect to the male sex role long predated the MSRI paradigm and are coincident with the rise of categorical thinking in the early nineteenth century regarding men and masculinity. The idea of a separate sphere for men, like that of a separate sphere for whites, is foreign to traditional thinking. It rests on an assumption of common identities rather than an emphasis upon a hierarchy of ascribed forms of behavior. In the nineteenth century categorization stressed the "natural" separation of men's and women's mental and emotional worlds, and it also reinforced social structures and ascribed behaviors which highlighted sexually based differences. Throughout this period economic individualism most defined men's distinctiveness as members of a separate social grouping and validated their masculinity. In the long run, however, categorization did not guarantee essentially separate spheres for the sexes any more than for the races although logically this is what it implies. The MSRI paradigm coincided with another crucial transition to an increasingly bureaucratized society in which the functional separation of men's and women's spheres has steadily broken down and men have become more and more involved with all sorts of complex hierarchical structures that have seemed to many to undercut individualism and hence masculinity. Rather than initiating a new pattern of thinking, this paradigm represents an attempt to shore up the process of categorizing people in terms of sex by validating scientifically the roles of nature and inward necessity.

Male Bonding--

As long as a man's involvements with other men in the world of success and power remain relatively impersonal, competition does not threaten his sense of individuality and a give-and-take cooperativeness allows everyone to further his own interests as far as possible. Impersonal relationships require a certain scrupulous concern about keeping one's distance and thus allowing people to keep theirs. David Riesman has described the "inner-directed" man as "capable of impersonal relations with people and sometimes incapable of any other kind."[35] The outward friendliness of "other-directed" people struggling to succeed in a complex bureaucratized world need not imply emotional openness. Impersonality remains a useful shield in guarding one's individuality in the midst of increasingly elaborate forms of interaction. At the same time men would like to believe that "comradeship and rivalry" can be easily reconciled, Michael Korda argues. Though this is seldom the case, they "still suppose, in a yearning romantic way, that the formula works somewhere."[36]

A modern office exists, Korda also suggests, "in part to reaffirm the bonds that exist between men." Women are excluded from "their privileges of conversational freedom, shared experiences and the all-important sense of membership."[37] Men are therefore capable of presenting a fairly solid front when challenged by women who boldly seek entry into their sphere. Nevertheless, the fact is that success-oriented American men are primarily loyal to themselves as individuals. Teenage boys, Clyde W. Franklin maintains, "learn that to be masculine means to become independent and relatively unreliant on, and to some extent unsusceptible to peer-group influence."[38] Older men have not historically thought of themselves as members of a group which levies special claims of allegiance, defense and furtherance. It was difficult for middle-class men of the industrial age in Europe as well as America, Peter Stearns argues, to bond together, for they had been "trained to be suspicious individualists." Thus they lost touch with "a sense of fundamental common enterprise" that had emerged early in the history of the human race.[39]

Probably the most ardent celebration of male bonding is Lionel Tiger's Men in Groups. Men naturally form organizational bonds, he argues, and these are central to social organization. He sees male bonding "as the spinal column of a community, in this sense: from a hierarchical linkage of significant males, communities derive their intra-dependence, their structure, their social coherence, and in good part their continuity through the past to the future." Tiger considers "human aggression in its social organizational sense" as "a propensity of males," who come together to realize "the male equivalent of child reproduction, which is related to work, defence, politics,

42

and perhaps even the violent mastery and destruction of others."[40] In almost every respect Tiger's world and the males in it reject the principles of individualism. What is valued is not personal success, self-reliance, independence and the freedom to determine the course of one's own life, but the subordination of the individual to larger hierarchies aimed at aggression, control and domination. Tiger does not suggest, moreover, that all males constitute a categorically defined social grouping. The bonds he describes link specific males in specific and formalized ways.

Tiger talks in general--though recognizably traditional--terms, and the question immediately suggests itself as to whether his views have any applicability to American society. "Elements of the traditional male role clearly persist," Joseph Pleck argues, "both in culturally conservative groups and in the personalities of many males, but these elements are becoming less dominant."[41] Traditional assumptions have slowly eroded over time, but they have persisted especially in those areas of American life most removed from middle-class expectations--in varying degrees among ethnic minorities, in the military and in sports. They are part of a world of hierarchy and status that some time ago may have been largely repudiated, but which still has a lingering appeal to most men's imaginations. The leveling and individualistic elements that are integral to the categorical view of American males have undercut traditional assumptions. At the same time the cultural category itself provides a framework within which attenuated traditional elements can be credibly retained. Thus while Tiger's concept of male bonding and patriarchal power has limited practical applicability to the lives of most mainstream American males, it appeals to a sense of masculinity which has not wholly lost its meaning.

In The Red Badge of Courage Stephen Crane describes the effect of military service upon a young recruit during the Civil War. In his first encounter with the enemy Henry Fleming "became not a man but a member," for "he felt the subtle battle-brotherhood more potent even than the cause for which they were fighting." On another occasion the men pause and immediately feel cautious: "They were become men again." Later "the impetus of enthusiasm was theirs again," and in their feelings of pride "they were men." Crane thus speaks of Henry and his comrades as being men in two different senses. In a modern sense to be a man refers to one's separateness, individuality and disposition to act rationally while in a traditional sense it refers to functioning as part of a hierarchical male organization. Clearly the latter is the more direct consequence of the fighting experience, and in moments of quiet reflection Henry recognizes that "he had proceeded sheep-like." Thus from an individualistic perspective there is considerable irony in the pride he comes to feel in his "quiet man-hood, non-assertive but of stur-

43

dy and strong blood."[42]   If manhood means being swept along by
feelings that bind one to other men and subordinate one to the
organization and its goals, the absence of choice and the loss
of individuality which Crane points up undercut the experience
and prompt the reader to see Henry in a much less heroic light
than he sees himself.

In Tennessee Williams' A Streetcar Named Desire Stanley
Kowalski places a high premium on his friendship with his buddy
Mitch and is responsible for aborting Mitch's brief romance with
Blanche instead of leaving him free to deal with her on his
own. Stanley's economic status may be lower-class, and his phi-
losophy--"to hold front position in this rat-race you've got to
believe you are lucky"--may downplay the belief that each man is
essentially responsible for his own fate. Still, he is ambitious, believes in himself, and is obviously loyal to America as
a land of opportunity. He bristles when Blanche refers to him
as a "Polack," for he sees himself as "a one-hundred-percent
American, born and raised in the greatest country on earth and
proud as hell of it."[43]   His focus on luck and male bonding has
strongly traditional overtones, but he sees no reason either to
doubt himself as a man or as a real American.

Don Vito Corleone in Mario Puzo's novel The Godfather also
uses traditional means to pursue the typically American goal of
success. He rises from poverty and obscurity and along with
many immigrants before him finds America indeed a land of promise. His major preoccupation is power, and to attain it he creates an elaborate network of very personal dominance-submission
relationships. His power is essentially feudal, based on ties
of personal loyalty and obligation. The Don is baffled by his
son Michael's outstanding war record because "he performs those
miracles for strangers." "Friendship is everything," he insists. His "closest companion and his closest friend" is his
"consigliori," who serves him in personal as well as business
matters and knows everything about him and so has the power to
destroy him.[44]   His is a world in which personal obligations
mean much more than the freedom to pursue one's goals on one's
own. His bonds with other males rest on loyalties, debts, ties
of ethnicity, and where necessary violence.

In marked contrast to his father, Michael wants his children to be Protestant because "it was more American." He does
not want them to be influenced by him as he was by his father:
"I want them to grow up to be All-American kids," he tells his
wife. He sees that his father's time has passed. Indeed even
the Don had recognized this. The world of guns and killing, he
had insisted, must be left behind in learning to be "cunning
like the business people."[45]   Michael understands that the world
he wants his children to be part of must be much more impersonal
and individualistic than the world of his father. He does not

44

reject power and status or traditional ties with other males up- on whom he depends, but he modifies their significance by blend- ing individualistic elements with them. In this way he simply carries his father's commitment to success to its logical con- clusion within the American context.

All the various actions and connections which insure suc- cess and which enhance power and influence within the mainstream are tacitly assumed to have their basic rationale in the promo- tion of individual welfare. Men cooperate impersonally in all sorts of ways which have the collective effect of promoting the interests of all American males--though not to the same degree in every case. As youths, Clyde W. Franklin notes, American males not infrequently "tend to form instrumental friendships, rather than ones based on emotional expressiveness."[46] Thus one can speak of mainstream male bonding and the furthering of men's collective power in two senses. It is evidenced specifically in formal as well as informal kinds of voluntary involvements with one another. A man retains his masculine credentials in associ- ating with other men by exercising a fair amount of control over his own life. Pride in one's ability to take care of oneself, self-reliance, a sense of the importance of defending one's sep- arateness by maintaining a certain psychological and even physi- cal distance from other males, keeping one's own counsel--all these essential elements of masculinity would have little mean- ing to males who expressed their masculinity in traditional terms.

In a second sense, all American males are brought up to regard themselves as members of a single social grouping and thus to share a generalized male identification, which in large part is built upon commonly accepted individualistic loyalties. Personal interests need not be subordinated to collective inter- ests because the two are assumed to coincide. A man does not consciously defend the interests of a male power structure as a soldier might those of his unit or an athlete of his team. He merely responds to a feeling of oneness with other males. The marvellous thing about such an identification is that it in- cludes all the like-minded. And in a society which defines so- cial unity in terms of like-mindedness, that is assumed to be everybody (male)--who is anybody.

Overview--

Masculinity in America has several individualistic compo- nents--personal achievement, independence, having to prove one- self. All emphasize control over the course of one's life, and so factors which undercut such control--physical endowments, de- pendence on women--are correspondingly deemphasized. Masculin- ity and maleness are closely linked in people's minds with one another and with the belief in the collective distinctiveness of all American males. Thus men are assigned to a single sexually defined cultural category that is translated into a social grouping beginning with the first lessons in sexual identity that each little boy learns. On one level males are expected to be what they "naturally" must be as a consequence of their biology. On a second level, however, masculinity is conceived in terms of a range of possibilities permitting each person to think of himself as a free and independent male individual. The generalized masculine expectations that apply to every man often do not mesh with the specifics of each person's behavior. Moreover, these expectations may make it difficult for American males to accept behaviors, such as emotional expressiveness and non-aggressive touching, or situations, like military life, that exemplify non-individualistic aspects of masculinity.

Power is a traditional attribute of masculinity that still retains its hold upon men's imaginations. It is closely linked in America with success, and both imply limitations upon a person's freedom and independence. Emphasizing the possibility of success for all who strive hard to attain it and persuasion as the most effective technique for exercising power over others links success and power with individualism as basic components of masculinity in America. To succeed one must be willing to accept certain voluntary limitations on one's independence and to be the object as well as the wielder of power in working with others. Such a balance is essentially a middle-class ideal and has less relevance to the lives of upper- and lower-class males.

Most aspects of men's lives in the twentieth century, including the pursuit of opportunity, have been affected by the bureaucratization of modern society. The challenge for individualistic males has been to maintain their sense of freedom and independence in contexts which have seemed increasingly to make this impossible. The solution would appear to lie in dealing with complex institutional structures in voluntaristic terms--in using them to help one realize one's own personal ends. Those who are drawn more toward power and success than toward independence and self-determination are likely to experience less personal conflict in such contexts. These larger changes in social organization are associated with a breaking down of the separate spheres for men and women which sexual categorization underscores. This has prompted advocates of the MSRI paradigm to emphasize inward necessity as the basis for a categorical definition of masculinity.

Individualism would seem to undercut male bonding by encouraging men to focus more upon themselves as individuals than upon their ties with other men. By contrast traditional views of male bonding stress the cohesiveness of tightly knit, hierarchically organized specific groups. Nevertheless, one can speak of male bonding within an individualistic context in two senses. Men cooperate impersonally and voluntarily in ways that further the interests of all males. Also there is a willing identification with other males as members of a single social grouping that can create a feeling of comradeship without any sense of loss of freedom or independence.

CHAPTER THREE

INVISIBLE WOMAN

Every society elaborates upon the reproductive and anatomical differences between men and women, and ours is no exception. Neither is there anything exceptional in the fact that ours is a society in which women generally are subordinated to men. Nevertheless, individualistic assumptions make the status of women a special problem by strongly emphasizing their collective distinctiveness and undercutting traditional modes of interaction. Male preeminence cannot rest essentially upon women's coerced obedience. There must be willingness, and this depends upon women's accepting men's views of the opposite sex as essentially their own. Undoubtedly American women have always been aware of a gap between their own sense of themselves and how men see them, and this gap has widened dramatically in the last two decades. Still, being acceptable to men remains the ultimate validation of femininity, and the "truly feminine" woman continues to be a person who wants to be what men wish her to be.

An emphasis upon sexual differentiation does not specifically prevent those who are categorized as the sexual opposites of men from applying individualistic values to their lives. At the same time individualism suggests that a real potential exists for interaction between men and women based on likeness of mind. In their relationships with men women must deal not just with the realities of reproductive biology nor with the persistence of traditional patriarchal assumptions, but also with individualistic expectations that apply to their sex within the framework of categorically defined differences.

Traditional and Categorical Approaches--

If the masculine value system requires a man to make his mark among men in the world, it also obliges him to link his personal fortunes with those of a single woman. At the same time it is taken for granted that he remains an individual and that marital responsibilities and family relationships constitute only a part of his life. By contrast marriage has at least until recently been seen as the only goal in life truly consistent with femininity, and thus both practically and symbolically it defines a woman and her femininity in all kinds of ways that are not true of a man and his masculinity.

As a legal and social institution marriage is based upon the hierarchical assumptions of pre-modern times. This makes it in theory at least a traditional relationship of two people of different statuses, each of whom performs appropriately different tasks and has special claims upon the other. From a radi-

49

cally individualistic point of view marriage as a formal institution means relatively little, for what should link two people
together is their love for and voluntary commitment to one another. Should these seriously diminish, then the union ceases
to exist and holding it together by some form of external compulsion is wrong. The traditional point of view is that marriage is not really a personal union but a social responsibility. Society has a right, therefore, to guarantee the stability
of marriage and the care of offspring through institutional
bonds backed by legal sanctions. The generally accepted interpretation of marriage in America blends the two points of view,
but not to the same degree for each sex.

As an institution marriage has historically affirmed the
superior status and patriarchal authority of the male in its
requirements of care, protection and governance of wives and
offspring just as it has the subordinate and dependent status of
women. For men it does not so straightforwardly fulfill individualistic requirements. The persistent assumption that they are
tied down and limited in marriage only makes sense if it is seen
as potentially a threat to such values as personal freedom and
self-determination. This anxiety is thus another example of the
ambivalent stance toward formal institutions which individualistic loyalties foster. Institutions are somehow necessary, and
yet also restrictive and thus of questionable validity. At the
same time the lesser degree of individualism associated with women's role in society means that marriage is seen as wholly fitting for them. They presumably are eager to lure nervous men
into making marital commitments because they do not share their
ambivalence about the institution. As dependents as well as
mothers and household managers, they benefit from the security
and stability which it is supposed to afford. Nevertheless, the
freedom to choose one's mate has been a characteristic of marriage in this country, as Carl Degler points out, since the late
eighteenth century.[1] Still, convention has mostly limited women's freedom of choice to the uses of indirection and the right
of refusal. Being refused may be an affront to traditional male
prerogatives, but along with a man's freedom to choose the person he wants goes the individualistic obligation to accept voluntarism as the basis of any union he enters into.

Traditional assumptions about male-female interactions
linger in a variety of attitudes and behaviors. Women are the
objects of the exercise of patriarchal power when men relate to
them as protectors, stern rulers, tyrants or possessors. The
view of women as possessions would seem especially compatible
with the assumptions that underlie the pursuit of economic opportunity. Helmut Schoeck has argued that "to expect man to
surrender his acquisitive urge is to expect him to give up his
possessive attitude toward wife and children."[2] Women are often
seen as having claims upon men as a consequence of their subor-

dinate status and their behaving in ways appropriate to that status. They are entitled to certain courtesies in public as well as private, to physical and economic protection, to the performance of tasks in their behalf that are not considered properly feminine. Such expectations logically apply only to relationships with specific men, and there is a distinct possibility of disappointment in many instances. Still, despite an increasing egalitarianism in the behaviors of men and women toward one another, it remains true that a woman who allows a man to change a tire for her, take her to dinner, open a door for her, or who dresses in ways which incapacitate her for activities men usually engage in will hardly be judged unfeminine.

Traditional views of the role of women in society and their relationships with men presuppose institutional restraints and social sanctions which promise order and predictability. Over time, however, these have eroded to the point where men mostly lack the authority and often the will to guarantee appropriate behavior on women's parts. Custom and external restraints have been largely replaced by inner controls for women as well as men, but not to the same degree. Traditional elements linger more with respect to feminine than to masculine behavior. Thus girls can be allowed to be tomboys while boys cannot be permitted to be sissies because outward pressures are counted upon to insure acceptable adult feminine behavior. The greater reliance on external controls permits, as it does in traditional societies, certain forms of role reversal under special circumstances. Another example is the greater latitude women of all ages enjoy regarding the wearing of articles of clothing of the opposite sex. Hence with respect to the importance of traditional elements there is an asymmetry in men's and women's role behaviors. In any context involving interaction on a personal level women are more likely to respond in traditional ways than men are. Although men may expect women to behave as subordinates, they will not necessarily feel obliged to place themselves under traditional constraints. Thus the essential element of reciprocity may be lacking, and so patriarchy is undercut and women's expectations often go unfulfilled.

Traditional differences in status are culturally defined and always have their justification in social utility and custom. The Mormon male is told that "fatherhood is leadership." Hence "it is not a matter of whether you are most worthy or best qualified, but it is a matter of law and appointment."[3] In Mormon thinking, strictly speaking, it is God's authority expressed through the values and institutions of the Mormon community which defines and enforces woman's role as well. It is not her intrinsic fitness as a female that determines that role.

In traditional societies the roles people play take time and patience to learn, for custom and tradition must be thor-

51

oughly taught. Individuals have little freedom to change or even to interpret roles because tradition and custom have a largely unquestioned validity, not because in some fundamental way they are unable to do otherwise. As far as sex roles are concerned, the categorically based assumption that these ultimately rest on innate differences between the sexes really has no meaning in a traditional context. It presumes that it is possible on some level to sever all connections between the individual and society and even culture, and this is precisely where a traditional order differs from an individualistic one. Sexual distinctions from a traditional perspective mean that anatomy is social destiny in the same sense as other accidents of birth determine one's status in society and the forms of behavior appropriate to it.

Because the Puritan social world was still conceived in largely hierarchical terms, a woman's traditional obligation to honor and comfort her husband was meant to insure order within the family. The Reverend Benjamin Wadsworth told his fellow Puritans that though a woman might be more intelligent or of higher status, "yet since he is thy Husband God has made him thy head and set him above thee and made it thy duty to love and reverence him." Like men women were willingly to fulfill the tasks appropriate to the position in society to which God had assigned them. At the same time the Puritans' allegiance to spiritual individualism and egalitarianism posed definite contradictions. Wadsworth reminded people that, in the words of the scripture, "there is neither Jew nor Greek, Bond nor Free, Male nor Female, for ye are all one in Christ Jesus."[4] Although God's grace was no respector of sex any more than of social class, in everyday life Puritans had no conscious intention of doing away with any traditional social distinctions. As Laurel Thatcher Ulrich has shown, the unwillingness or inability of ministers in the early eighteenth century "to transfer spiritual equality to the earthly sphere" caused them to anticipate a categorical conception of femininity by shifting "earthly differences to the spiritual sphere, gradually developing sexual definitions of the psyche and soul." At an earlier period they had acknowledged women's reproductive role "without giving a sexual content to the psyche and soul" by stressing "the experience of childbirth, rather than the nature of the childbearer."[5]

Arguably ascribed sex roles are as much arbitrary impositions on a person's right to determine a life course as social class or any other distinction based on accident of birth. Individualistic preconceptions encourage the questioning of all patently social barriers to self-determination. As individualism gained increasing currency at the end of the eighteenth century, women could no longer be convincingly distinguished from men simply in terms of their traditionally ascribed roles in society. Instead they came to be seen largely in categorical terms. Thus they were declared innately, collectively and wholly different from men. The process of fully elaborating categorically based theories of sexual and racial separateness took place at the same time and insured that all women, like all blacks, would henceforth be regarded as "naturally" and unalterably distinctive. Where distinctions exist for Americans they must somehow be "deserved." Viewing all women in terms of a single "natural" category shifted the focus away from traditional hierarchical assumptions without necessarily granting women equality with men or the freedom to structure their lives independently of the wishes of the opposite sex.

"In America, more than anywhere else in the world," Tocqueville noted, "care has been taken constantly to trace clearly distinct spheres of action for the two sexes, and both are required to keep in step, but along paths that are never the same."[6] Nancy F. Cott emphasizes the impact of economic and social changes which separated men's work from women's work. The latter "kept the traditional mode and location which both sexes had earlier shared." Increasingly men distinguished their work from women's by calling women's domain a separate sphere. "The demarcation of women's sphere from men's provided a secure, primary, social classification for a population who refused to admit ascribed statuses, for the most part, but required determinants of social order," Cott observes. Psychologically considered, however, this change in how women were seen did not suggest some kind of arbitrary imposition. It rested instead on a cultural redefinition of womanliness as part of their very natures. Most women accepted this view at least as fervently as men did. As Cott insists, "the more historians have relied on women's personal documents the more positively they have evaluated woman's sphere."[7]

Categorization disguised and yet also limited the power of men over women's lives, and at least partly for this reason women upheld the distinctions upon which it rested. Johnny Faragher and Christine Stansell have pointed out that women only reluctantly acquiesced in men's decisions to go west to Oregon and California at midcentury, for the move required leaving behind all the advantages of their separate sphere. The rigors of the journey soon forced women to work at male tasks, but sharing did not result in gender equality. Women lost their special privileges while "the men still retained dominance within their 'sphere,' despite the fact that it was no longer exclusively masculine."[8] While the belief that women are collectively and entirely different from men has been a basic element of American culture for nearly two hundred years, how such an assumption should be translated into social reality has remained a fairly open question that many have sought to answer in different ways. Not surprisingly, women have in varying degrees tended to favor some version of a separate-but-equal interpretation while

53

men--particularly outspoken conservatives--have sought to emphasize as much of traditional female subordination as categorization will allow.

Since custom does not enjoy unquestioned authority in
America, conservative males have been obliged to buttress traditional arguments with biologically based ones. Aubrey Andelin
insists that "a woman is very much in a subordinate position to
her husband." Andelin's authority for the man's position as
"undisputed head of the family" is "the Holy Scriptures." He
notes, furthermore, that while a man's position may be superior,
this does not mean that he is intrinsically superior to his
wife: "He is merely functioning in an office or calling." A
man's and a woman's duties are distinctly divided and should not
ordinarily overlap. The logic of this argument suggests that
women may in fact be capable of performing masculine functions,
but to do so is wrong because of custom and divine law. Andelin
does not, however, rest his case solely on these traditional
grounds. His insistence that distinctions based on the authority of custom do not imply distinctions in intrinsic worth opens
the way also for stressing categorical differences between men
and women, and so he turns to biological arguments. Thus we are
told that "by nature" a man "is strong, firm, steadfast and un-
yielding, whereas a woman by basic nature is soft and yielding."[9]

While traditional assumptions about women's proper role in
society cannot be consistently applied, they are not rejected
either. At the same time the insistence on categorizing them as
the opposite sex has served to rationalize beliefs and practices
that the authority of custom alone cannot support. The socialization process which aims at creating in women a strong need to
feel and to be perceived as unambiguously feminine, supplemented
by more traditional role pressures, is the final element in the
system of sex-related differences as it pertains to them.

Women as Opposites--

From a patriarchal perspective differences between the
sexes suggest complementarity of roles. Dominance is balanced
by submission, active by passive, reason by emotion, instrumental by expressive. Each sex requires the other, for behaviors
appropriate to one are incomplete without those of the other.
While masculinity and femininity have suggested opposite poles
of experience in almost all cultures, still in contrast to
characteristically American attitudes, "many philosophies view
each of the two concepts as one-half of a whole, neither of
which can ever be complete in itself."[10] Thinking of them in
terms of two mutually exclusive categories of being points away
from the complementarities of a traditional approach.

In America many feminine attributes represent negations of

masculinity rather than complements to it. To be economically successful or assertively ambitious from a conventional perspective undercuts a woman's femininity. It strikes men as appropriately feminine that women should put others first. They are not meant to be architects of their own destinies, and so it is acceptable for them to be subject to forces beyond their control. Neither are they expected to be independent and self-sufficient. Aubrey Andelin sees independence as "a virtue wherein one is relatively uncontrolled by others." It follows logically that "lack of independence on a man's part suggests a quality of femininity which in a man is decidedly unbecoming."11

Thinking in terms of categories operates primarily in a negative way by establishing what differentiates and separates one social grouping of people from another. Its main purpose is not to facilitate interaction but to account for essential differences in a culture which regards them with uneasiness and suspicion. The tendency to see femininity in terms of negations prompts men and even women to look down upon traits associated with it in whomever these may be manifested. It must be inferior since by definition it repudiates much that is really valued in the most important members of society. There is probably an inevitable tendency on the part of the powerful to scorn traits in those beneath them which they would not approve of in themselves and of those lesser in status to accept such judgments. Still, in traditional contexts such traits are appropriate in those whose roles require them. Individualism suggests with regard to everyone a fundamental alikeness, which categorically defined differences do not completely contradict. Thus it encourages men to disapprove on some level of feminine behavior even in women at the same time that in other ways they support it. Because it is not applicable to everyone, they are tempted to look down upon it on general principles. So are women at least to some degree, for it is hard to be sure that traits which everyone is taught to approve in men have applicability only to that sex. Conceptualizing women as a separate cultural category does not entirely solve this problem. Categorical thinking is a defense against basic human equality, and its essentially reactive character accounts for the often strident quality of the insistence that men/ masculinity and women/ femininity are polar opposites.

In exemplifying their femininity, women are expected to exhibit personal skills and to act in ways that in a male would call his masculinity into question. They are allowed to cry and in other respects freely express their emotions, and touching seems much more "natural" for them. Rarely are physical expressions of closeness between two women seen as immediately suspect because women are not assumed to have to guard their "space," be in control of all situations, and maintain a careful reserve toward other people. On a broader level women are seen as the special custodians of American moral values and domestic institutions. They keep the family together and uphold the various structures in the larger society which insure personal morality, domestic order and social cohesion. Once married and marriageable women arrived in California gold rush towns, it was understood that the days of unregulated masculine individuality were numbered. Settled households, churches and schools began to appear--not in opposition to men's wishes, for they had after all sent for or brought the women, but with their qualified support for the attitudes, values and outlooks which women themselves had cultivated as appropriate to their separate sphere.

Here women's role has been basically a supplementary rather than a complementary one. They represent values considered to be external to the practice of masculine individuality and in a sense independent of it. This prompts a mixed attitude on the part of each sex toward the other. As categorically different beings they exemplify qualities which highlight the difficulty of ever sharing fully with one another a basic likeness of mind. On the other hand, it seems desirable to uphold attitudes and values that either conventional masculinity or femininity does not allow for. This gives society a certain balance and enables each sex on a personal level to share experiences and ways of responding otherwise denied. C. A. Tripp argues that a young man's one-sidedness is very confining and so "to round himself out and thus correct his cultivated masculine eccentricity--that is, to regain much of what he has systematically eliminated from his personality and to savor softness in a hundred ways--he needs the company of women."[12] Women who live vicariously through their men can obviously gain analogous rewards.

Because the supplementary values which women have conventionally upheld are so removed from what is central to masculinity, they have been presented with the difficult challenge of adequately acknowledging the virtues of masculinity and yet also accepting and even taking pride in the very different virtues which underscore their womanliness. Men in turn must be able to honor the elements of femininity without in any way undercutting their own manliness. Not to take such virtues seriously enough is to defeat the very purpose of acknowledging them in the first place. To take them too seriously is to subordinate men and their masculinity to women and their femininity, and this threatens male supremacy as well as independence and self-determination. Putting women on pedestals is probably the easiest way to pay homage without placing femininity on the same level of real importance as masculinity. However the balance is achieved, it requires women's cooperation in the performance of their supplementary role. The practice of masculine individuality restricts men's ability to uphold feminine values just as the practice of femininity denies women the freedom to cultivate masculine values.

   As Peter Stearns has noted, because the nineteenth-century businessman lacked time to extend patriarchal power over all aspects of family life, he depended upon his wife "to provide the family with a sweetness and tenderness that the man felt necessary but beyond his powers to provide."[13] Ann Douglas argues that middle-class women in the Northeast preferred to stress their moral and religious "influence" (as opposed to the exercise of overt power) even though their role as consumers was equally important. In fact, Douglas goes on, "the two roles, saint and consumer, were interlocked and mutually dependent; the lady's function in a capitalist society was to appropriate and preserve both the values and the commodities which her competitive husband, father, and son had little time to honor or enjoy; she was to provide an antidote and a purpose for their labor."[14]

   Carl Degler believes that the conception of domesticity, in assigning a separate sphere of activity to wives, "was an alternative to patriarchy, both in intention and in fact." Men indeed "were quite willing to admit dependence upon their wives." Moreover, they had little objection to women's engaging in all sorts of activities outside the home, such as temperance reform, which were seen as appropriate extensions of their domestic role.[15] From a traditional perspective it could seem as though women's supplementary role had eclipsed their role as subordinates, thus undercutting a man's rightful claim to be master of his own household. Paul Bourget, a French observer, was prompted to wonder how it was possible that American men had "permitted their wives to shake off masculine authority more completely than in any other part of the world."[16] The absence of clearly formulated links between the separate spheres of men and women made such independence possible. Yet American males do not generally seem to have felt there was any real cause for alarm since the barrier between the sexes had not been breached by their wives. The logic of categorization suggests that men did not need to exercise the dominion Bourget had in mind in order to maintain their superiority over women. Assigning them, along with the values associated with them, to a separate sphere guaranteed their lesser importance without the necessity of explicit subordination. They mattered of course, but the influence they had on the more important world of men was necessarily limited.

   As categorical opposites of men, women in the nineteenth century had more maneuvering room in which to live their own lives than they had previously--but only within the limitations that categorization delineated. As Nancy Cott has shown, women came to embrace an ideology of passionlessness in the first half of the century that not only distinguished them collectively from men but also enhanced their "power and self-respect." This ideology functioned "as self-preservation and social advancement for women," and yet at the same time it also had the limitation of "allowing claims of women's moral influence to obfuscate the need for other sources of power."[17] Women who have continued to insist upon the moral superiority and authority of their sex and its values or have held themselves aloof from the ways of the world of men have thereby conceded the reality of sexual inferiority.

Even a man like Henry Adams, who fancied himself a critic of masculine values, in the final analysis accorded them a much greater validity and importance than feminine ones. In The Education of Henry Adams he detailed his lifelong effort to run "order through chaos, direction through space, discipline through freedom, unity through multiplicity." The domain of freedom in Adams' world was the domain of men, especially successful nineteenth-century businessmen, who throve in an environment which imposed few restraints. By contrast the domain of order was most fully exemplified by the Virgin and more generally by all women. Adams' attraction for what the opposite sex represented was matched only in its intensity by a deep suspicion that order, direction and unity are impossible human hopes which knowledge of reality systematically destroys: "Chaos was the law of nature; Order was the dream of man."[18] Ultimately, then, for him the masculine and individualistic values triumphed.

Nowhere in the twentieth century has the dichotomous and consequently separate and unequal distinction between masculinity and femininity been put more to the test than in the working world. Supporters of convention of both sexes have consistently opposed culturally redefining femininity and women's roles despite the actual social changes taking place in women's lives. The jobs which have come to be accepted as appropriate for women in fact relate to their "traditional" occupations, Elizabeth Janeway argues, only in terms of "the expectations projected onto them," not in terms of what women actually do.[19] In growing numbers, moreover, women are working in jobs involving close dealings with men which are not easily seen as simply extensions of the feminine role. Every effort is made to keep the masculine and feminine realms separate and to insure that women's successes do not, as far as possible, exceed men's. "From a man's point of view," Michael Korda notes, "a woman who works is always in some mysterious way less 'womanly' than one who doesn't. . . . The more successful she is, the more unnatural." Women who work are never allowed to forget the importance of not violating their "natural" femininity. This of course limits their opportunities, keeps them out of many positions, and requires all sorts of behaviors that men would find quite intolerable themselves to have to engage in. Men help to insure the femininity of working women by making them, according to Korda, in all sorts of ways "feel uncomfortable, on edge, hu-

58

miliated, powerless."[20]

While women's public roles, particularly in the working world, serve many useful social purposes, their utility from a conventional point of view rests on a clear sense that categorical distinctions remain viable. Where women actively compete with men in the economic arena, mainstream males rely directly on one another for support in maintaining a united front against encroachments which threaten to undermine the barrier between the sexes. In business Korda sees men's power "in direct proportion to their ability to separate women and keep them in dependent positions at arms' length from the workings of the system."[21] Fewer and fewer men nowadays insist on exclusive domesticity for their wives, and more and more of them have to deal with women in work situations when once this was unnecessary. As long as women continue to remain essentially loyal to the basic tenets of femininity, however, masculinity too will remain intact. If categorical differences imply certain restrictions on women's lives, these must be accepted as part of the "natural order." A woman should only want what will enable her to remain true to her basic identity as a sexual being.

Being Invisibly Supportive--

The ambitious individualist would never expect to find tranquility, comfort or emotional closeness in the larger world, but he does expect to find them at home. Here he can enjoy surcease from competition, repose and intimacy with someone whose purpose in life is to make him happy rather than to triumph over him. If categorization emphasizes fundamental differences between the sexes, it does not explicitly rule out the possibility of emotional closeness and likeness of mind. The complete separation of masculine and feminine spheres in the early nineteenth century was accompanied by a withdrawal of women from the quasipublic functions they had earlier performed into the privacy of the home. Here they were only to be concerned with personal services to husbands and children. According to Mary Ryan, in a world otherwise "unstable, impersonal, and rugged" a good wife "soothed the weary male on his return from work, refreshed him, and sent him back to his job with renewed vigor." Ryan notes that in the twentieth century marriage has come to seem increasingly a private arrangement, and women have been encouraged to devote more and more of themselves to learning to deal adequately with the men in their lives.[22]

Joseph Pleck argues that the modern male, in contrast to the traditional male, prefers the company of women. Thus "men now see heterosexual relationships as the only legitimate source of the emotional support they need."[23] Philip Slater suggests that "couples who cannot rely on a stable and supportive external social context must develop a more intimate relationship with each other."[24] Many social analysts have noted a growing emphasis in the twentieth century upon intimacy between men and women, but the importance of women as men's basic source of emotional support was stressed in middle-class contexts in the nineteenth century as well. Individualistic assumptions both prompted people to dichotomize masculinity and femininity and also encouraged less formal personal relationships between men and women than is true in traditional societies. In Nathaniel Hawthorne's novel The Marble Fawn Kenyon insists that "man never derives any intimate help, any heart-sustenance, from his brother man, but from woman."[25] A woman who provided such support was expressing the inherently nurturant qualities that categorization highlighted.

When one looks closely at the writings of contemporary advocates of feminine supportiveness, one cannot help noting how much effort goes into instructing women about their men's adherence to individualism and the importance of never violating its basic criteria. Helen Andelin advises women that a man needs a whole range of personal freedoms, including "the freedom to follow his own interests, to spend his time, money and energy as he sees fit, and in general to be the kind of man he wants to be." Any help a woman gives her husband in solving problems must be subtle and indirect so that he is not made to feel "ineffectual and incomplete as a man." Indeed one's husband must be "Number One" in one's life, which means also making "his interests, desires and responsibilities Number One."[26] Marie Robinson insists that the loved one becomes for a woman as important as herself, and she "makes understanding of him one of her most important activities." Though a woman may make sexual overtures, she must immediately "change her amorous direction" if she finds her husband preoccupied or too tired. He must never be made to feel sexually inadequate to her needs.[27]

Superficially these writers appear to be endorsing a traditional conception of female submissiveness. As an individualist, however, the American male has a greater need to be in control than to control and hence to feel that he is free to do what he wishes. The art of truly feminine supportiveness is to understand and accept such a male and to harmonize one's relating to him so perfectly that he will have no sense of a will contrary to his own. "Your husband needs you to see him as he sees himself," Marabel Morgan advises women. Her ideal "Total Woman" allows her husband "that priceless luxury of unqualified acceptance." Because traditional expectations and practices still persist, dominance and submission still exist to some degree in most relationships. The basic logic of individualism, however, calls not for a man to exercise conscious dominion over even an obedient woman, whose will is understood to be at least in some measure different from his own, but to share a relationship with someone whose will always harmonizes with his own.

Masculinity requires the freedom to lead one's own life, and a man who must rule over his wife is not free to devote his energies to his own purposes, however great the power he may exercise. Psychologically considered, insofar as a man is guided by individualistic assumptions, he does not rest his masculinity on the conscious exercise of power over his wife. A perfect wife sees to it that situations never arise in which her husband feels obliged to constrain her will to meet his own needs and desires. Morgan advises women: "Your husband wants you to want him sexually. He wants you to enjoy lovemaking as much as he does. If you fail in this arena, he is devastated."[28]

The relationship I am describing is a voluntary one, not a traditional one where authority and obedience are the basic modes of interrelating two people of different statuses. A traditional relationship does not suppose the harmony of wills that a voluntary one does. Obedience is primarily what is expected of the person of subordinate status, and this means essentially an outward conformity to what is required. It is sufficient that a woman do what she is supposed to do to please her husband and fulfill her duties, not that she desire only what her husband desires. By contrast, individualism above all calls for willing cooperation. I suggested earlier that to be an accomplished lover is thought not to be especially masculine in America. The reason is that employing arts of seduction does not fit a model of voluntarism. Women are socialized to facilitate men's individuality, and their femininity is evidenced by their willingness voluntarily to subordinate their wills to the wills of men. Morgan insists that "the conflict between two separate egos" in a marriage is the cause of "most of the problems." Unless a woman adapts to her husband's way of life, "there's no way to avoid the conflict that is certain to occur."[29] Accordingly Clyde W. Franklin maintains that "men are attracted to women to the extent that women's attitudes and values are in agreement with theirs regarding a man's 'place' and a woman's 'place' in society."[30]

Willingness on a woman's part satisfies both patriarchal needs insofar as male authority is acknowledged and individualistic ones in that the relationship is voluntary as well as supportive. For most contemporary mainstream males the latter needs have a higher priority. They prefer to see relationships with women in terms which have less to do simply with the performance of expected duties than with harmony of wills and voluntarily expressed concern for their well-being. Only when these are lacking is assertion of traditional prerogatives likely to come to the fore. Coercion might produce results, but it robs the male of the individualistic satisfactions that voluntarism--or at least the appearance of voluntarism--affords. Still, if necessary arbitrary authority can probably be invoked. As Peter Stearns observes, many men feel "that mutual-

61

ity is fine as a method of consensus but that in disagreement their will should logically prevail."[31]

Men who see themselves as free to govern their lives on their own terms must depend both on their wives' willing supportiveness and on a competency in the management of households and children which does not require much attention from them. Women are expected to be able to function independently within their sphere, and as wives, mothers and housekeepers their reputations rest on their ability and willingness to do so. Nurturance and nesting are "naturally" a part of their identity as categorical opposites of men. It is conventionally supposed that they need love and intimate relationships more than men do, and indeed cultural expectations regarding femininity dictate that women should invest more of themselves in domestic relationships. Contemporary observers frequently lament the husband's basic irrelevance as far as household affairs and child rearing are concerned. Some men seem to have become more involved in various ways over the last several decades. Still, as Stearns notes, "many a father asserts that he fully shares childrearing with his wife" even though neither the amount of time spent nor the child's sense of the situation justifies such an assertion.[32] If for the most part Americans take minimal male and maximal female involvement at home for granted, it is because both are so closely linked with the affirmation of fundamentally individualistic goals (for men).

When Tocqueville talked of individualism in America, what he had in mind was a society of individualistic males and their dependents. In the case of a frontier settler in Michigan, he noted, "family sentiments have come to fuse themselves in a vast egoism, and it is doubtful if in his wife and children he sees anything else than a detached portion of himself."[33] A similar analysis of the male-female relationship in marriage was later made by William Dean Howells. "When a man is married," he noted, "his wife almost ceases to be exterior to his consciousness; she afflicts or consoles him like a condition of health or sickness; she is literally part of him in a spiritual sense, even when he is rather indifferent to her."[34] In such a context the woman is really an extension of the male's ego, and his freedom demands that she be the one who makes all the daily adjustments that a relationship demands. Evan Connell's Mr. Bridge keeps a picture of his family on his desk. It is placed "so that it never interfered with his work but at the same time he could see the family as often as he liked." His family seems a mysterious accomplishment to him toward which he has contributed little, and his wife complains: "Half the time you don't know if I'm dead or alive."[35]

Here lies women's essential invisibility. The more fully they conform to the demands of masculine individuality, the less they have to be reckoned with. Helen Andelin suggests that "a woman need not be well educated or possess high intelligence to follow a clever man's discourse. In his pleasure at having himself admired, the man seldom notices that his conversation is not understood."[36] Clearly Andelin assumes that the male is relating essentially to himself, and so as a <u>person</u> the woman to whom he is talking is quite definitely invisible. The fact that the needs of masculine individuality are most fully met by a woman who is competent to handle everything that is expected of her maximizes her invisibility and frees the male most completely to attend to his own ambitions and concerns. Women may remain as beautiful objects or as capable partners, mothers and household managers, but especially within the twentieth century they have come to be seen as persons primarily dedicated to satisfying the emotional needs of their men. This places a premium upon self-effacement and affords little in the way of independent sources of satisfaction.

At least the appearance of intimacy and mutuality (and perhaps even something of the substance) can be maintained so long as the invisible person conforms to expectations, or in other words, remains invisible. Annoyance or hostility only results when the male is forced to deal with behavior which does not conform to expectations. Such situations call into question the compatibility of marriage and individualism, and American males are not disposed to accept this willingly.

Women as Individualists--

At the heart of the teachings about true womanhood lies the recognition that femininity is a way of acting which one must learn with some care in order to create effects that others (particularly males) expect. First and foremost women must always be the opposite of men. "Femininity is acquired by <u>accentuating the differences between yourself and men</u>, not the similarities," Andelin advises.[37] Clearly women must be aware of similarities and yet be willing to submerge them in deference to categorical expectations. Robinson's book is filled with worried criticisms of "clitoral" women, her metaphor for women who have wills and desires of their own. The vaginally centered woman, by contrast, is both literally and figuratively a person who surrenders herself to what men want. Robinson's thesis is a masterful tour de force in arguing that sexual surrender is both innately feminine and takes considerable effort to learn. Certainly men can be beguiled into accepting the results as genuine, for they have a strong investment in seeing femininity in "natural" and hence categorical terms. As both Andelin and Robinson make clear, understanding femininity in terms of artifice coexists with women's commitment to categorical thinking, thus making them much more self-conscious about their sex-related identities and sex roles than men are.

63

Femininity requires that women appear physically fragile and helpless in many respects. Andelin carefully advises them to "dispense with any air of strength and ability, of competence and fearlessness, and acquire instead an attitude of frail dependency upon men to take care of you." A man cannot be expected to take care of someone who can clearly take care of herself. A woman has to be both competent and dependent, and Andelin warns that while women need masculine protection in some areas, they must not expect men to rescue them from tasks at home that are clearly feminine.[38] Thus competence applies to feminine activities, weakness to activities that are masculine and should be performed by males.

The distinction between feminine strength and weakness is clear enough in terms of categorically defined expectations, but in practice the balance can tip in either direction. As long-- but only as long--as a woman adequately exemplifies her femininity in such ways as subordinating her own to the needs and wishes of her husband and family, a fair degree of competency and even self-sufficiency will not be seen as inconsistent traits. Conversely, weakness, incapacity and frailty carried to extremes go along with indirection and manipulation and are aimed at accomplishing the woman's will rather than the man's. Ironically for women who do not consciously seek to challenge feminine expectations, being weak and helpless indicates a certain strength and determination. Andelin insists, however, that with all a woman's helplessness and dependency, men would like the assurance "that she has somewhere hidden within her the ability to meet an emergency."[39] If when necessary she responds with support and strength, playing weak at other times to gain her own limited ends can be indulgently tolerated.

Whether in non-supportive ways a woman is too strong or too weak, she is expressing her own individuality in ways that contradict categorically defined expectations, and it seems that this is all too common a "failing" among American women. The advice and entreaties of the advocates of conventional femininity carry with them the unmistakable acknowledgement that even women who basically subscribe to mainstream role expectations are often unsuccessful in fully conforming to the wants and ways of their men. Probably relatively few men are "fortunate" enough to have completely invisible wives, but all men are taught to desire them. If they have to settle for less, they may become "distant and preoccupied" as Morgan suggests was the case with her husband before she changed herself into a "Total Woman."[40] The happy results which both she and Andelin promise from a return to invisibility on a woman's part suggest that such behavior fulfills very profound male needs. The average woman probably manages at least much of the time to approximate the conventional model of femininity. Otherwise she pays a high price in feelings of guilt and often in criticism from others.

Under such circumstances a man will endeavor to make the best of things since his wife basically agrees with his view of femininity even though she may not always live up to it.

Still, one cannot help supposing that there is a side of most men that responds with sympathy and interest to women who do come across as individuals in their own right, just as there is a side of most women that must find this alternative appealing. Nineteenth-century literature has many examples of such women, the intriguing brunettes whom conventional males find fascinating though in the end they marry the more ordinary blondes. The brunettes come to unfortunate ends generally. If the independent and individualistic woman is not to suffer such a fate, she must willingly surrender to convention. In the latter part of the century there was a particular interest in the American Girl, who exemplified many of the values prized by devotees of individualism. Like the tomboy she may not fully have conformed to role expectations, but she could hardly be blamed for emulating so central an American value, at least for a time--but only for a time--before settling into marriage.

William Dean Howells' novel A Chance Acquaintance describes one man's ultimately unsatisfactory encounter with such a young woman. Arburton is fascinated by Kitty and yet cannot really accept her as she is. Kitty has "a certain self-reliance" and from her uncle she has learned her democratic way of relating to people. Eventually we find Arburton "unconsciously speaking, as by authority, for both." In proposing marriage "he seemed to think that he had only to ask as a matter of form." In time Kitty consents but soon realizes that she cannot alter herself to be what he wants, and he cannot change either. "Perhaps you would try," she says to him, "and I know that I would, but it would be a wretched failure and disappointment as long as we lived."[41] She will not surrender her own individuality to become a "maturely feminine" conventional wife to him, nor will she try through indirection and manipulation to bend his will to hers.

Long before Howells' time Tocqueville commented on the freedom and individuality of unmarried girls in America. However, he also noted how fully and yet willingly (apparently) women surrendered this freedom in marriage "without struggle or complaint." They "seem to take pride in the free relinquishment of their will, and it is their boast to bear the yoke themselves rather than to escape from it." Under such circumstances it is not surprising that men "constantly display complete confidence in their spouses' judgment and deep respect for their freedom."[42] A woman who has voluntarily transformed herself into an ideal wife can be treated in certain respects thereafter as an individual because her individuality expresses itself in categorically appropriate ways. Thus women presumably act as they must in response to their deepest instincts and thereby willingly play out the role for which "nature" has destined them. Early in this century Charles Horton Cooley boasted that while European societies rule women by convention and coercive laws and even, among the lower classes, by blows, "Americans have almost wholly foregone these extrinsic aids, aiming at a higher or voluntary discipline."[43] To be truly feminine, however, women's desires must correspond with men's wishes and needs. Cooley's use of the term "discipline" was therefore appropriate.

Willing femininity leaves open the question as to whether individualism has much practical applicability to the lives of conventional women. Writing in 1959, David Potter argued that the American woman is "more of an individualist than women in traditional societies," but "she is by no means as whole-heartedly individualistic as the American male." He went on to cite a recent study which showed that "she still hesitates to claim individualism as a quality of her own."[44] Elizabeth Janeway maintains that in contemporary America only a few roles "carry with them as large an aura of expectations-to-be-met and norms-to-be-compared-with as ascribed roles did in the past." Woman's role is one of them, and "looked at from this point of view, is archaic." It "puts her at odds not only with the American ethos, but with the whole long trend of Western civilization toward individual freedom and individual responsibility."[45]

Carl Degler, on the other hand, finds that "the extension of individualism to women--the awakening to self--" lies at the root of the history of the family since the early nineteenth century. Thus "as women became more conscious of themselves as individuals, they also sought to control their fertility." This and other nineteenth-century manifestations of individualism that Degler describes occurred within women's separate sphere of activity, and he does not suggest that they were acting in ways inconsistent with their loyalty to their husbands and children. Unlike such activities as temperance, which were "other-serving," the suffrage was long opposed by the majority of women precisely because of its "individualistic or admittedly 'self-serving' aspect." Anti-suffrage arguments were based on "the fundamental assumption that the natures of women and men were different." Only feminists disputed the doctrine of separate spheres, and their statements clearly reflect the judgment that most American women were not truly individualists. In 1851 one wrote: "Would that women would learn to recognize their own individuality--their singleness of thought." Besides assuming that men and women are fundamentally different, categorical thinking also endorses the belief that women's femininity cannot meaningfully be separated from their marital roles. Thus Degler's conclusion that "philosophically and practically the family and women's individuality are difficult to reconcile" in important respects qualifies his thesis.[46]

Since the early nineteenth century categorical assumptions have theoretically accommodated individualistic and egalitarian views. Women are conventionally regarded as different from men rather than unequal to them, and within innately fixed limits they are granted the freedom to be self-determining individuals. While equality has always been an illusive goal, the general acceptance of the idea of separate spheres in the nineteenth century did give them a good deal of space of their own. The incorporation of American society, to use Alan Trachtenberg's term, has since then steadily extended various forms of institutionalized control over women's lives and thus limited their autonomy even though woman's separate sphere still retains considerable appeal as a cultural ideal. This has been true with respect to women's functions especially as mothers and housekeepers as sources of power and influence outside the home have increasingly impinged upon these activities.[47] Moreover, as Janet Saltzman Chafetz points out, "as virtually all semiprofessional and professional fields become more bureaucratic and 'scientific,' the few 'havens' for ambitious women that existed in such traditionally female occupations as library science, social work, nursing, and public school teaching are being taken over at the top levels by males."[48]

As long as women are seen and most see themselves as profoundly different from men, their individuality is circumscribed by the conventional insistence that their behavior must always exemplify this difference. There is, consequently, no easy way for them to function as beings who are wholly distinctive and subordinate in a society which assumes that likeness of mind and equality are the most acceptable bases of human interaction. Shulamith Firestone postulates that "a man must idealize one woman over the rest in order to justify his descent to a lower caste." A specific woman is thus singled out and viewed as a special and unique person though in fact she remains hidden (and therefore invisible) behind the male's idealization of her. Firestone also maintains that as far as women in general are concerned, the total separation of the sexes "encourages men to see women as 'dolls' differentiated only by superficial attributes--not of the same species as themselves." The standards of beauty encourage all women to look alike, and yet they are allowed "to achieve individuality only through their appearance." Thus "because social recognition is granted only for a false individuality," women in Firestone's opinion "are kept from developing the tough individuality that would enable breaking through such a ruse." Firestone's own individualistic presuppositions come out in her observation that "love demands a mutual vulnerability or it turns destructive: the destructive effects of love occur only in a context of inequality."[49]

For the most part, however, convention accepts only the kind of equality that categorization prescribes. Long ago John

Stuart Mill argued that women's "disabilities elsewhere are only clung to in order to maintain their subordination in domestic life; because the generality of the male sex cannot yet tolerate the idea of living with an equal."[50] Much more recently Michael Korda has suggested that "at heart, to the male chauvinist, every woman is his wife."[51] So it is that all paths lead back to marriage as the standard for defining true womanliness. One does not fully understand the feminine ideal in America unless one appreciates the kind of subordination that men's individualistic assumptions dictate. It must be self-effacing and willing on the part of people whose categorically based differences do not deprive them of claims to individuality and equality within appropriate limits. The mainstream conception of marriage does not permit a relationship of true equals though it must be freely and equally entered into. As a willing subordinate a faithful wife underscores her husband's freedom and loyalty to individualism and can do much to make his success in life possible. Masculinity asks for no more though it may settle for less.

Women's Power--

Because there has always been uneasiness about women's willingness to remain satisfied with their status as categorical opposites of men, the reliance upon external constraints has been greater for the former than for the latter. Externally reinforced categorical differences dovetail with the greater emphasis as well upon traditional elements. Many men over the years, moreover, have sought to dissuade women from pushing the logic of individualism beyond its proper bounds. In his novel The Sea Lions James Fenimore Cooper called upon nineteenth-century women to realize that their "real power and influence with men arises from their seeming dependence" and to condemn those "who are for proclaiming their independence and their right to equality in all things."[52] In our own day George Gilder has maintained that women "possess enormous power over men." He sees the most basic processes of civilization as "the subordination of male sexual impulses and psychology to long-term horizons of female biology." Men's sexuality is amorphous and unlike female sexuality lacks the kind of focus that naturally contributes to the furtherance of civilization. Compensating roles in the form of economic responsibility for wives and families are necessary, for without these men "disrupt the community, or leave it." If a woman understands "her enormous innate power over the man, his psychological dependence on her, and his need to compensate with external achievement," she will not assume that she should have "an equivalent career" for herself.[53] Men must remain outwardly in control of society, yet Gilder does not call on them to discipline and subordinate potentially unwilling women. Instead he seeks to persuade women to remain as voluntary guardians of the values of home, social order and civilization.

While individualistic loyalties among women may be circumscribed by their femininity, it is possible for them to take advantage of the traits they are encouraged to cultivate in ways which promise them status, security and above all personal power. Women know that men are highly dependent on them for the emotional support they offer and that men cannot readily compel or easily ask for this support without undercutting important elements of their masculinity. While this gives a woman no power in the larger world, it does give her enormous power within an intimate relationship. She can wound a man's masculinity precisely because it depends so much on her willing cooperation and so little on compulsion. Gilder considers the home as the place "where we express our individuality." In courtship a man offers this individuality to a woman, and "in his entire adult life, it may be only his wife who receives him as a whole human being."[54]

As Cooper and Gilder imply, the price for the rewards of femininity is to forsake any claims to genuine freedom and self-determination. Elizabeth Janeway argues that women cling to their "traditional" role primarily "because this role offers them power too: private power in return for public submission."[55] Many women seem to have found such terms tolerable, especially since these are compatible with categorically defined identities. American men have long encouraged women to take advantage of the power they possess by relegating them largely to a world in which personal power still matters very much. One can hardly expect women to have ignored its possibilities.

Overview--

Marriage in America defines a woman's life practically and symbolically to a much greater degree than it does a man's. As a formal institution it potentially inhibits the expression of masculine individuality but is seen as the most appropriate context for the expression of femininity. The larger element of traditionalism in the way the latter is conceived explains this difference as well as the greater reliance upon external controls to insure appropriate behavior on women's parts. From a traditional perspective anatomy is social destiny in that sex-related differences are understood to be culturally defined and socially governed. The early Puritans adhered to such a viewpoint, but by the end of the eighteenth century an individualistic questioning of social barriers to self-determination had led to a major cultural shift in how women were conceived. They were not granted the freedom to challenge sex-related social restrictions. Instead womanliness was seen as part of their very natures. All women were assumed to constitute a single culturally defined category which rested on a "natural" and therefore immutable distinction between men and women. Each sex was assigned its own separate sphere, which women as well as men accepted as part of the "natural" order of things. The categorical conception of womanhood reinforced many traditional elements, but it relied ultimately upon the authority of "nature" to underscore the view that women are not free to structure their lives independently of men's wishes.

While traditional thinking stresses the complementarity of the sexes, categorical thinking points away from such an emphasis upon balance and reciprocity. Many feminine traits are seen as negations of masculine ones, and this results in the practical inferiority of the former and the superiority of the latter. In many other respects feminine values and the female role are thought of as supplementary to masculine values and the male role. Women uphold many useful values that are external to the practice of masculine individuality, and their activities within their own sphere buttress those of their men. Truly feminine women are assumed to want to adhere to the distinctions and role expectations that categorization sets forth, not only in their domestic lives but also in their work lives outside the home.

While categorization emphasizes differences between the sexes, it does not explicitly rule out emotional closeness. Such closeness has been especially stressed in the twentieth century and linked with women's emotionally supportive function. Women are expected to relate to their men in ways that maximize the expression of masculine individuality and minimize men's awareness of a will contrary to their own. This emphasizes the voluntary nature of male-female relations and harmonizes much more fully with individualistic expectations than an emphasis upon coercive male dominance. Individualistic males indeed depend upon the emotional supportiveness of their wives and upon a competence in feminine tasks that leaves them free to concern themselves with the larger world. Women who conform to these expectations are essentially invisible and are likely to be noted mostly for their shortcomings rather than their accomplishments.

Because femininity is understood in terms of artifice as well as naturalness, women are much more self-conscious than men about their roles and the sex-related expectations that govern their lives. The ideal woman is neither too weak and helpless nor too strong and determined, for both extremes undercut invisible supportiveness. Still, both sexes have long been intrigued by women who exhibit a commitment to individualism in their lives. A separate woman's sphere in the nineteenth century gave women a good deal of scope for self-determination, which the incorporation of American society in the twentieth century has increasingly constricted. All along, however, categorization has confined the expression of women's individuality to what is considered appropriately feminine behavior. To guarantee such behavior men have relied on outward pressures as well as upon persuasion to circumscribe women's lives. In return for giving up personal freedom and self-determination conventional women have settled for personal power, which men's own individualistic commitments have in fact encouraged.

PART II

ON THE MARGINS

CHAPTER FOUR

HYPERMASCULINITY: THE QUEST FOR INVULNERABILITY

Each man himself knows if he fails to measure up in important ways to the requirements of the masculine code which assumes the categorical alikeness of all American men. By his own admission Philip Roth's Alexander Portnoy is such a male. The fact that he is not part of the American mainstream is both a source of constant anguish to him and an excuse for his masculine inadequacies. Portnoy believes that his family situation differs dramatically from the gentile norm, and he marvels at the "mix-up of the sexes" in his household. While his father has served the family in a "ferocious and self-annihilating way," his mother is domineering and able to "accomplish anything." He feels tied to his family even as an adult, and he believes his parents filled him with timidity rather than courage. Thus he has not developed the individuality and independence that masculinity in America is supposed to include. As a young man Portnoy had been consumed with admiration for blonde gentile girls and their "engaging, good-natured, confident, clean, swift, and powerful" athletic brothers, all of whom "are the Americans." His masculinity is largely given over to a futile attempt to be a part of the gentile world and thereby to have the presumed self-confidence of its males. He tells his psychiatrist that his compulsive sexual pursuit of gentile women really involves not so much them as their backgrounds, as if through sex he will "conquer America." "Bless me with manhood," he pleads.[1]

As far as deviant styles of masculinity in America are concerned, the range of possibilities is vast. All of these, however, are to be distinguished from another class of variations common in our literature. Here what sets men apart is their special interpretation of the mainstream masculine code and the implications of the dichotomy between masculinity and femininity. A complex balance of tensions tends to be replaced by selective and exaggerated ways of thinking and behaving. The result is a kind of marginality which nevertheless does not make the individual clearly an outsider.

The Hypermasculine Style--

Sometimes it is a quality of heightened anxiety as well as exaggeration that signifies a position at least on the fringes of conventional masculinity. William Reynolds' The American Father paints a picture of a male whose ambitious pursuit of success constantly involves him with a world "infested with competitors who do not wish you well and who are hoping to profit from your mistakes." He is almost exclusively preoccupied in his private life with possessing his wife, completely dominating her life, owning her in essence. Because he is "jealous of and competitive with" absolutely anything that suggests she is not totally concerned with him, he thinks mostly in terms of power and control. In his fantasies "incessant dominance-of-women themes vary with submission-to-women ones."[2] Dominance and submission in his world highlight an anxious need to maintain control over or completely surrender control to a totally different being. With few resources beyond himself to guarantee the submissiveness that is consciously desired, the quest for power can easily lead to feelings of powerlessness.

The male characters in Jack Kerouac's On the Road are completely caught up in a worship of freedom and mobility directly tied to the technology of the automobile. In all sorts of ways Dean Moriarty, the central figure of the novel, both embodies and exaggerates the basic elements of mainstream masculinity. He and Sal Paradise, the narrator, get "along fine--no pestering, no catering," and they eventually decide to be "buddies till we died." When Dean leaves Sal sick in bed in Mexico City, Sal considers him a "rat" but understands he has "to get on with his wives and woes."[3] Dean's preoccupation with himself and his own concerns carries an emphasis upon individualism to extremes, which Sal both admires and dislikes.

The attitude of these men toward women highlights their ambivalence concerning conventional values and expectations. Both idealize women as a refuge from the turbulent pursuit of personal aims, and both look forward to settled family lives. Sal hopes that some day the two of them and their families will live on the same street. These highly conventional expectations hardly accord with the reality of short affairs and broken relationships in which neither man seems to be able to find the kind of acquiescence and supportiveness in a woman that American males are encouraged to expect. Sal knows one affair is over when he realizes that the woman wants him "to be her way" and does not really understand him. Dean advises him to find someone "and cultivate her and make her mind your soul as I have tried so hard with these damned women of mine."[4] Hence for these two, women are not invisible and thus to be taken for granted. They are both frankly pursued and yet regarded with exaggerated uneasiness and suspicion.

The complete loyalty of both men to their own freedom and personal goals to the virtual exclusion of significant bonds with other males increases the importance of voluntary support from women at the same time that it prompts them to offer almost nothing in return. Hence the women's very real resentments. One of the says angrily to Dean: "You have absolutely no regard for anybody but yourself and your damned kicks."[5] Mutual disappointment and unfulfilled expectations cause the men to respond with hostility and uneasiness, frequent withdrawal of affection, and a strong emphasis upon women as sexual objects. At the same time their assertion of dominance has little in the way of larger social supports or material success to back it up. Though Reynolds' typical "Father" seems worlds apart from Kerouac's males in his devotion to marriage and success, the exaggerated need for attention and supportiveness from women is very similar. So also is the suspiciousness and eagerness to dominate and control them.

The masculine styles of these men exaggerate certain fundamental elements of the mainstream American code of manliness as well as its basic connection with individualism. In their different ways they form a link between everyday masculinity and a class of marginal figures who frequent the works of Cooper through London to Mailer and Kesey. All are males whose ties to institutionalized power and bonds with other males are very tenuous and who see in the external world a variety of threats to their freedom to be self-determining individuals. They are not concerned with power that is remote and cooperatively based. Instead what fascinates them is power which seems to depend on no one but the wielder of it. All, moreover, are inclined to fix upon the masculine/feminine dichotomy and to assume that relationships, however compelling, with total opposites are fraught with difficulties and dangers. All, therefore, embrace a style of masculinity which may be labeled hypermasculine because it exaggerates such aspects of conventional masculinity as competitiveness, aloneness, misogyny, dominance and control.

A typical early example is James Fenimore Cooper's Byronic hero "Skimmer of the Seas." A "free trader" or privateer who operates outside the bounds of conventional society, he stands in marked contrast to Captain Ludlow, whose authority is based on his acquired position within a formally organized social hierarchy. When Skimmer and his men aid Ludlow in battle, "it was the mind of the free-trader that controlled."[6] This approach to power carries the individualistic rejection of formalized social ties to its extreme. In the absence of impersonal cooperativeness personal magnetism, mental acuity or physical strength enable the loner to exercise power successfully. When the "Red Rover," a similar Cooper figure, speaks to a "crowd of fierce and excited spirits, there was not one so bold as to presume to brave his anger."[7]

Ken Kesey's Randall McMurphy in One Flew Over the Cuckoo's Nest pits his own personal power against the institutional power of the Big Nurse and the "Combine" she serves. As a woman she is appropriately willing to subordinate her own individuality and that of others to the demands of the "system" while McMurphy champions masculine freedom and independence. He makes it immediately clear to his fellow inmates that he is "accustomed to being top man." McMurphy's rebellious stance is only possible because he resolutely remains outside the world of middle-class constraints and obligations.[8] Lou Colfax in John Knowles' The Paragon steals rather than checks out a book from the school library because he "did not want to make that concession to regulation, restriction, order."[9] In the case of both men rebellion against power and authority wielded by others is the mirror image of a passion for domination.

"Desire for mastery was strong" in Jack London's Elam Harnish, nicknamed "Burning Daylight," "and it was all one whether wrestling with the elements themselves, with men, or with luck in a gambling game." At one time he contemplates exploiting the gold reserves of the Eldorado Creek basin in Alaska by washing away vast quantities of rock and dirt with high-pressure hoses and then dredging the creek bed in a brutal as well as massive attempt to subjugate nature.[10] Theodore Roosevelt, a contemporary of London's, embraced a similar ethic of exaggerated masculinity. "Manly" and "masterful" were two of the most common words in his writings, and according to Richard Hofstadter, "reflect a persistent desire to impose himself upon others."[11] Daylight believes strongly in his own luck, but this very belief is evidence of his sense that he is not really in control of the world around him. He pits himself directly against the Alaskan environment in feats of incredible endurance and wins, but there is no doubt as to which of the combatants is actually the more powerful in London's estimation.

Hypermasculine males in fact evidence a very strong fear of powerlessness, of losing control over their own lives. McMurphy says he has seen "ball-cutters" everywhere--"people who try to make you weak so they can get you to tow the line."[12] The fact that mastery is very likely to be precarious is directly related to the fascination with total power. Lou Colfax talks excitedly about diverting the Gulf Stream and learning to cultivate, fertilize and harvest the sea. At the same time he is enthralled by the "uniqueness, strangeness, beauty, power, vitality, uncontrollability" of a breaking surf and sees in a volcano "the ultimate, uncontrollable force on earth."[13] Thus absolute power fades into powerlessness for the male who would completely dominate the world around him.

Most forms of mastery cannot truly be realized without effectively dealing with other people. When Daylight becomes a financier and speculator, he forms alliances which are "purely affairs of expediency," and he "regarded his allies as men who would give him the double-cross or ruin him if a profitable chance presented" itself. His competitive involvements with other men, unlike his impersonal--though no less competitive-- battles with nature, make him hard and leave him with "faith only in himself." His first visit to the Sonoma Valley puts him in touch with those forces of nature which will ultimately redeem him. Significantly, a man who has left civilization to live there warns him: "The lust for power! It's a dreadful affliction."[14]

London links the world of nature here in California with that of Alaska, where Daylight first proved his masculinity. When he finally moves to the Sonoma Valley, he still has "work to perform, forces to combat, obstacles to overcome," and he proudly regains his athletic prowess and ability to best other men in tests of physical strength.[15] The personal exercise of power over nature and other men thus remains legitimate for London. Yet all along being a loner limits the power Daylight is able to wield. Unlike conventionally successful men he is basically unwilling to tolerate restrictions on his freedom in order to enhance his capacities for control. Indeed hypermasculine males are distinguished by an allegiance to complete freedom and self-determination that makes them extremely wary of other males as allies and of organized society in all its aspects. This is why their preoccupation with power is inherently so frustrating. The greater their insistence on complete self-determination the more powerless in a full sense they are, which only makes them want power all the more.

Initially Daylight is convinced that spontaneous involvements are only possible with other men. "Men and women," he reasons, "pursued each other, and one must needs bend the other to his will or hers." By contrast male comradeship implies no servitude: "It was a business proposition, a square deal between men who did not pursue each other, but who shared the risks of trail and river and mountain in the pursuit of life and treasure."[16] This idealization of relationships among men masks a hyper-competitiveness which allows for little in the way of male bonding and undercuts a categorically based identification with men in general. The power he seeks, however, aims at inducing other males freely to acknowledge his superiority. He has no real interest in dominating them through institutional means. His avoidance of marriage indicates that he believes it to be more than an impersonal business proposition. Unlike the conventional male, he is convinced that women want power and control in relationships as much as men do. Thus there will always be a contest of wills in which the male struggles for control-- not because it is socially appropriate that men rule over women, but because he needs to keep from being controlled in order to remain free to live his own life. Ironically beneath the sense that women are totally different from men lurks a respect for them as worthy adversaries and hence as possible equals.

There comes a time when Daylight no longer wants to remain aloof from women. His first inclination is to be boldly dominant since he is "used to forcing issues." Still, women are such "fluttery creatures" he is afraid that here "mere mastery

79

would prove a bungle." He courts Dede Mason with a surprising amount of sensitivity and candidly discusses with her his lack of expertise in matters of love. She appreciates his behavior toward her and yet also recognizes that "under his simplicity and boyishness he was essentially a dominant, male creature." He assumes the role of protector toward the woman he regards as a "comrade and playfellow and joyfellow." Once they are married "he lived his man's life just as she lived her woman's life. There was proper division of labor between them according to sex in the work they individually performed."[17] At times he comes close to treating her as an equal though at other times the old need for male dominance surfaces.

Other hypermasculine males are similarly reluctant to forfeit dominance, and yet the conventionally submissive female seems mostly to lack appeal. Early in their stormy relationship Charlotte Mills insists that she is very domestic at heart while Lou Colfax prefers to think of her as an aggressive actress with a strong drive fueled by "lots of male hormones." When she returns to town as a success in her career, Lou finds her "newly erotic and lovable" and also "newly challenging and distant."[18] What is intriguing about Lou is his need to dominate a woman who seems to resist his assertion of power over her. Hypermasculine males do not generally ally themselves with women who can be expected to fulfill their wifely and motherly duties with apparent willingness and solicitude. McMurphy has no lack of sexually accommodating female contacts, but they do not greatly preoccupy him. He has a strong interest in promoting his friend Billy's sexual assertiveness, just as he has in fostering the masculinity of the other inmates. To accomplish this he has to defeat the Big Nurse, the least accommodating female imaginable. Although he is ultimately defeated, there is a glory in his resistance to her and what she represents that makes her by far the most interesting and challenging woman in his life.

Norman Mailer's excessively masculine heroes come close to parodying the hypermasculine style. Mailer is perfectly candid about the fears and anxieties that lie behind his need totally to dominate women, and for him too women must be worthy adversaries.[19] In An American Dream Stephen Rojack's wife Deborah is a strong and passionate woman, whose voice could be "a master work of treachery" and who never really submits to her husband. During their last encounter she torments him with details of her infidelities, and when they fight she "tried to find my root and mangle me." His need for complete domination causes him to kill her; for, as he later speculates drunkenly, "women must murder us unless we possess them altogether." His next lover Cherry is acquiescent and supportive and utterly carried away by his sexual prowess, but Rojack remains uneasy about "the judgment which must rest behind the womb of a woman."[20] Her untimely death ends the possibility of some fuller relationship. However fervently Rojack may wish to be worthy of her, he is clearly more himself in situations which bring out his passion for dominance and power and allow him to express his misogynic inclinations freely.

Hypermasculine males want to be the sole recipients of a willing supportiveness which, however, they feel women can seldom be trusted to provide. As a consequence they seem to be filled with fear, anger and hatred which, as Kate Millett has suggested, can only be assuaged by (at least the fantasy of) violent acts of domination which render women wholly passive to their wills. Being "fortunate" in his choice of a woman to share his life, Burning Daylight centers his desires for domination on nature while Rojack conquers and even destroys the women who threaten his masculinity.

Hypermasculine males first became prominent in American literature at about the time when the pre-modern order had given way to one based essentially on individualistic values. These linked each man to the larger society through shifting hierarchies of power and attainment which in theory still left him free to direct the course of his own life. Social connections were buttressed by the sense of alikeness with other males which categorical thinking fostered. Assigning women to a separate social grouping facilitated their subordination to men and yet permitted apparently free and voluntary relationships between the sexes--as long as the masculine/feminine dichotomy was not pushed to its logical extremes.

For hypermasculine males an anxious and thoroughgoing dedication to individualism means that one must look solely to oneself for protection and support in a world in which dangers and competitive opportunities seem inevitably to go together. Ties with other equally competitive males are highly tenuous and seem to occur only as a temporary consequence of charismatic domination within specific contexts. Because social structures seem so threatening, compromising oneself through impersonal involvements must be strenuously avoided. There is relatively little sense that all men constitute a social grouping and thus share a collective identity as males. This is also true of assumptions regarding women. A disposition to take seriously masculinity and femininity as polar opposites is not matched by an acceptance of the ways in which categorization translates socially into practices and institutions which facilitate collective male supremacy. Hence each man is left alone to deal with women on a very personal and consequently (he fears) disadvantageous basis.

The Search for Freedom and Power--

The American West has derived much of its contemporary appeal from the widespread assumption that freedom and economic opportunity abounded there. As G. J. Barker-Benfield notes, the arena "for the ambitions of the American male imagination was divided between the free, exploitable resources of the West and the seas, and the obligations of heterosexual settlement."[21]   In contrast generally to colonial America, the West in the nineteenth century was a place where opportunities seemed not to depend very much on cooperative efforts with other people. This view exaggerated the aloneness of the individual and had little to do with such forms of social interaction as business enterprises and towns. Yet these came in time, along with churches, schools, wives and families. Thus eventually the "obligations of heterosexual settlement" caught up with the free spirits who moved west. Nevertheless, the appeal of the Old West as a special haven of male freedom and individualism remains to this day.

The tension between East and West involves two conceptually different value systems which however merge into one another, for the idealization of the West remains after the values of the East presumably have triumphed. While hypermasculinity seems especially appropriate to the untamed West, conventional masculinity belongs to the settled East. The persistent fascination with the Old West perhaps gives us a clue as to how these styles of masculinity are related to one another. If the masculine code of the East, which is built on the conventions and compromises of everyday life in an individualistic society, could be fully and comfortably accepted, the appeal of the West and the hypermasculine code associated with it would disappear.

While one can find examples of the hypermasculine style throughout much of the nineteenth century, its significance greatly increased after the closing of the frontier in the 1890's as what Joe L. Dubbert calls the "myth of the masculine past" took shape in people's minds.[22] This was part of the lingering interest in the "old individualism," but conventional assumptions were pushed to essentially hypermasculine extremes. The effect upon commonly held conceptions of masculinity in America has been so profound that for most people figures like McMurphy and Rojack seem more fully to epitomize what it means to be a real man than conventional males like Mr. Bridge.

The fascination with organized sports, which also began about the time of the closing of the frontier, represents another effort to project hypermasculine values into the forefront of the nation's consciousness. The version of masculinity which spectators over the years have experienced vicariously appears to blend individual freedom and personal power without any of the ambiguities and compromises of the conventional world. Referring to the early part of the twentieth century, Dubbert argues that "the aspect of power was what seemed most important to sports fans. The man who could hit the hardest, be his target another man or a ball, was certain to be ranked with the great men of history."[23] The gap all along has been very wide between the freedom and power apparently exemplified by sports heroes on the field and the actual lives of their fans, but this only suggests that on different levels the latter are responsive to both conventional and hypermasculine definitions of manhood.

It seems reasonable to suppose, furthermore, that the behavior of most men will exhibit varying degrees of allegiance to both styles, depending on circumstances as well as basic temperament or psychological makeup. Conditions which undercut feelings of masculine adequacy may produce compensatory behavior which rejects the balanced restraints of conventional masculinity. How predictably women act out their roles will also have an important effect. Independence and an unwillingness to play an invisibly supportive role may help to elicit hypermasculine behavior. By contrast conventionally feminine behavior probably insures in large measure conventionally masculine responses.

Hypermasculinity has long been closely linked with anxiety about what are feared to be widespread manifestations in America of independence and assertiveness on women's parts. Because it stresses male prerogatives without really relying on either traditional or categorical values or related social structures to buttress these prerogatives, men must depend only on themselves to remain dominant in all situations. If their loyalty to individualism is not compromised in any way, their resources for keeping women as a group and feminists in particular in their places are limited indeed. Their fears are compounded by the fact that they regard women as more like themselves than their mainstream counterparts do, and so they take for granted a desire for power similar to their own. Since they respect women as worthy adversaries, they are by no means confident of maintaining male supremacy in a world that seems increasingly more threatening.

Dubbert argues that sports in the Progressive Era "helped distinguish men from women just at a time when feminism and women's rights appeared most threatening." Even though some writers on the subject admitted that "athletics might be carried to an extreme in America, sport was accepted as a necessary antidote to feminine influence."[24] For the American male, according to Arnold Beisser, "athletics help assure his difference from women in a world where his functions have come to resemble theirs."[25] Unfortunately a special all-male arena does not change the fact that the barriers between men's and women's spheres have long been breaking down in American society. As Peter Filene has noted of the post-World War II period, "in terms of sexual stereotypes, it was a feminine world. The openly aggressive individualism of a robber baron or a would-be baron was out of place and out of date."[26] It is not surprising that hypermasculine males are more sensitive to this reality than conventional males, who have adjusted better to the other-directed ways of contemporary American life. Hypermasculinity thus readily lends itself to expressions of anxiety about masculine freedom, power and identity because of the supposedly "feminizing" influences of modern industrial society.

Robert P. Odenwald argued in the mid-1960's that the qualities society had come to reward had the effect of making "men less masculine--in the traditional sense," by encouraging "them to develop characteristics which have traditionally been considered feminine." Odenwald did not suggest that women actually controlled American society in his day--only that masculine values had been superceded largely by feminine ones. Nevertheless, it was only a short step to the dangerous effects of female dominance within the home. Odenwald lamented that mothers were exerting "an insistent feminizing influence on their sons." If women ruled the household, they did so, however, because men wished them to. "The typical executive," Odenwald observed, "is glad to have the management of his home and the making of basic decisions affecting his family's life taken out of his hands." Thus a woman is forced to assume male functions, and so "she cannot help but take on more of the traditional characterics of maleness."[27] Conventional males apparently did not share any of Odenwald's anxieties about the threat to masculinity posed by their wives.

The fact that hypermasculine males see women as bent on aggrandizing their personal power leads to a view of the male on the defensive with respect to all that women represent. Men seem to be dominated by anti-individualistic forces in American society which are readily seen as symbolically feminine. This suggests a connection with the parts women actually play in the home and in men's personal lives. To be dependent on women sexually and emotionally gives them the power to control men's lives. To compound the situation women inculcate feminine values in their sons, who are induced willingly to give up much of their individuality and hence masculinity in order to get along better in a world governed by feminine imperatives.

Hypermasculinity expresses an interpretation of individualism and an attitude toward organized society in which the desire to protect oneself and one's freedom leads finally to a self-defeating quest for complete control of one's world. As Jack Nichols points out, "domination can never be total, is always temporary, and is based on an illusion of power."[28] As long as American males can exercise power based on vestiges of patriarchal privilege, economic superiority, categorically validated preeminence and willing submissiveness on women's parts, it is not an illusion--but neither is it total. While desiring even more, the hypermasculine male has none of the resources of the really powerful, and without them power is indeed an illusion.

G. J. Barker-Benfield's study of male attitudes toward women in the latter part of the nineteenth century offers suggestive insights not only into hypermasculine attitudes, but into some of the men who exhibited such attitudes. The author argues that an emphasis upon male autonomy derives from the Puritan heritage and in time came to have precedence even over the family as a cultural ideal. Nineteenth-century men were drawn to separation, bachelorhood and compulsive recklessness. They threatened the social order, and their passion to control women was really an externalization of anxieties derived from their own compulsive focus on autonomy and competitiveness. As success became more remote and threatened after the Civil War, men's identities became even more vulnerable and so the concern to discipline women increased.[29]

It is not clear just how widespread such fears and concerns were among American men, but Barker-Benfield describes in some detail the views of three men who devoted their lives to controlling women. J. Marion Sims was a major figure in gynecological surgery, a form of extreme control over women's bodies pioneered by American doctors. The author sees "hostility toward women and competition among men" as basic "conditions for the rise of modern gynecology." Men in this profession indeed "exhibited mad impatience, addiction to chance, ferocious competitiveness with other men--and a paradoxical dependence upon them for judgment of success in self-making." As an obstetrician and gynecologist Augustus Kinsley Gardner felt especially threatened by and envious of the wealthy and successful "men on whose wives he was dependent for a living by definition always inferior to theirs." In his writings the Rev. John Todd carried on the crusade to discipline women. He is described as being very dependent on his wife for his success, and the author sees his insistence upon autonomy as a reaction to a fear of total dependence on the women in his life.[30]

Todd, Gardner and Sims all strike one as inordinately ambitious, driven men, who nevertheless remained clearly outside the circles of real wealth and power. The means they chose to get ahead in the world were simply not adequate to satisfy their ambitions. They related to other men almost solely in highly competitive ways and seem to have been little disposed to the kinds of impersonal cooperation and male bonding which further individual success in American society. At the same time, as professional men they were greatly dependent on the judgments of others in their fields of endeavor. Isolated, marginal in a sense, insecure and envious of men of real wealth and power, such men as these three readily related to the world in hypermasculine terms. Among other "marginal" endeavors that might have similar effects on those who pursue them is the literary profession. This may be one reason why hypermasculine figures have held such a fascination for American writers from Cooper to Mailer. To the degree to which other American males identify with these figures, they share a commitment to individualism which tends to dismiss sexual categories but not sexually based antagonisms.

Alternative Strategies for Invulnerability--

Bernard Malamud's Roy Hobbs in The Natural has certain affinities with Sims, Gardner and Todd. As a professional baseball player, whose aim is "to be the greatest there ever was in the game," he too seeks success in the midst of organized society and is highly dependent on others--in this case the fans--to validate his success. At the same time his independence forbids his cultivating them. He refuses to supply a reporter with information about himself, insisting: "My life is my own business." When hypnosis is proposed as a way of helping the team get back on a winning streak, Roy refuses to go along. "I want to go through on my own steam," he insists, highlighting how important it is for him to remain in control of his own life. He is strongly attracted to a woman named Memo despite the warning of her uncle that she will only undermine him. Roy feels he has reason to dislike women. "They burned me good," he maintains. He considers his mother a "whore" who ruined his father's life. In the midst of a slump he encounters an adoringly supportive woman named Iris, whose belief in him helps him to regain his powers. In time, however, he returns to Memo, for "he was sure that once he got an armlock on her things would go better." He has domestic fantasies of her, himself and their child, but realizes that the type of woman he has in mind "was more like Iris seemed to be, only she didn't suit him."[31]

Though he resembles typically hypermasculine figures in many respects, Roy is less power-oriented and tends to become more caught up in situations he cannot dominate. In his attempt to establish baseball records which will long go unchallenged, he strives for a kind of invulnerability in a world he has no real capacity to control. Roy's situation brings to mind Ernest Hemingway's bullfighters. What makes the bullfighter a hero for Hemingway is a flawless technique that leaves him in control within carefully defined limits. The fact that his control is precarious only makes him more admirable. He achieves a measure of invulnerability by eliminating extraneous concerns and concentrating on what he can master.

The coolness and reserve toward women so typical of the Hemingway hero also aims at controlling one's life by limiting the extent of one's emotional investments even more than conventional males do. Protecting oneself is important too, for involvements usually bring much pain with them. In one story an American fighting in Italy is advised instead to "find things he cannot lose."[32] What Hemingway has in mind is the invulnerability which a closeness to nature helps one to attain. In dealing with his fears of death, Nick Adams tries thinking about the women he has known and the kinds of wives they would make. After a while, however, he gives up because they all blur in his mind. "Finally," he says in contrast, "I went back to trout-fishing, because I found that I could remember all the streams and there was always something new about them."[33] Nick does not seek to dominate nature in the way Burning Daylight does though for both it provides a relatively safe place where one is free to be oneself. Style and a narrowing of focus enable the Hemingway hero to remain in control in nature without having to dominate everything around him.

A very similar figure appears briefly in Elia Kazan's novel The Understudy. Jim Piper, an Englishman living in Rhodesia, avoids deep involvements with other humans because "you have to be careful whom you admit to your life." He resents people who expect others to be responsible for them. "The least we can expect from each other," he says, "is 'I don't tax you, you don't tax me.'" Especially around women he "protects his elite order by laying down rigid rules of acceptable conduct." One woman particularly had been important to him, but "she began to be competitive and make demands." In the end he admits that he wants to marry and plans to come to America, where he will have "a place and a family and a future."[34] Beneath his reserve and apparent indifference to other people is a desire for a conventional life, but he carefully protects his individuality by seeking to be totally invulnerable. Kazan's point is that this is impossible. In contrast to Hemingway he believes that viable human involvements are both possible and necessary.

Louis L'Amour's Shalako Carlin recognizes that if a man cannot be totally invulnerable, by depending almost entirely upon himself he can be largely so. A drifter through the Southwest in the 1880's, "he trusted to nothing but his weapons, his horse, and the caution with which he rode." At the same time "he was without illusions; for all his care, death could come and suddenly." He rescues the hunting party of a visiting Prussian nobleman, who hates "the wild, irresponsible freedom and independence" of such men as Shalako. To Lady Irina Carnarvon, he seems "completely in command of the situation." He insists to her that "the more independent a woman becomes the less of a woman she is."[35] Subsequent events reveal that Irina is quite capable of being a dependable conventional wife. We are thus not surprised when she goes off with Shalako in the end. Throughout the story he never fails to control all situations in which he finds himself, and we can be sure that he intends that marriage will prove no exception. His willingness to marry is related to his acceptance of the fact that control can never be total. He is less defensive than Jim Piper or Nick Adams and therefore closer to the world of conventional masculinity.

The emphasis upon control and maintaining one's distance evidences a careful assessment of the world around. The assessment may not always be accurate and the strategies for achieving invulnerability may fail, but figures like Shalako, Jim and Nick are obviously highly self-conscious about the way of life they have chosen for themselves. In this respect they differ from other males whose relative invulnerability is achieved by an unconscious ability to block out anything that does not accord with their private realities. Even when outside reality breaks through and destroys their individual worlds, they try to cling to their illusions.

In John Steinbeck's _East_ of _Eden_ Adam Trask's idealized view of Cathy is totally at odds with what she really is, "and nothing Cathy did or said could warp Adam's Cathy." In the opinion of someone who has known Adam for many years, "an invisible wall cut him off from the world." His half-brother Charles, a loner who is able to deal with women only by keeping them at an emotional distance, has "the competitor's will to win over others, which makes for success in the world." Neither Adam nor Charles lowers his guard and lets himself really become involved with other people. In Adam's sons Cal and Aron the same pattern is reproduced. Like his Uncle Charles Cal is competitive and power-oriented. "Aron was content to be a part of his world, but Cal must change it." Aron's love of Abra makes her into a false ideal of purity. "He doesn't know me," she once remarks. "He doesn't even want to know me."[36] Adam and Aron are incapable of coming out of their private worlds even when the truth shatters their lives.

Jay Gatsby is something of a composite of Adam and Charles Trask though the reader sees mostly the self-contained dreamer. Hidden from public view is the ambitious, power-oriented underworld boss, who as a younger man had learned contempt for most women in part because "they were hysterical about things which in his overwhelming self-absorption he took for granted." His capacity for self-absorption enables him to create a world of illusion centering around Daisy. The two halves of his character come together in a life of gorgeous expenditure in which questionable means are entirely justified by his "incorruptible dream." Even his love, which refuses to see Daisy for what she is and assumes her recent past can be obliterated, has many elements of a hypermasculine quest for dominance. He is excited when he first meets her because "many men had already loved Daisy--it increased her value in his eyes."[37] Ultimately, however, his self-contained world is destroyed and Gatsby with it.

Unlimited personal power, an aloof control of one's reality or a private world that is impervious to outside forces--all are attempts to make the self invulnerable in a context without cultural categories to provide blueprints for male bonding and reasonably confident relationships with women. No single individual has the resources to guarantee invulnerability, but it is not surprising that men are much more attracted to such a goal than are women, who are not supposed to allow their own wishes or views to take precedence over those of other people. Even if invulnerability were to appear as desirable to them as to men, the special allegiance to individualism that is part of the masculine code makes it seem a more feasible goal for one sex than the other. According to Marcus Klein, the struggle to get beyond the necessity of human relationships is the secret history of the novels of Willa Cather. In 1936 she insisted that "human relationships are the tragic necessity of human life; that they can never be wholly satisfactory, that every ego is half the time greedily seeking them, and half the time pulling away from them."38

My Mortal Enemy is the story of Myra Henshawe, whose romantic elopement with Oswald Henshawe had caused her wealthy uncle to disinherit her. Charming and vital, "her chief extravagance was in caring for so many people, and in caring for them so much." Outwardly committed to her marriage, she nevertheless remarks: "Love itself draws on a woman nearly all the bad luck in the world." As the years pass, she becomes more angry and bitter about her life, which has not brought her the wealth, success and status she admits she wants. She feels more and more like her old uncle and denies the possibility of rising above time and place: "We think we are so individual and so misunderstood when we are young; but the nature our strain of blood carries is inside there, waiting, like our skeleton." She sees Oswald as a "sentimentalist," for he can look back on the past and continue to believe that their union has been a marvelous one: "It wasn't. I was always a grasping, worldly woman; I was never satisfied." Her suggestion that Oswald is much less vulnerable because he is protected by his romantic view of her and their marriage is an accurate one. She dies a bitter and lonely death. Oswald cannot deny this bitterness during her last years, but he maintains she has changed from the "wild, lovely creature" she was when they ran away together. "Nothing ever took that girl from me," he insists.39

The Ambiguities of Power--

Conventional American males realize that to have power as well as freedom and self-determination completely and without compromises is impossible. For hypermasculine males, however, nothing appears possible without power, which must above all be maintained in one's interactions with others. One may dominate them physically or psychologically, actively or passively by means of aloofness, withdrawal or obliviousness to their realities. One's world can be assaulted at any time, and this only increases the importance of a person's defenses so long as they can be maintained.

Philip Greven's <u>The Protestant Temperament</u> contains an analysis of a group of people in early America whose basic assumptions resemble in many respects those set forth in this chapter. He calls these people evangelicals, and as Calvinist fundamentalists one of their central preoccupations was the absolute sovereignty of God. Their thinking about God shaped their attitudes about power in general, for "power always meant <u>total</u> authority--authority which could not be compromised by the wishes or the personal needs of individuals." Parents' primary concern was to break the wills of their children, for "without total control, it seemed, there could be only total license and self-destruction." Greven argues that "evangelicalism generally flourished when individuals and households were most separate and self-contained." The authoritarianism within each household was not part of a larger structure in which patterns of dominance and submission extended outwards and upwards through the society. Just as God's power was wholly personal and completely independent, so was the power parents exercised. In other respects as well power for evangelicals had a very different meaning from what it had in strictly traditional contexts. Parents strove to exert control mainly through children's consciences, for obedience must be the consequence of an inward assent rather than merely outward compliance. Also power was not a beneficent part of the settled order of things--but an unfortunate necessity, a consequence of innate sinfulness. Parents always had to guard themselves against tenderness and indulgence toward their children because these were "subversive inner tendencies--which would overthrow all order and authority within families."[40] Thus power for the evangelicals lacked the cultural and social legitimacy it has in traditional settings.

Greven asserts that "the individualism of evangelicals was vitally important, for they confronted their God and their fates directly and alone." Throughout their lifetimes they were preoccupied "with the self and the perception of selfhood as the source of sin." Only by suppressing the self could a person live in harmony with God's will. Evangelicals who saw themselves as soldiers of Christ could attack sin in the world boldly, aggressively and intolerantly. They were provided with "a sense of self-assertion and of manliness," and yet "the ideal evangelical, nevertheless, was self-less and feminine." Greven sees one of the central sources of resistance on the part of evangelical males to the new birth as "their reluctance to relinquish their sense of masculinity."[41] Like later hypermasculine males they assumed that self-assertion is an integral part of masculinity and that it is linked with the exercise of unassailable personal power. Like the Hemingway hero they believed in a high degree of self-control and sought an order and a structure in their lives which did not depend on social institutions. Masculine power and self-assertion for them were ultimately undercut by their conception of grace; so like all the characters we have been considering in this chapter, they seem to have been torn between self-assertion and its complete negation.

Two other groups of people in early America come off better in Greven's account precisely because their concepts of power in institutional terms permitted a greater degree of self-affirmation. He describes the moderates as aiming not to suppress but to control the self. Unlike the evangelicals, moderates lived in extended family contexts. Children grew up with an awareness of "degrees of authority, of connections, and of obligations to superiors, inferiors, and equals." The authority of parents, while very real, was limited, and the emphasis within the family was upon love and duty. Moderates thus saw the world in organic and hierarchical terms, but they also emphasized aspects of individualism which pointed to the age of Tocqueville. They simply took for granted that individuals have the personal freedom to make self-control a meaningful option in their own lives. Most of them shared, moreover, "a deeply rooted ambivalence about the nature and the exercise of power, and a desire to ensure that all power, Divine as well as human, be limited and contained."[42]

If the moderates come off better than the evangelicals, it is the genteel who clearly come off best of all. Children of genteel families grew up in relaxed and loving contexts and learned to feel completely comfortable with themselves. Genteel men balanced feminine and masculine sensibilities and exhibited none of the uncomfortableness Greven finds within the men of the other two groups concerning the feminine component of their personalities. Their easy self-acceptance--so clearly meant to be admired--stemmed from the fact that they were born into a world in which their power and status could largely be taken for granted. They were deeply involved in all institutions of consequence in colonial society, institutions which "provided the settings and the contexts for the exercise of authority that were indispensable to their sense of superiority and eminence." They depended upon institutions and the deference of the lesser orders, for "both were essential to the self-image that gentility fostered."[43] Their positive sense of self was clearly the result of a comfortable and uncritical acceptance of a traditional way of life that was steadily undermined as the eighteenth century progressed. In Greven's analysis, therefore, the American Revolution has an implicitly darker side, for most-- though not all--of the genteel were, not surprisingly, loyalists.

Remnants of the structured hierarchical world that the genteel required for their way of life persisted, but in an increasingly individualistic society the alternative they offered had very limited relevance. Power had acquired much more dangerous and problemmatic overtones for most Americans as had the institutional structures that sustained it. In terms of the value system that was emerging, self-affirmation seemed to point in the opposite direction from the exercise of power. Yet if masculinity required freedom and self-determination, it continued to suggest a connection with power as well. How to reconcile the one with the other has remained a challenge which American men have had to face ever since. Hypermasculinity highlights the contradictions inherent within this effort.

Overview--

A common figure in many works of American literature ever since the transition to a modern individualistic society is the hypermasculine male, whose marginality reflects his special interpretation of the mainstream masculine code and the view of women as men's opposites. His behavioral style exaggerates such elements as competitiveness, aloneness, misogyny, dominance and control. Hypermasculine males do not have many personal or institutionally based ties with other males. Their desire for complete freedom and self-determination makes them suspicious of all such involvements, for they see the world as filled with threats to the self. Only unlimited personal power, they feel, can prevent their losing control over their lives. Their rebellion against the power and authority of others is simply an aspect of their passionate quest for domination. Not surprisingly, they see relationships with women as fraught with danger. On the one hand they feel constantly frustrated in their desire for total supportiveness. On the other they regard women as adversaries in the struggle for mastery within relationships--as persons who must be subdued or they will become the victors. Hypermasculine males represent an extreme version of individualism which rejects even sexual categories: men must deal with other men and with women directly and alone. Thus the quest for power in all aspects of life is inherently self-defeating, for such males lack the social resources to acquire and to exercise it effectively.

Hypermasculine males are symbolically associated with the West as a haven of masculine freedom. At the same time what they stand for appeals to more conventional males, who are symbolically associated with the East. With the closing of the frontier the hypermasculine male gained even greater prestige as a culture hero--so much so that to many he represents what real manhood is all about. A growing interest in sports in the twentieth century has centered upon athletic heroes who appear perfectly to blend individual freedom with great personal power. A hypermasculine point of view also informs many negative reactions to the perceived independence and assertiveness of American women. Such fears are in turn linked with anxiety about the feminizing impact of modern society on men's lives. Actual males may be guided by hypermasculine assumptions to varying degrees; ambitious professionals such as doctors and writers are particularly disposed to such an outlook.

If personal power seems to some males the route to invulnerability, other figures in literature seek it by limiting emotional investments and focussing only on what they are sure they can control. Still others remain oblivious to whatever does not accord with their private realities. Not surprisingly, men seem to find invulnerability both more appealing and more attainable than women do.

Calvinist fundamentalists (evangelicals) in colonial times closely resemble the hypermasculine male as he has been described in this chapter. They too were preoccupied with unlimited personal power, particularly God's power and the power exercised by parents over their children. At the same time power for them lacked cultural and social legitimacy, and they were torn between extreme self-assertiveness and the complete negation of the self. The challenge of reconciling power with personal freedom and self-determination has remained ever since at the very heart of the meaning of masculinity in America. Hypermasculine males, particularly in literature, dramatize this tension.

CHAPTER FIVE

HYPOMASCULINITY: THE IDEAL OF FREEDOM

Categorization is rooted in anxiety about the distinctiveness of people considered outsiders with reference to those making a judgment which categorizes them as well. Hypermasculine males share with conventional males only an uneasiness regarding women, not an acceptance of categories as cultural blueprints for dealing with sex-related differences. This anxiety dovetails with a feeling of being alone in a dangerous and competitive world, again without any conventional coping strategies. The possibility of an extreme version of individualism based on root anxieties within American culture suggests an alternative possibility based on its hopes and ideals. For want of a better term males of the contrasting type may be called hypomasculine in their chosen style of behavior, for they evidence little inclination toward competitiveness and dominance. Neither do they share the anxieties upon which sexual categorization is based. The ways in which such males deal with the social realities of sex-related differences, however, complicate the problem of reconciling these realities with the ideals that they espouse.

Special Male Friendships--

While male friendships have been idealized in many cultures, the importance of individualism has given them a special meaning in America. Male-female relationships cannot easily be based on a mutually shared allegiance to individualism since the categorization process complicates and limits its application to women. From boyhood on American males are encouraged to believe that other males are very much like themselves and so value freedom and independence as much as they do. Thus whatever male friendship entails, it must not involve any sacrifice of these principles.

Herb Goldberg's celebration of what he calls "buddyship" extends the contrast with the male-female tie and suggests a style of male bonding that is different from the impersonal bonds of conventional American males. He speculates that a woman is likely to be jealous of a buddy relationship because it "has more room for freedom, is less possessive, and does not have the components of jealousy and role rigidity that often exist in male-female relationships." The "mutually supportive, nourishing, no-strings-attached aspects" of buddyship are especially rewarding and are not based on any legal obligation to stay together.[1] There are no fixed expectations, no suggestion of dominance and submission, nothing that links the two people specifically either to organized social structures or to all other males as members of a social grouping--only an insistence on men's capacity to form pair bonds based on freedom and mutuality. Buddyship does not evidence any of the effects of the pursuit of economic opportunity--competitiveness, skepticism about trusting other males, the quest for power. It stands for relationships of caring equals, and nothing undercuts equality and caring more surely than the pursuit of success. For buddyship to be more than just an ideal it must occur under conditions which make economic opportunism irrelevant to the relationship itself. "To achieve brotherhood means to go beyond everyday power-based modes of relating," Tony Silvestre insists.[2]

American literature has many examples of such special bonds. Jack Schaefer's novel <u>Shane</u> centers around the relationship between Joe Starrett and Shane though to some degree Joe's young son Bob, who tells the story in retrospect, is also included. Joe is a fairly conventional American male, an industrious and ambitious Wyoming farmer who represents the forces ultimately destined to advance the course of civilization in the West. Shane remarks to Joe's wife Marian that "give him time and he'll be mayor." Joe opposes the local cattle baron and "the power in the valley in those days" because "there are," in his words, "some things a man can't take." On one occasion Shane helps him tear out a tree stump. "There's no wood ever grew can stand up to a man that's got the strength and the will to keep hammering at it," Joe insists.[3] Shane, who is staying with the Starrett family, lends his assistance as a matter of courtesy and friendship, but he does not share Joe's passion to triumph over nature.

As a loner with a mysterious past, Shane is not part of the local society. He remains reserved and "withdrawn beyond a line of his own making" toward everyone but the Starretts. Joe intuitively understands and respects Shane's reserve, for a man is "entitled to stake his claim to what he considers private to himself alone." The two work "together more like partners than boss and hired man." Thus theirs is a relationship based on freedom, equality and mutual respect. It seems to transcend all elements of competitiveness between the two of them. Joe refuses to react angrily when he realizes that his wife is attracted to Shane, for he freely acknowledges that Shane is the better man of the two.[4] Shane personally shares neither Joe's stake in conventional masculinity nor his commitment to family and organized society, yet he becomes deeply involved in the struggle between the farmers and the cattle baron. He is not interested in power for himself and acts entirely alone. He is capable of using violence but in a way which suggests no love of it nor of the power that it could bring. His concern is solely to help Joe and indirectly Joe's family and friends as well. When he is finished, he asserts his allegiance to personal freedom and leaves as Joe knows he must.

Although Shane stands apart from society, he seems to

identify with what Joe represents. With "a real man behind him," Shane observes, Bob has "the chance another kid never had." Clearly he is referring to himself and implies that if it were a matter of choice, he would like to have been the kind of boy Bob is. But, he continues, "a man is what he is, Bob, and there's no breaking the mold." Still, the friendship allows him some measure of vicarious participation in Joe's world. It is true as well that Joe and his family find in Shane many appealing qualities. Bob early notes that "Shane knew what would please a boy." Shane puts him at ease by dealing with him as an equal. Marian quickly comes to like Shane too. "He's so nice and polite and sort of gentle," she tells Joe. "Not like most men I've met out here." Shane is able to talk with her about fashions in Cheyenne and obviously can enter into her interests in ways that Joe cannot. Bob finds talk of fashions "foolish to me to be coming from a grown man. Yet this Shane was not bothered at all."[5] His camaraderie with Marian is probably what prompts Joe to feel that Shane has masculine powers he lacks. Shane does not, however, behave in an expectedly masculine fashion toward her. Though each seems attracted to the other, he in no way seeks to exploit this attraction. Marian is free to make her own decisions, and she appropriately remains committed to her husband and son.

Shane's ability to break through convention in dealing with all three members of the Starrett family is doubtless important in explaining why each responds to him so readily. Sex and age differences, as well as masculine defensiveness, do not matter to him, yet he does not seem in any conscious way to rebel against convention. Between him and Joe there is a deep understanding; it is almost as though the two men exhibit different aspects of the same personality. The closeness between them seems very important, but to project it into the future suggests all sorts of possible complications. Shane must leave for all their sakes, not just for his own.

In John Knowles' novel, A Separate Peace, Phineas and Gene (who narrates the story) are paired in much the same way that Shane and Joe are. Like Shane, Phineas is the hypomasculine figure who does not adapt well to structured situations governed by established rules and regulations. He "considered authority the necessary evil against which happiness was achieved by reaction." Though he often ignores his school's rules, he really wants to be good. He clearly likes people very much, for flows of "simple, unregulated friendliness" are one of his reasons for living. He has great charm and manages to win over everyone he meets. He organizes a group of his friends on occasion to play an improvised game based on rules which are "his own, not those imposed on him by other people." He obviously prefers spontaneous forms of interaction, and his rules are not really efforts to control others or exert power over them. In contrast to the hypermasculine male he is unconcerned with personal power and quite lacking in competitiveness. Once when he and Gene are by themselves in the gym, he breaks a school swimming record just to see if he can do it. Gene is astonished because Phineas is not interested in duplicating his feat in public and realizes that unlike his classmates at Devon School he seems "too unusual for rivalry."[6]

In contrast to Phineas, Gene is typically masculine in his competitiveness and desire to succeed. After their friendship deepens, Phineas calls Gene his "best pal." Gene recognizes this as a "courageous thing to say," for "exposing a sincere emotion nakedly like that at the Devon School was the next thing to suicide." His own masculine reserve prevents him from saying anything in reply even though he wants to. It is just at this time that Gene becomes suspicious that Phineas is deliberately trying to undermine his scholastic achievements by inducing him to slack off. This prompts him to study all the harder in order to achieve the academic counterpart to Finny's athletic stardom. Rivalry is the name of the game for Gene, and it comes as a shock to him to realize that all along Phineas has genuinely felt that study for Gene comes as easily as athletics for him. "Now I knew that there never was and never could have been any rivalry between us," Gene acknowledges.[7] He is jealous of Phineas for being above competitiveness, and this undoubtedly prompts him on the spur of the moment to make Finny lose his balance and fall off a branch into the water and seriously injure himself.

Gene realizes that all along his purpose must have been "to become a part of Phineas." In the end he also understands that "Phineas had thought of me as an extension of himself." Knowles is thus quite explicit in depicting such a male pairing as two sides of the same personality. In retrospect Gene feels that Phineas symbolizes the careless innocence of youth, which cannot last once the boys become involved in World War II. Phineas desperately wants to join the fighting, but Gene tells him that he would not be any good in battle. His openness and friendliness would come to include the enemy as well, and so he would make "a terrible mess . . . out of the war." Phineas had a way, Gene comes to understand, of "sizing up the world with erratic and entirely personal reservations, letting its rocklike facts sift through and be accepted only a little at a time, only as much as he could assimilate without a sense of chaos and loss." Unlike Nick Adams and Jay Gatsby, Finny's selective approach to reality seems aimed only at the freedom to be himself in a world he does not challenge but is not entirely at home in either. Only Gene is able to break his "harmonious and natural unity," and the indirect result is Finny's death.[8]

Though Phineas and Shane seem superficially different,

both are really private people, who at the same time open up under unstructured circumstances. They seek no power or dominance and are conspicuous for their lack of competitiveness. These traits enable them to form close male bonds. Joe is more able than Gene to relate on such terms, which is why his friendship with Shane goes more smoothly. Gene cannot transcend his conventional masculine competitiveness even though he is not proud of it, and this undercuts his relationship with Finny all along. Both authors find the hypomasculine style intriguing, yet both are convinced that a conventional style is more realistic. Knowles' conviction seems much more grudging than Schaefer's, which is probably why Gene is flawed and Phineas is not. Schaefer clearly endorses the triumph of convention; so by contrast, it is Shane who is flawed rather than Joe. It has never seemed to me that the capacity for violence is necessarily linked to Shane's other traits, yet the fact that he can take care of himself has a great deal to do with his ultimate survival. Phineas, however, has nowhere to go but death.

Enter Women--

The most important as well as the earliest hypomasculine figure to appear in our literature is James Fenimore Cooper's Leatherstocking. In his role as the Pathfinder, Leatherstocking's ordinary expression is described as one of "simplicity, integrity, and sincerity, blended in an air of self-reliance." Like Shane he is capable of fighting and killing, but he insists that "peace and marcy," not "bloodshed and warfare" are his "real gifts." Though he has lived most of his life beyond the pale of organized society, he clearly values the ties he has with the Indian Chingachgook and the young frontiersman Jasper Western. He places a high priority on his own freedom and independence and has no inclination to exercise power over other people. At the same time he relates to others on basically egalitarian terms. Like Phineas he confronts social practices and conventions against which he does not openly rebel and yet which at the same time he does not personally uphold. Regarding class differences, "the most surprising peculiarity about the man himself," Cooper says, "was the entire indifference with which he regarded all distinctions that did not depend on personal merit."[9] Like Phineas, also, he freely acknowledges his affection for his special friends Jasper and Chingachgook.

His Indian comrade, however, belongs to a very different culture. The Pathfinder tries to balance acceptance of cultural differences with the individualistic assumption that such differences should be transcended by personal ties and an emphasis upon likeness of mind. As a Mohican chief Chingachgook has "gifts and traditions to tell him what he ought to do."[10] The Leatherstocking, who has "white gifts," accepts in him as an Indian actions that often clash with his own "white" values. This

99

conception of "gifts" encompasses a double awareness on Pathfinder's part. On the one hand, he accepts with reference to
himself as well as others cultural assumptions and dictates
which in large measure are conceived in categorical terms. On
the other hand, he often does not act in accordance with these
dictates but rather prefers to cross the barriers of class, race
and culture as only someone completely devoted to individualism
might try to do. He respects Chingachgook's "red gifts," yet
the two come together freely as equals who have much in common.
Differences are not obliterated, but it is similarities that
form the real basis of their friendship.

Leatherstocking feels that appropriate gender behavior also comes under the heading of "gifts." His problem in courting
Mabel Dunham is to win the affections of someone who "has her
gifts, too," but whose "gifts" are "not rude like ours, but gentle, and womanish, as they ought to be." Pathfinder is concerned that there are significant differences between the two of
them in terms of age, background and tastes. He tells Mabel's
father, Sergeant Dunham, that his "gifts" are not Mabel's
"gifts" and that "like loves like." The Sergeant's response is
a model defense of conventional distinctions: "If like loved
like, women would love one another, and men also. No, no, like
loves dislike." What Pathfinder is proposing, however, is a relationship based on freedom and equality and which presupposes
mutually shared interests and values. He tells Jasper that he
has no doubts about his ability to provide for Mabel's physical
wants, but he wonders whether in the long run from him she will
have "knowledge enough" and "ideas enough, and pleasant conversation enough." He fully understands that a young woman "must
wish to marry a man that is nearer to her own age and fancies"
than himself.[11]

There is little doubt that Pathfinder could win Mabel by
being reasonably aggressive in his suit. At the same time his
general assessment of marriage is conventional enough to cause
him to hesitate about giving up his independent way of life. He
worries that in seeking to establish a permanent home near the
settlements for Mabel and make her comfortable he will give in
too much to "a craving after property." Pathfinder remains
split between conventional views of marriage and categorically
defined feminine "gifts," which he cannot in practice accept,
and respect for Mabel's individuality and her freedom of
choice. When he learns that Jasper loves her but has said nothing because of his regard for his friend, Pathfinder insists
that Mabel hear everything and "have her own way." The girl of
course loves the younger man, and Pathfinder reluctantly gives
up his suit, telling Jasper, "you'll make her happier than I
could, for your gifts are better suited to do so."[12]

Leatherstocking's conception of "gifts" cannot be so suc-

cessfully invoked here as elsewhere because gender-based categorical expectations make differences a more complicated challenge than he is prepared to accept. He can deal with members
of other races or classes essentially as equals when he chooses
because the "gifts" that make them different are not fundamental
to his interactions with them. These can in a sense be put
aside. Clearly there is a part of Pathfinder that would like to
deal with Mabel in the same way, but he does not assume that either sex can or should disregard the conventional expectations
that define women as categorically different from men. Thus womanly "gifts" would form an important basis of marital interaction. Pathfinder's insistence upon genuine likeness of mind
rather than invisible supportiveness as the crux of his relationship with Mabel cannot be reconciled with the categorical
assumptions he is unwilling to repudiate. He has no alternative, therefore, but to give up his suit.

While maintaining that Jasper has more appropriate "gifts"
than he, Pathfinder accepts with reference to his friend the importance of the masculine/feminine dichotomy that the Sergeant
dwells upon. The marriage will be based on different "gifts"
appropriate to each sex as well as similarities with respect to
age and interests, thus underscoring the fact that categorization highlights differences and yet is flexible enough to allow
for at least an approximation of likeness of mind. For himself
Pathfinder simply reaffirms his commitment to a free and independent life which allows him to focus on more comfortable relationships. He says to Jasper: "I know few love me better than
yourself, Jasper. Chingachgook is, perhaps, now the only crea-
tur' of whom I can say that." As the more conventional member
of this male bond, Jasper returns to civilization and becomes a
successful merchant while Pathfinder is left initially with an
almost overwhelming sense of "his isolated condition in the
world."[13] Having doubtless expected something closer in his relationship with Mabel than from his male comrades, he finds it
much harder to accept her decision to go her own way.

Leslie Fiedler includes Cooper's hero among the typical
male protagonists of American literature who are seeking to
avoid "the confrontation of a man and woman which leads to the
fall to sex, marriage and responsibility."[14] Such an interpretation accepts conventional definitions of masculinity and femininity by implying that however attractive the innocence and
freedom of someone like the Leatherstocking, maturity obviously
demands that these be given up for the responsibilities of work,
marriage and family. Cooper's treatment of the Pathfinder's
courtship dilemma suggests, however, another interpretation.
The desire for relationships based on freedom and equality may
be a genuine one though it is difficult to achieve because it
challenges categorical assumptions. Although Pathfinder in theory accepts the values of his culture, in practice he cannot re-

ally adhere to them. In this sense he may be neither a fantasy figure nor simply an immature male, but a person whose inability to conform represents an important comment on the meaning of sex-related differences in nineteenth-century American culture.

Although their situations differ markedly, the Pathfinder and J. D. Salinger's Holden Caulfield have much in common, particularly as regards relating to women. Holden's prep-school roommate Stradlater seems to possess all the conventional masculine attributes boys are taught to admire. Holden envies his athletic abilities, his "damn good build" and his being "pretty handsome." Yet Holden is also critical of his vanity. Holden's feelings are equally mixed about Stradlater's technique with women, which he feels aims at overwhelming dates with an apparent but false sincerity and charm. Part of Holden shares this attitude toward women, an attitude which justifies the male's right to use them as he wishes. In New York he tries his skills on three women in a bar. He finds one of them both stupid and an excellent dancer, and this leads to the arrogantly masculine observation that "a really smart girl either tries to lead you around the dance floor, or else she's . . . a lousy dancer."[15] Still, he fails as a chauvinist on the "make."

While Holden's conscious assessment of women is very conventional, his deepest instincts lead him to behave in unconventional ways. His platonic friendship with Jane Gallagher is something he prizes a great deal. "You don't always have to get too sexy to get to know a girl," he observes. He has remained a virgin partly because, he says, he always stops when a girl tells him to. From a conventional point of view this may seem rather naive, but it also means he respects a girl's expressed wishes and thus takes her requests seriously. He tries to gain some practice with a prostitute, but only feels depressed and unresponsive. Holden sums up his predicament with women in this way: "I can never get really sexy--I mean _really_ sexy--with a girl I don't like a lot. . . . Boy, it really screws up my sex life something awful."[16]

Like the Leatherstocking's, Holden's conventional views of women dictate ways of responding at variance with his deepest inclinations, which are personal and egalitarian. He lacks the confidence in himself, however, to be effective in the former style of relating, for he continues to judge women as well as himself by conventional standards. He admits that he is a poor fighter, who is "not too tough," and he worries about being "yellow."[17] Because he does not fit yet is not sure about any alternative values, he often feels lonely, more so even than Leatherstocking. Both are marginal figures who are not so much social rebels as unable to respond in typically masculine ways. Nowhere is this more obvious than in their dealings with women.

102

The Hypomasculine Style--

Hypomasculine males have much in common with hypermasculine ones. Both are uncomfortable with the structured social world of impersonal involvements and formal responsibilities. Instead they prefer one which revolves essentially around personal ties. John Knowles' Cleet Kinsolving in Indian Summer insists: "I'm only usually interested in things that apply to me personally."18 Both male types place a high premium on freedom, and both dramatize the importance attached to the individual in America and the closely related skepticism about fulfillment through organized social structures. One regards these with suspicion and feels that only in conscious opposition are freedom and individuality realizable goals. The other is actually more removed from the ordinary pressures of society, for he simply goes his own way without really adhering to the conventions against which the hypermasculine male constantly struggles. Both therefore belong essentially to the West rather than to the East.

These two masculine styles differ most significantly concerning the question of power. To acquire and wield as much personal power as possible is the central concern of the hypermasculine male and of no concern to the hypomasculine male. Power for the most part is a social phenomenon, and the latter is simply not sufficiently immersed in the formal processes of society to make it a significant factor in his life. Moreover, he eschews power and competitiveness because these necessarily imply limitations on the individual's freedom and on the applicability of equality. It is possible to speak of two aspects of the hypomasculine male's personality. There is a kind of formal self that abstractly accepts the categories and values of his culture and the structures of his society. Sometimes he even acts as their guarantor. Leatherstocking insures the survival and even success of his middle- and upper-class friends, and Phineas remains an eager supporter of the war. Still, the deeper, more personal self cannot effectively operate in terms of social conventions and cultural categories even though these are not really repudiated.

In his own rather special way Joe Buck in James Leo Herlihy's Midnight Cowboy shares the conventional disapproval of homosexuality. His logic in going to New York to become a hustler is that "the men back there is just faggots mostly, and so the women got to buy what they want." His subsequent encounters with the gay scene leave him uneasy and even depressed though because of financial necessity he is a reluctant participant from time to time. Still, in dealing with individuals he is sensitive and compassionate and can muster none of the hostility that most conventional males feel obliged to express. Years before Joe leaves for New York he has a brief sexual relationship with a young man named Bobby Desmond. Three weeks later, when Bobby gets married, Joe is unaware of what this immediate embrace of conventionality means and so is disappointed not to be invited to the wedding. Clearly categorizing people in terms of sexual object choice means relatively little to Joe. Like other hypomasculine males, he does not choose to be a loner. He desires companionship, but he lacks the acquired social skills to initiate personal relationships. As a young man he seeks to make friends simply by hanging around a person who interests him "in the hope a friendship would come into being."[19]

Hypomasculine males tend not to attach much importance to differences based on race or class. They see people essentially as individuals apart from social contexts, and unless one accepts the validity of such contexts, race and class have very little personal significance. Cleet Kinsolving is "prejudiced, if that was the word for it, in favor of equality," and so he is bored and confused by such differences as Northerners and Southerners, officers and enlisted men or even the specialness of the Japanese though he is living in the period just after World War II.[20] Hypomasculine males generally exhibit a marked sensitivity toward others, not so much on a rational as on an emotional level. This follows from the fact that they operate in mostly personal terms and thus do not rely on conventions but on their own intuitions and feelings in responding to other people. They want to relate voluntarily and as equals and are usually hesitant to force themselves on others. This is why the ideal relationship with another male is characterized for them by mutual consent, freedom and equality.

Potentially the same thing could be true with regard to women. Temperamentally hypomasculine males are not inclined to favor conventional forms of masculine dominance in their dealings with women, and their allegiance to egalitarianism points the way toward cutting through categorically defined gender barriers. Yet somehow conventional expectations persist, and it never seems quite possible to deal with women on the basis of freedom and equality. To these males--and evidently to their creators as well--women belong too much to the world of conventions, formal social order, laws and regulations to imagine them in a wholly personal context. Men by contrast can presumably leave this all behind--at least temporarily--and so even conventional males are capable of dealing with hypomasculine ones in ways which underscore the importance of the individual and his capacity to form voluntary and egalitarian ties. The freedom, innocence and even boyishness of hypomasculine males suggest an imperfect integration into mainstream American life. Imperfect integration in turn means that however much such males may wish to relate freely with others, these others will be influenced by conventional values and behavioral expectations that shut them out. This leads frequently to a profound sense of loneliness.

Private Robert E. Lee Prewitt's dying thought in James Jones' novel _From Here to Eternity_ is that the world is a "lone-some place." He has been repeatedly struck by how isolated each human being is. Once he feels "the sense of loss and the alone-ness, the utter defenselessness that was each man's lot, sealed up in his bee cell from all the others in the world." Like many hypomasculine figures, he is a wanderer. His move to a new Army unit brings home to him "the essential rootlessness of yourself and all men like you." Prewitt is always looking for ways of reaching out to people and communicating with them, but he can really do this only with his bugle. He realizes that he cares about others, even those in his company who harrass him because he will not join the boxing team, for they "were men and, being men, could not help but mean something to him, who was also a man." While he has a stronger sense of identity with other men as members of a social grouping than most hypomasculine males, he is not deeply immersed in the conventional male value sys-tem. When he falls in love with a prostitute, he is unperturbed by her social status or by the fact that she has money and he does not.[21]

Prewitt really loves the Army and constantly describes himself as a thirty-year man. His basic problem, however, is that he cannot accept, much less practice, the political skills which others see as crucial to succeeding within the military establishment. When he first joins his new unit, he is advised to "jockstrap" in order to "get on the gravytrain." He, how-ever, has his own reasons for not wanting to engage in any more boxing and steadfastly refuses to bend to the pressures designed to get him to change his mind. Initially Captain Dana Holmes, the company commander, appeals to his presumed loyalty to the Army as an institution. "In the Army," Holmes insists, "its not the individual that counts." He hints at the pressure he him-self is under from his superiors to produce winning athletes, for "no matter how high you get there is always somebody over you." He is a perfect example of a man whose ambition to get ahead takes precedence over his individualistic loyalties. He knows he has to curry favor with important superiors, and he carefully does so. His first sergeant recognizes that Holmes has the makings of a very successful general, for "good generals had to have the type of mind that saw all men as masses, as ab-stractions that they worked on paper with." Prewitt stands in total contrast to this mentality. He tells his friend Stark that all he wants is to be left alone. In today's world, Stark answers, nobody is left alone. One must use politics to get and keep what one wants. To Prewitt, if this is true, then "a man himself is nothing."[22]

Adjusting to Realities--

At the same time that writers pay tribute to figures who

transcend culturally defined barriers, they are aware that conventional values and institutions not only persist but must somehow be dealt with. Most yet not all would concede as well that these perform useful functions. Cooper's Leatherstocking Tales are an elaborate exercise in honoring the best of both worlds, and in one way or another all authors are obliged to pay some degree of deference to organized society. While the hypomasculine male remains an appealing ideal embodiment of pure individualism, he is at the same time a figure whose very marginal status cannot be left unresolved. Cooper places the Leatherstocking beyond the pale. Though he may have temporary contacts with members of organized society, he is left behind when they return to marry, have families and prosper economically. Shane rides off into the sunset though he hints that he would like to remain had circumstances made him another person.

In _Indian Summer_ we meet Cleet Kinsolving in Kansas. He senses "a give and take and flow here which was completely absent in the rigid world he had grown up in" back in Connecticut. His boyhood friend Neil Reardon, the son of a multimillionaire, induces him to return to the East to work for the Reardon family. Cleet consents but in a typically individualistic fashion insists that "people should be able to take care of themselves." For Neil "life was rivalry," and so "a good battle of wills or muscles or anything else" in his opinion "was the healthy, American way to live." The result is that he has "no friends, except his peculiar, unlettered, shrewd, erratic, dreaming, lifelong pal, Cleet." Cleet feels himself being drawn into the value system of the Reardons and even comes to wonder whether they "were perhaps finally giving him a sense of responsibility and teaching him to fit in to life as normal, successful people lived it." Nevertheless, his hypomasculine values win out and he leaves for Kansas with just his duffel bag, which "contained everything he owned," including an atlas "because Kansas might be only a stage in his journey."[23]

The fear of entrapment which motivates Cleet to "fight to remain what he had always been" indicates a certain affinity for conventional masculinity.[24] Figures like Phineas, Prewitt and Holden Caulfield function too far outside the aggressive and competitive bounds of everyday masculinity to fear entrapment. If anything their concern is quite the opposite. Cleet has just enough of a power orientation in him to be drawn to what the Reardons represent. Thus to maintain his freedom he must fight against entrapment. Like the Leatherstocking and Shane, Cleet can only remain true to himself when he separates himself from the world of conventional masculinity. Death--as in the cases of Phineas and Prewitt--as well as distance can preserve the integrity of the hypomasculine style, but in both instances its essential incompatibility with the everyday world seems to be conceded.

106

Attempts to bring hypomasculine males themselves into the conventional world, by contrast, remain tentative and rather vague. Herlihy makes it clear that Joe Buck's marginal status is the result of growing up without either a mother or a father. His desire to be a cowboy is his attempt to recapture a time when he had a father-substitute in a male friend of his grandmother. His fantasies of blonde women who will love and care for him are likewise an attempt to find a mother-substitute. Both of these elements come together in his desire to be a cowboy hustler in order to set up role-reversal situations in which women pursue him. After he has teamed up with Rico Rizzo (Ratso), who is "the natural leader of the two," he is content simply to put himself in the hands of his street-wise friend. As Rico's health declines, however, Joe assumes more responsibility. He arranges a trip to Florida, and on the bus he tells his friend that he intends to throw away his boots and go to work because he is "no kind of hustler." He likes feeling responsible for Rico and looks forward to having a job and a home of his own, friends and a wife "not necessarily a blonde either or any one particular kind of woman," but someone who "would be glad to have a man to take care of her, one who was good at love making." Rico's dying in his arms does not alter Joe's sense of responsibility for his friend even though the story concludes with him "scared now, scared to death."[25] Nevertheless, he has at least begun to commit himself to a conventional life and to adopt the masculine values that such a life requires. Beyond this the reader cannot be sure, but Herlihy suggests that in wanting to abandon a hypomasculine style, Joe is taking his first tentative steps toward real manhood.

Minimizing the competitive and aggressive aspects of masculinity allows more scope for emotion and gentleness, especially toward other males. This raises a problem for some writers concerning the masculine credentials of their characters. Cooper takes pains to assure the reader that the Leatherstocking is quite capable of fighting effectively when he has to, and Shane proves to be no coward when the chips are down. Jack London's short story, "The Heathen," deals with the lives of a conventional white male, Charley, and a hypomasculine Pacific Islander, Otoo. Considering London's own racist proclivities, this special friendship, cutting across racial lines, is fascinating though it is true that Charley always remains in a dominant social position. London points out that Otoo is no fighter, but also insists that he is no coward: "He was all sweetness and gentleness, a love-creature, though he stood nearly six feet tall and was muscled like a gladiator." He is brother, father and mother to Charley and his influence makes Charley a better man. "I cared little for other men," Charley insists to the reader, "but I had to live straight in Otoo's eyes." Though Otoo has no personal ambition for himself, his interest in Charley's affairs keeps the careless young man from failing, and in the end he loses his life to save Charley's. "And I could see in his gaze the love that thrilled in his voice," Charley says. Nevertheless, the conclusion offers a final reassurance that both men lack nothing in the way of masculinity: "And so passed Otoo, who saved me and made me a man, and who saved me in the end."[26]

In Herman Melville's Moby Dick a somewhat similar relationship exists between Ishmael and Queequeg, and here too the person of color is responsible for saving the white man's life. Ishmael is much less typically masculine than Charley, and the question remains open as to whether his approach or the defiant hypermasculinity of Captain Ahab is more appropriate in a hostile or indifferent world. By the time he wrote Israel Potter Melville was even more skeptical about a hypomasculine style. Though Israel can be a "dare-devil upon a pinch," still he seems "to have evinced, throughout many parts of his career, a singular patience and mildness." He is easily swayed by charismatic leaders but refuses to submit to the tyranny of a brutal foreman. As time passes Israel seems more and more carried along by circumstances which first take him to England during the American Revolution and then conspire after "a rash embarkation in wedlock" to keep him there for half a century.[27] During the desperate years of the Napoleonic wars Israel never sinks to a level of beggary, thus vindicating his American independence. He does not rail against his circumstances and he has no attraction to power as a means of controlling the world around him. The result in Melville's eyes is that he is simply a victim.

Israel is very different from others whom he meets--Benjamin Franklin, whose crafty conventional masculinity Melville despises; Ethan Allen, the symbol of Western independence; and John Paul Jones, "who never had been, and never would be, a subordinate."[28] Melville is by no means the only writer who has been attracted to both hyper- and hypomasculine males. This dual attraction suggests a fundamental connection between the two approaches, both of which embody more complete affirmations of individualism than mainstream masculinity. In many respects hypermasculinity represents the collapse of the optimistic expectations of hypomasculinity. The individual is left with only personal power to confront an unredeemed world whose influence over him increases as his sense of being able to separate himself from it wanes. Shane already manifests an inclination to respond in hypermasculine ways. It is important to bear in mind as well that the evangelicals, with whom I dealt in the last chapter, had a millennial vision which has much in common with hypomasculinity.

The Uncertain Appeal of a Marginal Figure--

As I have previously observed, historically the emphasis

upon success through individual achievement has different origins from the emphasis upon equality and individual freedom. Hypomasculinity is an expression of the latter tradition, and its continued appeal suggests a reservoir of opposition to the dominant cultural tradition. If this opposition is not carried too far, hypomasculinity is most easily dealt with as a kind of self-indulgence which must be put aside in favor of a male's mature integration into American society. The alternative is to cling to an unrealistic innocence which puts one outside the bounds of normal masculinity. Still, there is probably a side of most men that continues to be drawn to a way of life which rejects competitiveness, success and the quest for dominance, which prefers relationships that are mutual and voluntary and believes that these can be based on an equality which transcends race, class and even perhaps sex. Depending on how fully a man is immersed in conventional values, this ideal will vary in its intensity. It seems logical to suppose that its hold is greater on those whose conditioning in the success ethic is for whatever reasons imperfect. More emotional openness toward specific other males, when it manifests itself in the lives of hypomasculine males, draws to some extent upon a categorical identification with one's own sex but goes beyond it as the guardedness fostered by rivalry dissipates.

If there are varying degrees of commitment to a hypomasculine style, there remain varying degrees of uneasiness about it, even on the part of men who have taken pains to deal with it in literature. In terms of everyday realities it <u>does</u> seem a bit unrealistic. It hints at a kind of softness, and no American male is invulnerable to criticisms about the adequacy of his masculinity. Hypomasculine characters themselves remain very much aware of conventional society and its demands. While the male pairs we have examined suggest a certain attraction on the part of the conventional male for what the hypomasculine male represents, the reverse is also true. Because the hypomasculine male is a marginal figure, he is likely to exhibit the ambivalent attraction of someone on the outside toward the supposed comfortableness of a more conventional (normal) life. These males therefore do not wholly reject a value system that they are nevertheless unable or unwilling to live up to. Nowhere is this more evident than in their attitudes toward women. Somehow the choice here seems to be restricted to the alternatives of conventional involvement or freedom to be oneself. One cannot have both.

Just as the basic realities of women's lives make the goal of invulnerability seem much more problemmatical to them than to men, so the possibilities of personal freedom seem especially to belong to males in America. In her introduction to Edith Wharton's novel <u>Summer</u> Marilyn French argues that in contrast to Henry James "Wharton, a woman, was far more aware of the power of the environment over the individual" and also "of the impossibility of getting beyond the bodily and social consequences of sex." Yet at the same time, French also points out, Wharton believed that "the 'real unpardonable sin' was the denial of life. And by life, she meant largely sexual experience, but also an existence created by the self rather than by society."[29]

Summer is the story of a young country girl's affair with a city man. Charity Royall is sensible and realistic, and she immediately is aware of the sexual power she has over Lucius Harney. She however refuses repeatedly to take advantage of this power or to employ conventional feminine wiles to manipulate him in any way. One night she watches Harney through the window as he tries to make up his mind whether to go away or not. She realizes that if she were to go to him then she could easily seduce him, but this is not what she wants: "If he wanted her he must seek her; he must not be surprised into taking her." Clearly Charity wants a relationship based on freedom and mutuality, and this makes her acutely aware of the fact that "education and opportunity had divided them by a width that no effort of hers could bridge." When she learns that she is pregnant, she understands that she can compel Harney to marry her, but she recoils from the prospect of a forced union. She has seen far too many miserable marriages that were undertaken "to make things right."[30] At the same time a perfectly free union is not a realistic possibility under the circumstances. Harney remains at liberty to determine the course of his life while Charity can only consent to her guardian's offer of marriage.

Even for a man the realities of everyday life can undercut all the hopeful expectations that hypomasculinity incorporates. Jane Kramer, a journalist, has written an account of a forty-year old cowboy living in the Texas Panhandle. Henry Blanton believes completely in the cowboy code of the movies and in "a hero's West." His belief remains unshaken no matter how much his own life and the lives of his father and grandfather have "conspired to disabuse him." Intellectually Henry recognizes that success is closely bound up with such social realities as education and access to power and influence. Otherwise, he admits, a man's "going to end up nothing but some other man's dumb cowboy."[31] He believes in ambition and the survival of the fittest, yet he lacks the necessary interpersonal skills and the drive. He is thus condemned to remain an employee, who is constantly taken advantage of by his superiors.

Blanton had proposed to his wife Betsy right after he had been corrected in front of a college English class by a girl whom he had told "that, as he understood the Bible, women were supposed to listen respectfully to men, not speak out against them." Years later he did not forbid Betsy to work though he arranged with her employer to have time off whenever he needed

110

her on special occasions to cook for his men, for "a cowboy's wife had her duty to her husband and to the ranch that paid him." Blanton tells Kramer that "a cowboy can't stand a domineering woman," and he is pleased that when he is away Betsy always gives orders to the hands in his name. If his outward interactions with his wife are conventional enough, inwardly he prefers to remain detached. "Cowboys don't like the company of women much," he insists. "We don't really have much in common with them."[32]

Blanton prides himself on his independence, noting that in contrast to union members cowboys "may not be as well off as some financially, but we're more independent." At the same time he is sensitive to others and kind and helpful in many personal ways. As a real person rather than a literary type, he does not perfectly fit the model of the hypomasculine male--especially in his belief in success despite his inadequacies in this area. Betsy sums up his frustration and sense of falling short of his goals: "Not having your own place, being someone else's foreman, running someone else's cattle--that's second-best, isn't it? Least, to Henry it is." He cannot really be like Joe Starrett, but neither can he be like Shane. The result is something unsettled about his character, a tendency "to a kind of inept excess."[33]

Hypomasculine males in literature are only representations, but they do suggest an interest in a version of masculinity which is non-competitive and non-power-oriented and that persists despite the rational conviction that it is either suspect or at least unrealistic. The closer one feels to the requirements of conventionality, the more impossible it must seem. Still, it remains an intriguing possibility, which is probably more comfortably dealt with in literature than in life.

Overview--

Hypomasculine males signify an idealization of individualistic freedom and a way of life which has little to do with either success or dominance over other people. Such figures are frequently paired with conventional males with whom they form close personal friendships emphasizing mutual freedom and equality. The hypomasculine male easily crosses barriers of class, race and culture to form highly personal ties without however explicitly rejecting these conventions. Often he shows a similar interest in egalitarian relationships with women, but from his point of view categorical assumptions about the opposite sex and related sex roles cannot be ignored and so prevent the realization of this desire.

The same authors have often been attracted to hypermasculine as well as hypomasculine males. Both types place a high premium upon personal independence, and both are very skeptical about involving themselves with social institutions of all sorts. Hypomasculine males, however, do not rebel against convention but instead tend simply to go their own way, and they are not drawn to power as a means of self-preservation. They exhibit a split between a kind of formal self that accepts mainstream American conventions and a deeper self that cannot function in such terms. Because relationships with others are conceived in very personal terms which place little premium upon context, social barriers can be transcended with apparent ease-- but only as long as women are not involved. Hypomasculine males thus are not really integrated into everyday life, and for this reason they often feel shut out and very lonely.

The marginal status of hypomasculine figures prompts their creators to try to resolve the tension between what they represent and the values and practices of the dominant society. By dying or leaving the hypomasculine male can preserve the integrity of a style of life which is clearly seen to be incompatible with conventional masculine expectations. Efforts to transform him in accordance with these expectations, however, are tentative and unconvincing. Because such a male does not exhibit many behaviors that are generally associated with masculinity, his masculine credentials can be seen as suspect and in need of validation.

The interest in hypomasculinity suggests a reservoir of skepticism about many of the values associated with conventional masculinity. It belongs to the secondary and more radical tradition of individualism in America rather than the mainstream one. Probably most males are attracted to what hypomasculinity stands for though in varying degrees depending on how immersed they are in the dominant masculine value system. At the same time hypomasculinity implies a marginal status that takes its toll on those who adhere to its values. The realities of everyday life undercut their realization, and this is why hypomasculine males are most easily dealt with as literary ideals rather than as realistic role models.

CHAPTER SIX

THE SPECTRE OF HOMOSEXUALITY

While public attitudes toward homosexuality have changed in the last few years, deeply rooted negative judgments have not disappeared. Homosexual acts have always been proscribed in America, but only within the last century has homosexuality emerged as a quality of being which defines the inner essence of a category of people who are thereby distinguished from the heterosexual majority. The credibility of categories based on sexual object choice rests on the conviction that, contradictory evidence notwithstanding, everyone can be meaningfully characterized as either heterosexual or homosexual.

The Impact of Individualism--

If Americans would prefer that everyone's sexual orientation were unambiguously heterosexual, they are willing to settle for the appearance of conformity and likeness of mind in this regard. People are under considerable pressure to disguise any homosexual inclinations and (if they are unwilling to check them) to conduct themselves in all but the most private situations as if they were heterosexual. This pretense has long had the effect of rendering the majority of homosexuals invisible, and so for the most part they disappear from people's awareness. In many instances nowadays this is no longer true, but it is safe to say that most Americans under most circumstances find invisibility preferable to any sort of openly gay identification.

Homosexuals are often assumed to be different by choice. If they really wanted to be sexually normal, they would be--or at least with effort, could become so. As long as they persist in refusing to be like other people, at least some of the anger toward them reflects the feeling that only their own perversity sets them apart. The ultimate source of this line of thinking is doubtless the long-standing belief in the sinfulness of homosexual acts. Logically the concept of sin means that everyone on occasion has homosexual feelings just as everyone at some time or another has feelings of avarice or hatred or rage. Because sinners are most readily distinguished by their acts, the emphasis upon external behavior has basically traditional overtones. Colonial Americans, John D'Emilio argues, did not "conceive of homosexual acts as different in essence from other sexual transgressions--such as adultery, fornication, or bestiality --that occurred outside the sanctioned bonding of husband and wife."[1] The illness theory, which gained precedence as psychiatrists increasingly replaced but did not entirely supercede ministers and priests as moral guardians, makes a similar assumption that homosexual tendencies do not clearly set some people apart from others any more than tendencies toward depression or anxiety do.

These two approaches contrast with what has become the dominant tendency to categorize certain people as homosexuals and to use the term homosexuality to describe the reality that defines them. Typically this version of categorical thinking reflects the anxious judgment that homosexuals are wholly and negatively distinctive. There can be no gradations, for difference serves, just as in the case of people of mixed blood, to classify them as completely other. Anyone who has had homosexual experience is likely (if the fact is known) to be regarded as a homosexual though there is some acceptance of the proposition that situational homosexuality (as in prisons) and adolescent experiences ought not to count. During World War II, Wainwright Churchill points out, officials in the armed services labeled as a homosexual any serviceman known to have had a homosexual encounter.[2]

Homosexual responses are presumed to define people in critically important ways which justify assigning them all to a separate social grouping. What is involved is not, as in traditional cultures, simply behaviors or roles, but rather one's very being. As Carol Warren notes, "homosexuals are viewed generally not just as people who do a certain type of thing, but, rather, as people who are a certain type of being."[3] A profound conceptual shift had occurred by the late nineteenth century, D'Emilio points out: "Some men and women _were_ homosexuals. The label applied not merely to particular sexual acts, as 'sodomite' once had, but to an entire person whose nature--acts, feelings, personality traits, even body type--was sharply distinguishable from the majority of 'normal' heterosexuals."[4] Conversely, John Boswell observes that "Roman society almost unanimously assumed that adult males would be capable of, if not interested in, sexual relations with both sexes."[5] In traditional contexts, where the focus is upon external behavior, homosexual acts--whether they are permitted or forbidden--are not thought of as manifestations of a person's inner essence. There are no words even to correspond to our nouns homosexual or homosexuality even though there are adjectives to distinguish homosexual from heterosexual acts. Dennis Altman thus concludes that "the creation of a specific person known as 'the homosexual' is a product of modern Western societies and runs contrary to traditional mores and values in even strongly homoerotic societies."[6]

Though one encounters the feeling that the right person of the opposite sex can reverse someone's homosexual orientation, this assumption is more often applied to lesbians than to male homosexuals. One reason seems fairly obvious. If a woman's seductiveness is not sufficient to lure a gay male into responding to her, her femininity limits how far she can go in bending him to her will. In fantasy and often in fact as well, masculin-

114

ity labors under no such constraints. It is not uncommon for "straight" men to imagine themselves persuading a gay woman to leave a lesbian bar with them. Heterosexual males generally find lesbians as interesting as they do challenging, and a flourishing business in lesbian pornography caters exclusively to them. Because (presumed) lesbians in these circumstances serve male interests--whether as objects of seduction or merely of desire--they are functioning in appropriately feminine ways. Only by refusing to satisfy men does the lesbian assert her individuality, call into question her femininity and thereby attach a homosexual label to herself. On a deeper level different assumptions about how easily sexual preferences may be altered suggest the large admixture of traditional elements in the American cultural conception of femininity. Because femininity is viewed in terms of acts subject to outside control as much as inner dispositions which behavior merely reflects, lesbian acts do not define a woman in so absolute a sense as homosexual acts define a male. Hence male homosexuality in America is much more vividly and emphatically categorized than lesbianism.

One finds traces here and there of traditional attitudes toward male homosexuality. In Lionel Tiger's world of hierarchical male relationships initiation ceremonies "frequently involve partial or complete nudity of initiates, and in many there are homo-erotic implications of greater or lesser clarity."[7] More specifically, in prisons passive homosexual partners are stigmatized in ways aggressors are not. Similar forms of role playing are sometimes exhibited by members of gangs who may set out to "teach" some "queer" a lesson by sodomizing him. Even those who engage in homosexual encounters under much freer conditions often distinguish acts that are role-appropriate and therefore acceptable from those which are not. Many do not even regard themselves as homosexual if they always observe these distinctions. In general, however, categorical assumptions on men's parts do not permit easy distinctions on the basis of overt behavior because the tendency is to focus on a person's frame of mind and to assume that behavior merely reflects one's inner disposition.

Homosexual acts presumably require the subjection of one man to another as heterosexual acts require the subjection of a woman to a man. Sex as far as mainstream conceptions are concerned is inextricably linked with the exercise of power, and the objects of sexual power cannot have unrestricted claims to individuality. Women's sexual subordination appeals to American men's sense of traditional male superiority, but their aversion to sexual relationships with other males is not based on patriarchal assumptions. We assume that all males--as males--are equals and so cannot be subordinated to other males except in the most carefully defined and impersonal ways. A man cannot remain independent and free, the equal of all other males, if he is the object of another man's sexual power. Nor under most circumstances are males allowed to wield such power over those who are supposedly their equals.

In some traditional societies, by contrast, certain modes of homosexual encounter are permitted precisely because they accord with accepted views of differences and inequalities among men. Since some males are appropriately subordinate to other males and so in homosexual situations play a "feminine" role, homosexual subordination does not undermine a basic principle of social order. John Boswell points out that in early imperial Rome "a very strong bias appears to have existed against passive sexual behavior on the part of an adult male citizen." Sexual passivity was associated with political impotence: "Those who most commonly played the passive role in intercourse were boys, women, and slaves--all persons excluded from the power structure." Similarly among the Germanic tribes at a later period "no man could be sexually passive with another and retain the respect accorded a fighting adult male." Again "this does not mean, however, that younger males, slaves, captives, or men with no desire to enjoy warrior status could not be sexually passive and meet with acceptance."[8] In such cultures the basic distinction was not between men and women as biologically different beings, but between a "masculine" or superior status (that included only some men) and a "feminine" or inferior status (that, admittedly, included all women, but a great many males as well). The distinction was not unalterably dichotomous as it is for contemporary Americans, nor was everyone within a given status considered fundamentally like everyone else.

As long as sex is conceived in terms of power and same-sex encounters are not forbidden, hierarchical relationships among males accommodate themselves quite easily to homosexual forms of interaction. Though homosexual acts have always been condemned in America, the steady attenuation of traditional assumptions regarding masculinity has made individualistic considerations increasingly important as a central element in the masculine value system. At the same time sex has not lost its association with power. Thus it continues to imply the subordination of one person to another--which in homosexual contexts is unacceptable for males of any age. Because even a very young male has claims to masculine individuality, the homosexual encounter that creates the most aversion in America--and is perhaps the most acceptable in traditional homoerotic societies--is one involving a younger and an older male. It cannot be merely a concern to protect the immature that prompts this hostility, for young females are protected by no really equivalent taboos from the statistically far more frequent advances of older males.

The ideal of male friendship must also be protected from any sexual taint, which by definition denies the possibility of freedom and independence for both parties. In Cat on a Hot Tin Roof Tennessee Williams analyzes Brick's attempt to honor his friendship with Skipper as both pure and asexual. Maggie insists that this was the ultimate tragedy of the relationship between the two men "because it was love that never could be carried through to anything satisfying or even talked about plainly." Brick recoils at her suggestion that Skipper's feelings had a real element of physical desire which he could never acknowledge openly. Later Brick asks his father: "Why can't exceptional friendship . . . between two men be respected as something clean and decent without being thought of as . . . Fairies?" Big Daddy accuses him of not being willing to face the truth with Skipper to which Brick answers: "His truth, not mine!"[9] An idealized relationship leaves Brick free to control his life as a sexual one would not. Skipper may not have had as great a commitment to a purely asexual friendship, but he strove as long as he lived to honor Brick's conception. Had Maggie not forced the issue, it seems quite probable that both males could have continued indefinitely in a male-male bond that was free and pure.

Sexual subordination within a lesbian relationship hardly poses the same kind of problem from a mainstream perspective. It is not the fact that one person may be unequal or the object of the other person's power that makes such relationships seem wrong. Rather it is the illegitimate exercise of power that is condemned. A frequently employed story line in lesbian fiction deals with the triangular struggle between one woman and a man for the affections of a second woman. That the male most often wins only proves that power is rightfully his to wield. The object of his desires is "saved" not from being dependent and unfree but from subjection to someone who has no recognized prerogative of dominion over her.

All in all, individualistic assumptions in American culture greatly complicate attitudes toward homosexual acts and feelings. What in traditional contexts are simply carefully circumscribed or explicitly proscribed ways of interacting sexually with someone of the same sex become matters of one's very being as a person. One is seen as intrinsically different and yet is expected to appear "normal." Because individualism is applied less rigorously to women, lesbianism seems a less complicated matter and the chasm between normality and perversion easier to bridge. If men's confidence in this assumption has been undermined in the last two decades, it is because many women have taken upon themselves more individualistic attributes than in the past.

Homophobia and Sexual Conformity--

Because homosexuality and heterosexuality are seen in cat-

117

egorical terms as two completely separate and mutually exclusive orientations, homosexuality in the twentieth century has functioned as an important negative standard by which heterosexuality is measured. Sexual normality presupposes a whole set of attitudes toward and responses to homosexuality which make a person constantly aware of what to avoid. Thus role conformity becomes a good indication of one's probable heterosexuality.

To many people homosexuality is a threat to marriage, monogamy and the family. Homosexuals are criticized for shirking familial and procreational responsibilities, and one catches just a hint that it is unfair of them not to assume these burdens when others must labor under them. The cultural emphasis upon categorically defined alikeness dictates that all males, without exception, should be acceptably masculine just as all females should be acceptably feminine, and so all ought to be married and parents as well.

From the perspective of conventional femininity male homosexuality represents a rejection of the sexual desirability women are taught to value in themselves. To some degree heterosexual men may see in lesbianism a rejection of their masculine desirability as well, but in a larger sense it suggests a refusal to acknowledge men's preeminence and fulfill their needs. Heterosexual women who value their femininity are obliged to condemn lesbians for scorning all that they stand for. Men who are presumed to reject their masculinity and women their femininity refuse to honor either American culture's most important categorical distinction or the social consequences that flow from it. Even if their numbers are not large or their presence very obvious, they are likely to be condemned by those who remain loyal to conventional sex-related expectations.

Homosexual males are not full participants in the enterprise of furthering collective male power, for they reject the most personal manifestation of this power--sexual dominion over women. Since most remain invisible, however, their outward behavior helps to reinforce the ethic of male superiority. Remaining invisible means sharing all the public privileges that come from being male in American society, and so they are offered a very powerful inducement to support the sexual status quo. Unless there is a presumption of sexual normality, however, there can be neither acceptance on the part of other men nor rewards for loyalty to one's sex.

The conformist implications of anti-homosexual attitudes are clearly evident in the worry on many people's parts that homosexual views and feelings might gain adherents if any measure of acceptance were accorded them. Thus while committed homosexuals are obviously objects of hostile anxiety, such anxiety is by no means limited to this small minority. Frequently expressed fears concerning homosexual seduction reflect an assumption that especially younger males are potentially vulnerable to direct pressures or even such indirect influences as homosexual pornography. A close consideration of the anti-homosexual position, particularly with regard to males, however, reveals that its real focus is general conformity to categorically defined expectations, not specifically sexual relations involving one's own sex.

Peter and Barbara Wyden's book, <u>Growing</u> <u>Up</u> <u>Straight: What Every</u> <u>Thoughtful</u> <u>Parent</u> <u>Should</u> <u>Know</u> <u>about</u> <u>Homosexuality</u>, was issued in 1968 as a warning to parents to be on the alert for the slightest signs of homosexual tendencies in their sons. "Pre-homosexual" boys are clearly identifiable by their "unmasculine" ways of behaving, the authors insisted. In order to become "well-adjusted heterosexual males" boys must be able to admire and identify with their fathers." Equally important in helping "a small boy grow up to be masculine" is the mother's acceptance of her role and her "respect for the father's role as head of the family." The authors' basic proposition was emphatic: only boys who are encouraged to become conventionally masculine can avoid the possibility of becoming homosexual. "In sexually normal homes," the readers were told, "the definition of 'la grande difference' is taught naturally and early. Girls are given dolls to play with. Boys are told, 'Boys don't cry.'"10

The theory behind this argument is simple enough. Heterosexuality can only express itself properly through accepted male role behavior, for such behavior embodies what is "naturally" masculine. Males who fail to play by these rules have no appropriate channels of heterosexual expression. Their sex drive thus flows into unnatural channels, which always remain inadequate substitutes for true masculinity. Parents whose role behavior is unconventional fail to equip their sons to fulfill "normal" masculine role expectations and so lay the groundwork for the development of homosexual tendencies. So-called weak or absent fathers are poor role models while overly assertive, seductive or dependent mothers do not teach their sons how to deal with women in ways which underscore masculinity. The logical avenue of help for pre-homosexual males is therefore to aid them in learning to feel and to act in appropriately masculine ways. They will then be able to deal comfortably with women and thus will have no need of "unnatural" homosexual substitutes.

Professional psychiatrists and psychologists who have sought or still seek to "cure" male homosexuality operate on basically the same premises--which, as Joseph Pleck's analysis makes clear, are important elements of the Male Sex Role Identity paradigm. He notes that the method of selecting items for scales which attempt to measure individual sexual characteris-

119

tics "in effect assumes that the same characteristics that differentiate adequate sex role identities with each sex also differentiate men from women and heterosexuals from homosexuals." Hence the simple equation of characteristics deemed inadequate for well adjusted males with both femininity and homosexuality. It follows logically that "in most popular discussions about insecure or inadequate sex role identity, concern about homosexuality is not far below the surface."[11] Many lay persons and still some professionals continue to believe that homosexuality can be cured. Such a belief reflects a way of thinking at odds with the assumptions upon which categorizing people in terms of sexual object choice is based. The fact that categories help to create the realities they describe--in this case people whose identities revolve around their choice of sexual partners--may explain why the cure-rate among homosexual patients has always been notoriously low.

Homosexuality--particularly male homosexuality--in America is assumed to be lurking beneath the surface wherever and whenever any departure from conventionally acceptable masculine behavior occurs. Endeavors, such as ballet dancing, interior decorating and hair styling are inherently suspect. The fact that there are committed homosexuals in all walks of life in no way alters the common practice of judging a male's masculinity (that is, his probable heterosexuality) in part by his choice of occupation. The same thing is true of mannerisms and ways of behaving. Those which appear to be the opposite of assertive, decisive and self-reliant are widely assumed to be indications of homosexuality. Males who, for a variety of reasons beyond their control, are prevented from fulfilling at least some of the expectations of masculinity, may encounter difficulties in assuring either themselves or others of their heterosexuality. Indeed any evidence, no matter how temporary, of masculine inadequacy--impotence, fear, inability to find work, failure to succeed--may suggest, however illogically, a taint of homosexuality. Robert Brannon points out that "surveys have shown that a majority of all men have been worried about being latent homosexuals at some point in their lives."[12]

Rationally considered, male doubts about heterosexuality which arise in connection with temporary impotence with women or job problems do not create in and of themselves a sexual preference for other men. This indeed is not the issue, for what causes a fear of homosexuality is not perceived homosexual feelings or responses, but simply any evidence of a failure to live up to cultural expectations of masculinity. "Homophobia" aims, as Gregory K. Lehne has pointed out, not to inhibit explicitly homosexual feelings or practices, but to goad the majority of males to conform to the demands of the conventional code of masculine behavior.[13] In other words, homophobia has become a crucial contemporary element in affirming masculinity in categorical terms. If manhood must be constantly proved, the price of falling short is to risk being labeled homosexual. Some indication of an anti-homosexual stance is therefore an expected component of every supposedly normal male's pattern of behavior. Openly expressed, it often serves to bolster a man's own feelings of masculinity and may enhance his heterosexual standing in the eyes of his peers. Anti-homosexual feelings may be restricted to verbal judgments of greater or lesser severity. Perhaps most subtle of all is an apparent tolerance, which affirms one's own heterosexuality (lest anyone get the wrong idea) while insisting that one has nothing against homosexuals as individuals.

One especially conspicuous example of the effect of homophobic imperatives can be found in the way American men relate emotionally and physically to one another. Displays of closeness--affectionate touching, warm feelings, caring--easily raise the spectre of homosexuality and are therefore usually avoided or at least carefully muted. Jack Nichols insists that the homosexual taboo sours and distorts "male friendships, making them less expressive, limited, apprehensive, casual, cool, and full of competitive, dominating tendencies."[14] Indeed, as Robert Brannon has observed, "the unspoken fear which bedevils friendships between men is, of course, the fear of being seen as a homosexual."[15] In many societies feelings which we would label homosexual and the physical expression of them are not prohibited. These feelings need not necessarily be eroticized; so there is no inevitable link between them and patently homosexual desires. Americans, however, generally think that there is, and so men feel obliged to keep themselves aloof from other men in order to preserve their heterosexual reputations.

While women are not assumed to operate under similar constraints, they are still obliged to recognize limits that must not be transgressed. Self-consciousness about the necessity of observing such limits is a twentieth-century phenomenon that has followed in the wake of books and articles that began appearing about the turn of the century on women's "perversions," "inversions" and "disorders."[16] As Caroll Smith-Rosenberg has shown, close and loving relationships between pairs of women in the nineteenth century were considered "both socially acceptable and fully compatible with heterosexual marriage." The women involved, their husbands and families simply did not share "the twentieth-century tendency to view human love and sexuality within a dichotomized universe of deviance and normality, genitality and platonic love."[17]

The emphasis upon the externalities of behavior means that only actions which patently flout the canons of femininity are likely to prompt some sort of accusation of homosexuality. This was certainly true in the case of feminists in the late 1960's

121

and early 70's, and many were especially anxious to reassure society that they were really heterosexual. Even today most women
who seek to push beyond role limitations in one area feel constrained to demonstrate their feminine allegiances elsewhere and
hence their heterosexuality. It is difficult to recognize that
the accusation of homosexuality is more often a political action
referring to public role behavior than a moral judgment referring to private sexual behavior.

Still, the fact remains that the spectre of homosexuality
looms less over women's consciousnesses than over men's because
women in large measure are born into their status as females.
Inappropriate behavior may be censured and even punished, but
one does not easily lose one's status because of it any more
than a peasant or a nobleman would. For males external behavior
is not really a matter of acting as one is expected to act but
of evidencing one's inward state of masculinity. This leads to
an anxious scrutiny of actions that is much more rigorous than
when the emphasis is solely on what one does. Women are thought
to be more subject to the dictates of biology, and all sorts of
social pressures make them constantly aware of the seriousness
of role violations. Being outwardly more free, men could in
theory rebel more easily--if they wanted to. Needless to say,
the fear of being considered homosexual is an inducement to conform that comparatively few are able to resist.

Homophobia and the Loss of Individuality--

Ever since the Kinsey studies revealed that a sizeable minority of the adult population has had some homosexual experience, one of the most intriguing questions about homosexuality
is why it is generally regarded with such aversion in America.
"Surely we cannot continue to imagine," Wainwright Churchill
insists, "that homosexual interests are rare among American
males, or even that the tendency to act upon these interests is
rare."[18] Similarly it is difficult to suppose that homosexual
interests are rare among women though the Kinsey studies indicate a much lower incidence of responsiveness and of experiences. Still, societies are often intolerant of behavior which
is both common and at the same time contrary to certain basic
values. Like homosexual activity, premarital and extramarital
heterosexual relations are seen by many as inconsistent with a
high valuation of marriage and the family. Nevertheless, the
latter involve legitimate passions, however illegitimately they
may be expressed. Homosexual feelings by contrast are generally
presumed to be in and of themselves illegitimate because they
represent negations of heterosexual feelings. They are wrong to
have in the first place though of course it is even worse to express them in practice.

It may be argued that much of the negativism about homosexuality is a reflection of the emphasis within the Judeo-Christian heritage upon procreation as the only real justification for sexual intercourse. Because homosexual couplings have no procreative possibilities or overtones, they remain unnatural acts in the eyes of a great many people. American anti-homosexual attitudes are much harsher than attitudes in Western Europe, however; so a common religious tradition cannot adequately explain the generally more negative judgments on this side of the Atlantic. In the mid-1960's Wainwright Churchill came to the conclusion that "in the United States male homosexuality occasions more social and personal anxiety than in any other civilized society known to science." He found that cultures that are positive about sex in general tend to be much more tolerant of homosexuality than cultures which are generally negative.[19] Certainly ours is a sex-negative culture. Still, heterosexuals can be as abandoned and promiscuous as it is possible to imagine homosexuals as being. While the former may be condemned by guardians of official morality, they are not categorized and made the objects of aversion that the latter are.

C. A. Tripp observes that in societies where homosexuality is more or less accepted, "there is little or no tendency to assume that homosexuality implies effeminacy, or that effeminacy necessarily indicates homosexuality."[20] Quite the opposite is assumed in America. Since masculinity and femininity are considered to be mutually exclusive categorical opposites, the link between failures of masculine self-assertion and the feminine realm is thought to be very direct. Ruth E. Hartley has noted that because males growing up in American society are constantly pressured to assume "the outward semblance of non-femininity," avoiding womanly ways for many "takes on all the aspects of panic."[21]

Passivity, will-lessness, an absence of self-assertion are at the deepest level what men associate with femininity and in turn with male homosexuality. Will-less surrender of the self to outside forces, complete loss of individuality, is a possibility that American men fear and subconsciously or consciously feel they must guard against. On some level all must at one time or another have been tempted to stop trying to prove themselves. This is the homosexual potential in every American male. Since there is so much room for falling short in proving oneself as a man and since failure is so readily associated with homosexuality, men are bound to feel anxious about possible homosexual tendencies in themselves. Whether through a lapse of will or want of effort or because of forces beyond his control, any man can conceivably slip into a condition of "homosexuality."

Because a man must constantly prove himself with women, the assumption follows easily that deficiencies elsewhere in his life carry over into dealings with the opposite sex. George F.

123

Gilder feels that millions of men are open to homosexuality. "Failure in love or work may so deject a man that he feels incapable of rising to a relationship with a woman. He finds he lacks the confidence for the rudimentary acts of self-assertion --even the rudimentary selfhood--needed for any heterosexual exchange."[22] This line of thinking assumes that no proving of oneself is required in dealing with other men on a sexual level --just a surrender of one's self-assertiveness. Indeed it is not clear exactly how or even if one actually becomes a practicing homosexual under these conditions. A kind of asexual withdrawal from other people might be more logically predicted though possibly a "feminine" passivity opens the way to easy seduction. If the real problem, however, is a will-less surrender of individuality, Gilder has every reason to be concerned about a potentiality in every male which only the most careful vigilance can presumably keep in check.

Homosexuality functions as the categorical negation of heterosexuality in the same sense as femininity functions as the negation of masculinity. On this level of response the possibility of complementary and supplementary links between masculine and feminine realms fades as men face a threat to manhood which is externalized to focus on male homosexuality but cannot really be separated from attitudes concerning women as well. No matter how hard one tries, it is difficult to fulfill the demands of masculinity and not look down upon femininity and thus women, upon homosexuality and thus homosexuals--not from a patriarchal sense of social superiority, but from an inner need to keep one's masculine individuality intact. This need has grown in the twentieth century as men have felt themselves increasingly "feminized" by bureaucratic forms of dominance. Needless to say, resisting this threat is synonymous with preserving oneself from any homosexual taint.

Although the terminology of homosexual categorization originated in Europe in the late nineteenth century, the thinking it reflects has fulfilled American needs ever since. Clearly it underscores the importance of the masculine/feminine dichotomy. While openly antifeminist thinking is one way of calling attention to categorical distinctions that social realities are in many ways undercutting, another way is to displace anxieties onto the homosexual/heterosexual dichotomy. Donald Sabo and Ross Runfola see opposition to the gay rights movement "not primarily as an effort to preserve heterosexual sexual morality, but as an attempt to resist any further erosion of the distinctions between males and females and any further altering of their sexual status in the direction of equality."[23] In the twentieth century a categorical definition of masculinity has been preserved by increasingly emphasizing homosexuality rather than femininity as its opposite polarity, thus tacitly recognizing the lessening of the social distance between the special spheres of the two sexes. As long as these spheres remained reasonably intact, there was no disposition to categorize homosexuality, and this is why it did not become important until the second major turning point in the history of sex-related differences in America.

The logic of conceptualizing gender in dichotomous terms has an indirectly homosexual implication within an egalitarian context. Emotionally close relationships between equals of the same sex were widely idealized during the nineteenth century. At the same time they were not seen as threats to what came to be called heterosexual ties because gender roles included marital obligations which retained strongly traditional elements. As these elements weakened, some additional pressure apparently seemed necessary to validate sexual relationships between opposites and unequals and discourage the possibility of any between people who are equal and alike. The heterosexual imperative, therefore, largely replaced but also supplemented traditional expectations regarding intimate relationships between men and women. Categorizing people by sexual object choice thus buttressed marriage, the family and women's sexual subordination to men not as outward behavioral expectations but as evidence of sexual normality. Homosexuality and heterosexuality as cultural symbols have meant in the twentieth century that a person--particularly if he is male--cannot logically have strong emotional feelings for anyone of the same sex and the opposite sex as well. Males especially understand as they emerge into adulthood that, in the words of Donald H. Bell, the "denial of homosexual feelings by strictly limiting our intimacy with other young men" must accompany "the need to assert a growing heterosexuality." Thus "in return for the love of women we surrender feelings of closeness with members of our own sex."[24]

As with males the deepest meaning of lesbianism stems from its symbolic association with the opposite sex. This makes the lesbian an exemplar of individualism as the male homosexual is its negator and begets mixed feelings on the parts of both heterosexual men and women. For men there is a great fascination, in the words of Del Martin and Phyllis Lyon, for "the unattainable, independent woman who is not an adjunct or appendage to a man."[25] She deserves a certain respect because she represents values all Americans are taught to revere, yet at the same time she stands as a challenge to men's patriarchal authority and their personal need for unsolicited female supportiveness. If she can be conquered, men will have met the challenge she poses at the same time that they show respect for what she symbolizes. To conventional women, the lesbian is a threat in that she invites others of her sex to an assertion of self that is inconsistent with what is considered acceptable femininity. Still, they cannot surrender to what she represents in the sense that a male presumably can in a parallel situation. Also there are other ways of asserting individuality which women can follow with less danger of social disapproval. Thus the symbolic link between individualistic self-assertion on the part of women and lesbianism is much more tenuous than the tie between the failure of masculine self-assertion and male homosexuality. One cannot help concluding, therefore, that homosexuality is a much deeper threat to heterosexual men than to women in America.

Encountering Homosexuals--

Jack Kerouac's Dean Moriarty and some of his friends get a ride with "a tall, thin fag" who drives "with extreme care." Dean labels the car a "fag Plymouth" and an "effeminate car" because it has "no pickup and no real power."[26] Many people share Dean's opinion that homosexual males are all pseudo-women. Although obviously effeminate homosexuals are scorned and even abused by heterosexual males, they are not very threatening. Under the right circumstances they can be fairly easily dealt with because they are clearly different from other males and so conveniently confirm stereotyped expectations. Although all female impersonators are not homosexual, most people assume that they are. Their performances are popular with many conventional men and women precisely because they pose few threats to heterosexual sensibilities. Until fairly recently the supposed rejection of one's manhood has so inevitably been assumed to be part of being gay, that many people have refused to believe homosexual commitments or even interests are possible where there is no evident effeminacy on the part of the participants. Howard Brown tells the story of a young man who found only incredulity in his minister when he tried to talk of being gay. "I was tall and strong and a good athlete--I'd won a lot of ski meets and I was a quarterback on the football team--and I came from a good family, so I couldn't possibly be queer," he told Brown.[27]

The traditional assumption that male-female role behaviors characterize all sexual relationships lies behind the equation of homosexuality with role inversion. Thus a homosexual coupling must logically involve only one such inversion. Common conceptions of lesbian relationships take for granted the roles of the mannish "dyke" or "butch" and the appropriately feminine "femme." Hence the aggressive, assertive role is supposedly carried out by the pseudo-male, who is also the true homosexual in the relationship. Male homosexual couplings, however, pose an interesting conceptual problem for the heterosexual world, for the person most committed to homosexuality is presumably the pseudo-female, whose role logically forbids taking the active part.

The answer to this dilemma lies in another view of male homosexuals not as innocuous nellies and "drag queens," but as aggressive seducers and child molesters. They are the homosex-

126

ual counterparts of the women who dominate and often enslave men in the countless fantasies that fill the pages of certain male magazines. There is a widespread assumption that gay men have designs on unwilling males everywhere and are eager to win converts to their persuasion. No matter how much the actions of violent and unscrupulous heterosexuals may be deplored, there is a deep-seated feeling that males can be violated in a way no woman can. Where a man's will triumphs, a woman's femininity remains intact no matter how brutally or insensitively she has been treated. In parallel circumstances a male's masculinity does not. Moreover, the assumption that all males carry with them a vulnerability to homosexuality brings with it the anxious supposition that even a single sexual encounter can irrevocably cause a person to turn his back on heterosexuality. Although this supposition is neither logical nor factually accurate, it makes a good deal of emotional sense to many people.

Spending the night in the apartment of an older male acquaintance and his wife, Holden Caulfield awakens and suspects his host of making tentative sexual advances. He hastily leaves and notes: "When something perverty like that happens, I start sweating like a bastard." Such fears have been nourished in part by a school adviser in talking to Holden and his friends about how many "flits" there are: "He said you could turn into one practically overnight, if you had all the traits and all. He used to scare the hell out of us. I kept waiting to turn into a flit or something."[28]

In <u>Vengeance</u> <u>Is</u> <u>Mine</u> Mickey Spillane's hypermasculine hero Mike Hammer encounters a strange woman named Juno with "a supernatural loveliness as if some master artist had improved on nature itself." Hammer always refers to her as a goddess and cannot rid himself of the suspicion that there is something wrong about her. On one occasion Juno takes him to a "fag joint." This is Hammer's reaction to what goes on inside: "Maybe ten eyes met mine in the mirror and tried to hang on but I wasn't having any. There was a pansy down at the end of the bar trying to make a guy who was too drunk to notice and was about to give it up as a bad job. I got a smile from the guy and he came close to getting knocked on his neck." When Hammer finally accuses Juno of being a criminal, he still assumes that she is a woman. She, however, staggers him with a blow to the face and puts up a violent struggle though in the end he kills her. Only then does he realize the source of his resentment and even revulsion toward her, for "<u>Juno</u> <u>was</u> <u>a</u> <u>man</u>!"[29]

As a "drag queen" with masculine power and strength, Juno is clearly dangerous in a way that an effeminate homosexual would not be. Though in different ways, both Hammer and Holden feel threatened far more deeply than one might logically suppose ought to be the case. It is almost as if they feel trapped and fear they will be unable to resist when clearly they have only to walk away or say no. Their situations are complicated by an apparent assumption that they are irresistible to homosexual males though Hammer is candid in admitting that he is not a handsome man and Holden feels physically quite inferior to his athletic roommate. Males who express similar fears about advances from homosexuals share both this deep sense of vulnerability and also the assumption that they are highly attractive to potential seducers. The possibility that they might be simply ignored seems not to occur to them.

The attitudes of a great many heterosexual males about encountering male homosexuals can be best understood in terms of their perspectives on male-female encounters. This is where their experience lies, and so a kind of unconscious analogizing occurs. In such situations a man asserts impersonal sexual superiority over all eligible women. By responding in some appropriate way a woman validates his claims to manhood and sexual preeminence. While a male's interest may range from casual to very strong, he assumes it is his right to manifest interest and to expect an appropriate response. When this is not the case, American men tend to become angry and confused rather than clever and resourceful in overcoming opposition. Men take for granted women's willing responsiveness, and so they do not see their advances as compelling women to respond. In more involved encounters there is a sense of mutual give and take that can even cause a man to feel that the woman has led him on. If she denies this, he is likely to insist that he never would have made an advance at all had he not sensed some encouragement. At least on occasion men may look with a certain amount of envy on women and imagine that it would be nice to be able to wait for the other person to make all the advances and take all the risks. To some degree, then, a man may identify with woman's role as surcease from all the demands of masculine assertiveness though under most circumstances this identification is never carried far.

When many men either contemplate the possibility of casual interaction with male homosexuals or actually have some kind of encounter, they quite clearly suppose that the intent is to "feminize" them. They assume that homosexuals are as bent as heterosexuals on establishing a kind of impersonal dominance over those who are sexually available. Probably it is not accurate to suggest that heterosexual males really assume that they are extremely attractive to male homosexuals. The former by no means restrict their sexual cues to only the most beautiful women, for their purpose is really to manifest potency and power, not taste in feminine beauty. By analogy homosexual males, in wanting to "feminize" them, presumably seek them out impersonally simply because they are available males. The capacity for identifying to some degree with women makes heterosexual men feel very vulnerable to assumed homosexual designs. They fear being caught up in the dominant male's interest just as they assume women are. Since their identification is a very ambivalent one, they also feel panic, for they have cultivated none of the skills at evasion that enable women in fact to resist most if not all unwelcome male advances.

Rarely are heterosexual males likely to be physically overpowered or forced to submit sexually. What they react to is not fear of assault but of powerlessness before the actions of another male whose professed interest alone is enough to "feminize" them because it is experienced as a psychological assault on their masculinity. Their reactions are compounded by the assumption that a man's sexual interest is inevitably keyed to a woman's responsiveness. If women can be blamed for sometimes leading men on, surely the same logic can be turned against a man placed by another male in parallel circumstances. If a gay male evidences sexual interest, obviously he must have felt some encouragement however subtle from the other male. Even the faintest forms of encouragement can be interpreted as evidence of secret homosexual urges.

Occasional or even fairly frequent homosexual encounters on the part of males who see themselves as essentially heterosexual are probably based on a very different premise--that they are not "feminized" but retain their essential masculinity. Because their actions are voluntary, they are not inclined to feel that they have freely surrendered their manhood. Actual experience may have little connection with abstract conceptions of homosexuality as a threat to their manhood. So it is quite possible for them to subscribe to a code of masculine behavior that stigmatizes actions which in fact they commit.

Crossing into Forbidden Territory--

In Norman Mailer's Why Are We in Viet Nam? D. J. and Tex spend a night together in the Alaskan wilderness, and the awesomeness of nature itself has something to do with a heightening of their sexual desires for one another. D. J. raises "his hand to put it square on Tex's cock and squeeze . . . D. J. who had never put a hand on Tex for secret fear that Tex was strong enough to turn him around and brand him up his ass, sheer hell for a noble Texan." Tex is equally hesitant to "prong D. J., because D. J. once become a bitch would kill him." Filled with sexual desire, "they hung there each of them on the knife of the divide in all the conflict of lust to own the other yet in fear of being killed by the other." Neither makes the ultimate move, and finally each knows the moment has passed. They emerge as "killer brothers" whose destination is war. As a typically competitive male D. J. notes that in one respect he has "it slightly over Tex--the Measure Your Dick Department." The two engage in a great deal of homosexual banter, and we are told: "They is crazy about each other. They even prong each other's girls when they can." But this is followed by the assurance that "they is men, real Texas men, they don't ding ding ring a ling on no queer street with each other."[30]

Mailer's treatment certainly lends itself to the interpretation that insecurity about masculinity is closely related to a marked predisposition to homosexuality. This argument, however, does not take into account the fact that most American males to some degree are similarly insecure. If the failure of D. J. and Tex to act on their feelings for one another leads to externalized aggression, this is a trait which they share with most heterosexual males. Any common-sense definition of heterosexuality must include these two, but it must also recognize that contrary to categorical assumptions it is extremely difficult to divide all males into two separate groupings labeled homosexual and heterosexual. Because categorization in terms of sexual object choice fulfills important collective and individual needs, however, Americans are reluctant to abandon it even though many kinds of evidence contradict this way of thinking. Indeed all cultural categories are abstractions which are meaningful only if individual differences are ignored.

Anti-homosexual beliefs tell males who would like to see themselves as sexually normal that any failure to live up to conventional masculine expectations leaves them open to the suspicion of being homosexual. They learn to be wary of intimacy with other males lest this in any way encourage homosexual feelings or acts. Close and satisfying male-male ties need not be explicitly eroticized and often are not in societies in which men are less anxious about emotional and physical closeness with other males. Doubtless this is true in individual instances in America too, but in general men are encouraged to inhibit feelings toward other men which are easily triggered and therefore difficult to suppress altogether. Robert Brannon argues "that the male role so totally prohibits tenderness and affection toward members of the same sex that few men can live a normal lifetime without experiencing supposedly forbidden feelings."[31]

Common sense also suggests that interactions and involvements which have sexual consequences are not "unnatural" either. It seems likely that most of the males on the Kinsey scale who have had some homosexual contacts but remain generally heterosexual over the course of their lives have simply engaged in acts they have found pleasurable. These acts do not rule out sexual feelings for women. Nevertheless, guilty emotions are probably difficult to avoid, and ironically becoming oneself something of a critic of homosexuality is one of the simplest ways to assuage guilt.

In still another way it is easy to cross into the forbidden territory of homosexuality. C. A. Tripp argues that in societies where male aspirations are seen in non-competitive terms, homosexuality tends to be low whereas the opposite is true in a society like ours. "A boy," he notes, "who for any reason develops an intense admiration for another male may soon find his adoration drifting toward the erotic."[32] A male does not have to become a committed homosexual to respond with some degree of eroticism to males whose attributes he is taught to admire. This is undoubtedly the case with D. J. and Tex though the result is an extreme anxiety about losing their manhood.

There would seem to be no real resolution of the dilemma conventional males face with respect to homosexuality. The categorical approach to masculine and feminine values and the tendency to regard women as unequal and inferior despite egalitarian professions does not make for easy and comfortable interactions between the sexes. Categorical assumptions further suggest that because all men are alike, they understand each other better and ought to be more at ease with one another than with their opposites. At the same time men have come increasingly to depend on their relationships with women to validate their own masculinity even as the media continue to celebrate the Marlboro Man's many present-day incarnations. Add to this the threat of somehow falling short of proving his manhood which a man is often likely to feel, the homophobic anxiety that is encouraged to guarantee his masculine performance, and the likelihood at some time or in some way that he may stray across the line into forbidden feelings or acts. The result is a difficult course for anyone to follow. It is little wonder that homosexuality remains an awesome challenge to masculinity which simply cannot be dismissed as an eccentricity of a small and quite separate minority.

Overview--

Homosexuality still causes a great deal of anxiety in America, and most people continue to prefer that gay men and women remain invisible as much as possible. Homosexual inclinations have been seen as evidence of both sinfulness and mental illness, but neither view clearly distinguishes one group of people from the rest of society. By contrast the dominant tendency in twentieth-century America has been to categorize everyone in terms of sexual object choice. People with homosexual desires are seen as wholly different from the heterosexual majority not just because they may act differently in sexual contexts but because they are fundamentally and intrinsically distinctive. The greater emphasis upon a person's inward state associated with masculinity means that homosexual acts are considered a surer indication that a male is a homosexual than are lesbian acts in the case of a woman. The premium placed upon

131

individualism in America explains why it is intolerable for males to wield sexual power over other males or to be the objects of such power. This is not the case in many traditional societies, where differences in power and status expressed in sexual terms are fully accepted. In such contexts the crucial distinction is between those of superior status (some males) and those of inferior status (females and many other males). As far as lesbian relationships are concerned the exercise of power per se is not the issue, only its illegitimate use by someone not authorized to wield it.

In the last hundred years homosexuality has increasingly become an important negative standard for assessing heterosexuality. The critique of homosexuality stresses violations of role behavior rather than same-sex physical encounters. Thus the MSRI paradigm equates characteristics deemed inadequately masculine with both femininity and homosexuality. Not surprisingly, therefore, homophobia in America functions essentially to insure heterosexual role conformity especially among males and to a much lesser degree among females as well. The difference can be explained by the fact that women are essentially born into their status while males must earn theirs, and so claims to masculinity are more easily forfeited.

The special aversion to male homosexuality in America stems neither from the Judeo-Christian religious tradition nor from the sex-negativism of American culture but rather from the symbolic link with role inversion. It suggests passivity, willlessness, loss of individuality and self-determination. Since all males are considered vulnerable to such a condition, every male has within himself a homosexual potential. It is not surprising that concerns in the twentieth century about institutional threats to masculinity have focused also on the growing danger of homosexuality. With the breakdown of separate spheres for men and women there has been an increasing disposition to emphasize a categorical definition of masculinity by stressing homosexuality rather than femininity as its polar opposite. Strong emotional feelings for someone of the same sex were much less threatening in the nineteenth century to both men and women because of a greater traditional stress upon marital obligations as part of role expectations. Lesbianism, like male homosexuality, is symbolically associated with traits assigned to the opposite sex. In the case of lesbianism this means in large part an emphasis upon individualism. Because there are other avenues of individualistic self-expression open to women, however, the connection between role inversion and lesbianism is rather loose.

Effeminate males may be held in contempt by heterosexual males, but they are not very threatening. Homosexuals seen as seducers and child molesters produce a very different response. Fears expressed by heterosexual males regarding encountering ho-

132

mosexual males focus on feelings of vulnerability, of being powerless as women are assumed to be powerless before men's asser-
tions of masculine preeminence. The intent, they feel, is to
"feminize" them. Their anxiety is compounded by the fear that
their own unconscious homosexual impulses may be responsible for
encouraging homosexual males to make advances.

Categorically based expectations regarding sexual object
choice make no provision for the complexity of sexual and emotional feelings and responses in the personal lives of actual
men and women. It is very easy for men especially to experience
emotions which are perceived as inconsistent with sexual normality, and this causes a good deal of guilt and anxiety. Thus for
a variety of reasons homosexuality is a threat which cannot be
lightly dismissed by those American males who by any common-
sense definition of the term must be considered heterosexual.

CHAPTER SEVEN

ON BEING GAY IN A "STRAIGHT" WORLD

Joe Christmas in William Faulkner's novel Light in August does not know for certain whether he is white or black. In a racist society, where everyone must be assigned to one or the other social grouping, this presents serious problems of self-definition. Because Americans place a similar emphasis on classifying people by sexual object choice, each person feels constrained to define himself or herself as heterosexual or homosexual--as "straight" or gay. Since the choice often seems arbitrary, some people resist making it. The more exclusively one feels sexually attracted to members of the same sex, however, the more one is compelled to accept the label homosexual. Categorizing people in these terms blurs sexual distinctions. In some respects, therefore, gay men and women are treated in similar ways simply because they are gay, and for this reason they will share similar attitudes and responses. In other respects, as men and as women they have different experiences and see themselves differently.

Invisibility and Gay Identity--

A strong homosexual commitment implies an interest in others of the same sex which is consciously erotic. While most gay males would probably be satisfied with such a statement, gay women would be inclined to stress the more general idea of affectional preference. Del Martin and Phyllis Lyon argue "that being a Lesbian is not merely indulging in physical acts or love-making." Rather, "for the woman involved it is a way of life, encompassing the structure of her whole personality."[1]

At whatever age one becomes aware of homosexual feelings one soon realizes that they must remain hidden from general public scrutiny if one does not want to become an outcast in most people's eyes. "I wasn't particularly embarrassed about it, nor ashamed," one person has observed of his early interest in other males. "But I learned quickly to lie about it in order to survive."[2] Any substantial gay commitment is thus commonly preceded by a good deal of experience in disguising a part of one's life that undoubtedly gains an exaggerated importance precisely because it must remain hidden most of the time. Even today most committed gay people are fairly careful about how much of themselves they reveal to other people and under what circumstances they do so. "Most American lesbians live in the closet to one degree or another," Sasha Gregory Lewis argues.[3] Those who are most fearful of being found out even pride themselves on how successful they are at "passing." Others who are less anxious still realize that it makes little sense to insist always on identifying oneself as gay. C. A. Tripp argues that "a person

has to find ways to retain his spontaneity and yet avoid fla-
grant confrontations with people who do not agree with him."[4] A
large part of being gay in America is learning to lead a double
life without feeling really torn apart.

Since most gay people are not outwardly distinguishable,
they are free to be part of the larger society in ways that members of visible minorities cannot be. Their rather special
freedom to pass must seem an advantage to those who have to deal
with limits imposed on them solely by virtue of their physical
distinctiveness. Gay men have certain obvious advantages as far
as economic opportunities and male privileges are concerned.
Even when lesbians disguise their identities as gay people, however, they cannot avoid all the social consequences of being women. The fact that they are doubly oppressed certainly limits
their options and affects their sense of themselves in different
ways from gay men. While the "straight" world reacts much more
negatively to gay men than to gay women, lesbians are more likely to feel powerless and at the mercy of that world. Moreover,
because the defection of gay men is taken so seriously and other
men feel so threatened by them, they "count" more than lesbians
do. Gay men have long tended to be bolder in their sex lives
than gay women, and in outward ways they have probably been more
persecuted. But inwardly, I think, lesbians have more fully
felt the burden of being sexual outsiders.

Tripp has observed that there is a real difficulty in
looking at homosexuality as a "behavioral category," for it includes people "who are defined more by social opinion than by
any fundamental consistency among themselves."[5] Nevertheless,
the impact of social opinion on everyone with homosexual interests profoundly affects people's lives. They are strongly en-
couraged--though they are not obliged--to think of themselves as
homosexuals and thereby to identify themselves in terms of a
particular cultural category. "The acquisition of a homosexual
or gay identity," Paul C. Larson observes, "is a process by
which self-attributions, perceived rejection by 'straight' society, growing self-definition as homosexual, and associations
with gay people begin to coalesce into a coherent sense of
self."[6] Sexual orientation is accepted as a crucial element of
one's identity as a person and as a characteristic which makes
one like everyone else who has a same-sex orientation. One thus
identifies oneself in terms of both sex and sexual object choice
as a gay man or a gay woman. The two categorically based identities fuse in the common observation that it is easy and comfortable to make love to someone of one's own sex because one
"naturally" knows what will please another person just like
oneself.

All gay people pay a price in internalizing in varying degrees the negative judgments that are the basis for categoriz-

ing them as sexually abnormal beings. Only with a good deal of effort can one free oneself from these self-judgments and yet function within the larger society as much as one's goals in life require. Outwardly gay men must know how to be conventionally masculine, but inwardly they have more in common with women and members of ethnic minorities, who must live by rules that they themselves do not really make. Like all negatively categorized people, gay men and women cannot avoid the social effects of the categorization process though they have some measure of control over how it applies to their lives. Their identities as gay people are in large measure imposed upon them, and this makes them much more self-conscious about who they are and the roles they play than are heterosexuals. This self-consciousness is equally true of their identities and behavioral roles as men and women in American society, for they know these cannot be taken for granted as naturally free expressions of one's inner being. Only the positively categorized--particularly heterosexual males--are likely to feel that belonging to a social grouping is simply an expression of what they "naturally" are.

The Gay Community--

The negativism associated with the labeling process means that only among other gay people will a person feel under no obligation to disguise his or her sexual interests. Where society's tendency to stigmatize prompts homosexuals to secrecy, Carol Warren argues, "secrecy tends to intensify the split between the gay and straight worlds."[7] Specifically in the case of gay males one can speak, in Martin Hoffman's term, of a "gay world"--a loose confederation of institutions and activities that link people together in ways that enable them to meet and interact with others they know share their sexual orientation.[8] Evelyn Hooker prefers the term "homosexual community." Though not all gay people in any particular area will be part of such a community, still, like any community, it is made up of "an aggregate of persons engaging in common activities, sharing common interests, and having a feeling of socio-psychological unity" in varying degrees.[9]

The origins of the gay world go back to the urban setting of the 1870's, according to John D'Emilio, as "the interlocking processes of urbanization and industrialization created a social context in which an autonomous personal life could develop." In contrast to an earlier period "affection, intimate relationships, and sexuality moved increasingly into the realm of individual choice." Gay men as well as women gradually found ways of meeting each other and so "staked out urban spaces and patronized institutions that fostered a group life."[10] Because sexual orientation is the only thing which gay men necessarily have in common, the primary institutions of the gay community have long been designed to facilitate sexual contacts and to a lesser degree friendly socializing. Casual observers of the gay scene are likely to get the impression, therefore, that homosexual males are concerned only with sex, for many other dimensions of their lives do not belong to the gay world and so go unnoticed.

The various parts of the gay community meet different needs and thus appeal to different people. At the fringes are various informal meeting places such as public restrooms and sections of parks or beaches where brief sexual contacts are made. An excellent study of restroom sex is Laud Humphreys' Tearoom Trade. Humphreys found that "men of all racial, social, educational, and physical characteristics meet in these places for sexual union" to constitute "a sort of democracy that is endemic to impersonal sex." In contrast to the premium the heterosexual world officially places on investing sex with personal meaning, tearoom participants seek to avoid involvements and to keep contacts impersonal. Thus there is a need for a special ritual that "must be both noncoercive and noncommittal." A basic rule is never to force attentions on anyone. Each encounter moves through a series of stages based on "enough silent communication to guarantee mutuality." Another characteristic of most of these encounters is the lack of rigorous role playing. Here Humphreys notes that as long as he held to "ascribed masculine/feminine, aggressive/passive labels," he "found it difficult to conceptualize the switching of roles that occurs in some of the encounters." He came to understand that various roles played are parts the actors step into and out of rather than (categorically based) "sex roles as such."[11]

In the picture that Humphreys paints the outside lives of the participants have no real bearing on the sexual world of the tearooms, which they enter as individuals. Each makes his own way, and no one can depend on anything but such personal qualities as ingenuity and physical appearance. Thus it is not surprising that Humphreys characterizes these situations as democratic. Each person is left quite free in his selection of partners, and no one seems to be concerned with either fixed behavioral roles or the exercise of substantial power or control over others. Some rules of the game are required to permit noncoercive encounters to take place and to screen out unwary outsiders who may wander in. Only the like-minded are invited to participate. In The Sexual Outlaw, an account of many of his own gay experiences, John Rechy notes in his description of a tearoom scene: "A hostile presence enters the restroom. He is totally unaware of the sex-charged currents."[12]

Moving more toward the center of the gay world, one finds other structures that are either less impersonal or more visible than places of ephemeral encounters like the tearooms. Steam-baths and bars have a basically sexual reason for existence although they do permit informal socializing also. Private social gatherings, gay streets and neighborhoods, gyms, restaurants and coffee houses place greater stress on non-sexual aspects of socializing. This is also true of institutions that have grown up mainly in the last decade or two such as churches, political action groups and social organizations. All emphasize the independence, freedom and functional equality of the males involved --and of the females as well in the case of those newer organizations that include or are made up of gay women. Martin S. Weinberg and Colin J. Williams note that in gay baths "sexual invitations follow an etiquette involving simple and non-abrasive rituals" that are rarely "forceful or persistent."[13]

Every gay male hopes that those who interest him sexually will reciprocate his interest, but few dispute a person's right to reject any unacceptable overture. Two people determine if there is a mutual interest usually by a series of subtle cues (called "cruising") that often though not always preclude the necessity of any overt rejection. Each person preserves himself from being too vulnerable in situations where everyone is similarly free and equal. Non-sexual friendships develop but not easily, and many gay people themselves are critical of what Evelyn Hooker has called the "sexual market" operating in places like gay bars, where "agreements are made for the potential exchange of sexual services, for sex without obligation or commitment."[14] Still, everyone seems basically willing to grant others the freedom to pursue their own interests in voluntaristic settings. Elsewhere in their lives gay men may be affected by contrary ethnic, religious or social values, but in the gay world people are obliged to function essentially as individuals.

Lesbians too enter the homosexual realm as individuals. Once there, however, they establish voluntary ties to friendship groups that are stronger than similar ties among male homosexuals. Such groups, Sasha Gregory Lewis notes, have functioned as a survival alternative for decades. "They form the lesbian's extended family, and through interlocking networks between friendship groups, form the largely invisible lesbian subculture." There are lesbian bars which have been over the years "an almost universal point of entry into the lesbian subculture." These are places where friends and acquaintances gather as well as "the first place a woman might meet a potential lover."[15] The lesbian world has never been organized to facilitate casual sexual involvements of the sort that are still the most conspicuous aspect of the gay male community. If ties among both gay men and women are essentially voluntary ones, lesbians do not tend so strongly as gay men do to bring the values of the marketplace to their relations with others like themselves. Gay women's relations are less impersonal and place a greater emphasis upon more enduring kinds of commitments.

Power and Freedom in the Gay World--

The premium upon individualism which gay men learn as a consequence of growing up as males in American society is compounded by the realities of a special world where few larger ties exist and those that do are entirely voluntary. Still another factor adds to the importance of individualism within the gay community. In contrast to the heterosexual world sex tends not to be equated generally with power. Without larger social supports to enhance a gay person's power, the resources for exercising it are very limited as they would be in parallel instances if heterosexual males had only at their disposal such power as they were personally able to wield. Good looks can give a gay male a certain amount of power over others, as can money. Still, gay men largely lack the means to exercise power very effectively over their friends and lovers.

They also lack a strong desire to do so. As individualistic males they have no real investment in functioning as objects of sexual power nor too much interest in being wielders of it either. Since in most instances neither party to a gay encounter is expected to subject himself to the other person, power cannot be the real basis of attraction. There is some interest in rituals of dominance and submission on the part of a small minority of gay males. John Rechy points out that much activity that is assumed to be sado-masochistic involves merely the acting out of fantasies through such devices as costumes. Actual participants in "S & M" observe definite times and boundaries. They are "like actors in a play, performing only on stage--stepping out of their roles once the play is over." Such activity is always willing: "both the 'S' and the 'M' agree mutually to participate. There is no force to join, there is no outside seduction."16 Most gay men, including Rechy, do not find sado-masochistic behavior attractive, but from the perspective of the participants there seems little disposition to view such acts as either reflecting or reversing the innate right of members of one social grouping to inflict pain and the obligation of others to accept it.

Much more typical of attitudes toward power is a statement contained in The Spada Report, a survey of gay male sexuality. In explaining the appeal for him of a particular type of sexual encounter, one man notes that "no one is dominant, nor submissive." This in his opinion "is the most egalitarian sexual act possible--and as such, the most pure homosexual act there can be."17 As a group gay men exhibit remarkably little attraction for such forms of personal power as physical force, coercion and violence. In gay bars, for instance, fighting is relatively uncommon while precisely the opposite is true in "straight" bars. Some people would insist that homosexual interests are directly related to the blocking of normal male aggressiveness, but one might also argue that openly expressed sexual interest dissipates the kinds of aggressiveness so typical of figures like Mailer's D. J. and Tex. Gay men place their highest priority on their own and other males' freedom, self-determination and masculine independence. These can only be preserved by a kind of tacit agreement to keep power substantially out of the sexual realm.

John Rechy insists that he cultivates a tough appearance because it attracts people sexually, and, he adds, "I do equate sex with power." He has a constant need to exercise his sexual power over other people, and this makes him highly dependent on their reactions. If he is uncertain of another's response, he prefers to walk away rather than to risk rejection. Once, when he is "cruised" by two attractive men, he is terrified by "the possibility that they might prefer each other, not him." The reason is that "even with all the night's conquests, one rejection might crush him." To a degree that is not typical of most gay males Rechy's freedom and independence are limited by his vulnerability to other's responses. At the same time he cannot really constrain others to fulfill his desires as the truly powerful can; all he can do is to glory in his ability to attract men who must be willing initially to respond to him. He is highly selective in his choice of partners; and while he finds rejection painful, he never questions another man's right to reject him. Moreover, he takes for granted that those who do not interest him will accept with reasonably good grace his rejection of them. On one occasion he ignores a man who has followed him, and "the man moves desolately away."[18] If his conception of sex as power limits his freedom in some ways, he nevertheless operates in a world in which everyone accepts voluntarism as the basis for sexual encounters. His masculine style of behavior rests essentially on this freedom even though it does not always make him comfortable.

There is no real counterpart in the gay world to the affirmation of sexual superiority that heterosexual males seek from nearly all women they come in contact with. The visual encounters between gay males that routinely take place foster only personal reactions--gratification at being found attractive or at eliciting an interested response, annoyance at being ignored or else "cruised" by someone considered unattractive. It makes little sense to think of one person as playing a dominant role and the other a submissive one. Neither is "feminized," rendered subservient and expected to acknowledge a basic difference in power and status. Both males are free to respond or to ignore each other. Obviously this reflects sexual situations which involve the same kinds of people rather than members of different social groupings.

In a more general sense as well, homosexuals do not wield

141

much power collectively over other homosexuals. As in Tocqueville's America the weight of opinion and the dictates of fashion are strongly felt. Moreover, within the gay world entrepreneurs as well as community leaders and political organizers exercise some power. But this is in large measure related to their skills in dealing successfully with the world of heterosexual male power. For the most part the gay community is too loosely organized, too private still, too restricted in the ways in which it involves homosexuals to afford many opportunities for the cooperative exercises of power that enable heterosexual males to control one another in many respects as well as the world around them. As long as gay males accept being categorized in negative terms, they remain split between privately identifying themselves with other homosexuals and publicly and invisibly identifying themselves with other males.

At the same time a gay man never feels wholly a part of the male power structure. What power he exercises must seem at least in some ways inauthentic. He must deny part of himself to wield it, and it is always in danger of being stripped away. It is possible, moreover, that growing up as outsiders may mean that many are less likely to acquire the taste for power or the skills to exercise it effectively. Though this is changing, the easiest road to success for those not wholly committed to playing "straight" has been in marginal areas where little real power is involved and one's heterosexual credentials tend to be less carefully scrutinized. White male privilege has never been threatened by successful actresses or black athletes, nor by successful gay entertainers or fashion designers.

Seymour Kleinberg argues that many gay men have gone into areas such as women's fashions and the movies where they have exercised considerable power over people's tastes. Excluded from the world of male power, "gay men turn to women in culture to exercise their appetite for power," Kleinberg maintains. He seems particularly to have in mind older and more elegant homosexuals who, he says, "imitated women because they understood that they were victims in sisterhood of the same masculine ideas about sexuality." Kleinberg feels that "effeminacy acknowledged the rage of being oppressed in defiance" whereas the more masculine styles of younger gay males deny "that there is rage and oppression."[19] If a sense of powerlessness with regard to the larger masculine world is related to angry identification with women, the compensatory forms of power gay men have exercised have never posed a serious threat to heterosexual male supremacy.

Gay men have long been ambivalent about denying or accepting the validity of the emphasis upon effeminacy that is central to the categorical conception of homosexuality. Howard Brown hopes for new role models for young homosexuals, who "would certainly not confuse homosexuality with effeminacy as I and too

142

many others had done."[20] In Brown's younger days it was not uncommon for gay men to feel that in private situations they must consciously cultivate effeminacy as a badge of sexual orientation. Outrageous "camping" proclaimed a homosexual identification that one generally sought to disguise in public. An openly effeminate minority has always been a part of the gay world. Their behavior appears to involve a combination of affirmation and parody of feminine values--a willingness to accept in themselves what males in America are told to reject along with an uneasiness about what is accepted and even self-mockery because of this acceptance. A great many more gay men would probably strike the careful heterosexual observer as at least somewhat effeminate. This may be because such men often have not learned to purge themselves systematically of any behaviors categorized as feminine. It may also be due to the fact that aggressiveness is much less common among them.

The majority of gay males, nevertheless, look down on the effeminate minority and often will have nothing to do with them. Nowadays especially many are proud of a "macho" image, and some bars and other gathering places cater almost exclusively to males in leather or levis. At the same time, however, the effect that is created is hardly conventionally masculine. Men meticulously dressed as construction workers, cowboys or motorcyclists are in fact posing, or "camping," to be more technical. They are actors playing roles which they both like and yet still parody by exaggerating various facets of masculinity. At some level these men are questioning a definition of masculinity in categorical terms by acting as if it is mostly a behavioral standard that one deals with in one's own ways rather than a manifestation of biological imperatives that reflect one's very essence.

In general less role-rigid styles of behavior are the norm among gay males. While it is impossible to avoid the masculine-feminine dichotomy with its unequal valuation of the two elements that make it up, those who cultivate very masculine or effeminate styles of behavior do so in ways that suggest that they do not take these styles altogether seriously. Most gay men, moreover, opt for styles in both sexual and non-sexual contexts that blur the conventional distinctions to a greater or lesser degree. Each has a certain freedom to choose his style, and thus he cannot help realizing that any choice he makes is inevitably arbitrary. He often chooses special styles for such limited purposes as pleasing a partner or attending a party. In no case is sex-role behavior simply accepted without question or reservation. One respondent in The Spada Report finds intercourse "a great way to express the masculine and feminine parts of your personality" by assuming both roles at different times. There is a kind of rough sense among gay men that the more flexible and versatile one is as a sex partner, the more accepting one is of being gay. The more someone remains within the orbit of conventional expectations, the more likely he is to restrict himself to ways of behaving and sexual acts that are generally considered appropriately masculine. What it might mean to be "straight"-identified in a gay setting is revealed in an observation in The Spada Report that one must expect emotional reserve to characterize the behavior of such males: "Some men are almost completely heterosexual, so those types I don't require affection from."[21]

Gay men are exposed to the attractions of power and privilege as well as of individualism, but for many reasons they lack the means and often the will to follow through on the former as heterosexual men do. Thus as a group they function in ways closer to the pole of freedom than to the pole of power. Even those who find power appealing lack the institutional means to implement it effectively, and, moreover, they lead lives which place a higher premium upon freedom. This emphasis on freedom also is expressed in less role rigidity than among conventional males.

Among gay women roles have tended to be more carefully spelled out along masculine and feminine lines than among gay men. This may be the result of the fact that all women are socialized to live less individualistically than men and to accept relationships based on status and power differences which they clearly recognize. Decades ago "in public gay life, women felt that they were pressured into maintaining butch-femme roles and that the maintenance of such roles was one major characteristic of old gay life," Deborah Golemen Wolf argues.[22] In the 1950's Del Martin and Phyllis Lyon had founded the Daughters of Bilitis, a lesbian organization of white-collar semiprofessionals, who, according to John D'Emilio, were "disenchanted with a bar subculture, whose population included many women who labored in factories and appeared butch in dress and behavior." The butch-femme dichotomy had long been part of lesbian bar culture, he points out.[23] By 1972, however, Martin and Lyon insisted that the butch-femme concept of relationships had gradually been declining for nearly two decades though "the stereotype has not yet vanished."[24]

Role flexibility nowadays is greatest among those most affected by gay liberation and feminism. Letitia Anne Peplau and Hortensia Amaro feel that "feminist lesbians may be more conscious of the power dimension in close relationships and more concerned about equality as a goal than are nonfeminist lesbians."[25] Dennis Altman argues that rigid role playing has declined in the last ten years among gay men as well as gay women. "For both sexes," he says, "homosexual sex is becoming more a matter of equal action and equal response."[26]

Gay Couples--

A fairly common view of gay males is that they are all caught up in a promiscuous commitment to sexual variety. Spada chooses to avoid the word "promiscuity" in his study "because it suggests indiscriminate and random choice of partners." Instead he feels that "a gay man's sexual relationships no matter how frequent, need be neither."[27] Intimate relationships of varying lengths do exist. Paul C. Larson feels that short-term relationships should be seen "not as failures of coupling but as alternatives to coupling."[28] Altman insists that "what often appears to straight critics as an obsession with sex is more accurately a preoccupation with constructing relationships that can meet our needs for both security and independence, commitment and variety."[29]

C. A. Tripp believes that in contrast to heterosexual couples "a fundamental rapport between same-sex partners not only permits them to hurdle huge social distances but often to be especially stimulated by them." He seems to have in mind a categorically based affinity which transcends differences "in age, race, background, or social level."[30] Homosexual couplings generally assume a "fundamental rapport" rather than the attraction of opposites. Spada sees "the egalitarian nature of most male homosexual partnerships" as "by far the dominant theme emerging from the responses" to a question asking men to characterize their emotional involvements with other men. The emphasis upon alikeness and equality makes it possible to accommodate allegiance to freedom and individualism, for like-mindedness means that unity is possible without sacrificing either. "I basically want to be free; free to do the things that I want to do," one Spada respondent notes. Another observes: "I find men and their independence very refreshing. My lover and I share all."[31]

Bonds of like-mindedness and mutuality rest lightly on those involved and on the whole tend to be more fragile than conventional marriage bonds. In order to have a goodly measure of individualistic freedom, heterosexual males surrender a fair amount of power to women under certain circumstances. The support and intimacy which women provide give them a great deal of indirect power in relationships--but not much freedom. Maximizing freedom and individuality for both gay partners greatly restricts the power either has to get his own way if disagreements arise. It also makes walking away easier--especially since no legal bonds exist. Power is the most effective means of either resolving conflict or minimizing its impact. While heterosexual males have obvious power advantages, women too have power. Each therefore has weapons to deal with conflict and hopefully gain some advantage from it. Women, moreover, are socialized in the arts of compromise and indirection and so may gain their ends without upsetting a man's claim to be the head of the household. Where a male's economic or physical power is unassailable, conflict may have little meaning short of desperate actions on a woman's part. Because inequalities and the uses of power are closely linked, the impact of conflict is not necessarily fundamental and may result in advantages for one or both parties. It is not surprising, therefore, that conflict will not seem so disastrous as it does in relationships where power is largely avoided.

Tripp notes that gay males are relatively intolerant of clashes in relationships and are not good at dealing with friction. At the same time "they often are good at avoiding conflict by other means," mainly by being "quick to detect a mismatch at the time they are first choosing a partner."[32] Where there is a high priority on likeness of mind conflict is much more serious because it strikes at the very essence of such a union. In traditional marriages by contrast custom and authority provide the real glue, and there is no premium placed on like-mindedness. The widely stressed categorical differences between the sexes in America have made like-mindedness here too a highly elusive though still attractive marital goal. Because gay male relationships are much closer to an egalitarian and wholly individualistic model than most heterosexual ones, conflict must be resolved in fairly easy and open ways. If discussion and persuasion do not restore essential agreement, separation is the only recourse. As long as there is fundamental agreement, gay male relationships persist in the absence of any real power advantages available to either party. If the contrast in terms of relative fragility between such relationships and heterosexual ones seems to be lessening nowadays, it is because the advantages of power diminish as freedom and equality become more important for women as well as men.

Because gay relationships exist outside the bounds of general social approval, the larger society does nothing to buttress them and much directly and indirectly to undermine them. The fact that the gay community is organized to facilitate easy and impersonal sexual contacts is a constant challenge which can only be met on an individual basis. There is no necessary assumption among gay males that absolute sexual fidelity is crucial. Dennis Altman insists that "a long-lasting monogamous relationship is almost unknown."[33] The individualistic basis of relationships which are held together solely by the feelings and wishes of the participants is further enhanced by the absence of any real preconceptions of roles to be played. Usually both people are self-supporting and have long been accustomed to taking care of themselves in all the little ways heterosexual men generally depend upon women to provide. Whatever roles emerge reflect individual preferences and mutual accommodations. Each person's individuality is much less likely to be obscured by role expectations than in heterosexual relationships. Moreover, there is no inevitable presumption of inequality based on physical differences. Self-determination, freedom and equality belong fully only to men in America, and as males gay men demonstrate this in a special way.

Paul C. Larson points out that the authors of one study "concluded that the cultural model around which most gay men structure their relationships could better be termed 'friendship' than 'marriage.'"[34] Commenting on "a fairly equal give-and-take approach to sex" and "a fairly egalitarian approach to decision making," James A. Doyle concludes that "most gay couples who live together stress the ideal of equality and role flexibility to a greater degree than do most heterosexual couples."[35] Each person retains his individual separateness, and there is more acceptance than among heterosexuals of the fact that life goes on after relationships end. Bruce Voeller argues that some data on homosexuals suggest that in contrast to heterosexuals "they seem to be less devastated . . . by the fear of facing old age alone or by the loss of a spouse."[36] This implies an acknowledgement of a kind of ultimate separateness which loyalty to individualism among heterosexual males is not assumed to require.

In contrast to gay men lesbians seem much more predisposed to close permanent ties with one other person. New relationships are entered into less casually and more slowly, and friends play a more important role in introducing someone to a prospective mate. In general, Sasha Gregory Lewis observes, most lesbians "tend to pursue the ideal of a long-term, committed, and usually monogamous relationship." Loyalty to this ideal is especially strong among older lesbians and those least affected by feminist views. Thus it is among younger lesbians especially that one finds "women who create egalitarian intimate relationships with a high degree of satisfaction and opportunity for individual growth."[37] The result of the premium placed on freedom and independence by lesbian feminists and of their strong opposition to role playing, therefore, is an emphasis upon individualism and egalitarianism which results in less permanent kinds of relationships. Wolf argues that a major cause of breakups among members of the lesbian community in San Francisco is the unwillingness to tolerate possessiveness.[38]

In her account of the dissolution of a relationship with another woman, Kate Millett deals extensively with the unresolved tension between power and freedom. Power clearly rests, in Kate's opinion, with her lover Sita. Kate describes herself during a sexual encounter as "utterly commanded." In other aspects of the relationship as well Sita comes across as the decidedly dominant partner. She is always eager "that the controlling power of action be in her hands." Both women have careers of their own, and there is no assumption that Kate should play a conventionally feminine role. Nevertheless, her own confusion and uncertainty about her life make her highly dependent on Sita for love and support. At the same time she recognizes the ambivalence of her commitment: ". . . my longing for New York and my own life, my utter horror of staying here permanently or for any length of time."[39] To have real freedom within the context of a close relationship in which power figures so prominently involves contradictions she can never reconcile.

Relating to the Opposite Sex--

Especially in years past gay men and women, notably in smaller cities and towns, often socialized together. The presence of both sexes lent an air of plausible heterosexuality to such gatherings and was a useful protective device. Many activities and organizations growing out of the gay liberation movement have also brought gay men and women together in a variety of ways. One would expect a fair amount of fellow feeling and even of friendliness born of a sense of common oppression although sexual interests lead in different directions. Significantly, most lesbian feminists have come to recognize a greater bond with other women than with other homosexuals who are male. One reason is that they sense a very strong tendency on the part of gay males to behave toward them in fairly conventional ways. Much of the larger society's hostility toward male homosexuals is rooted in sexist prejudices that give gay men a stake in feminism. Understanding this stake is a more complex task, however, than reflecting attitudes toward the opposite sex that they have grown up with.

In part what heterosexuality involves is learning to attach erotic significance to various aspects of women's inequality. A man comes to eroticize passivity, weakness, fragility, even in many cases childishness, and in some cases the condition of total subjection that rape represents. Men can never be absolutely confident of maintaining their masculine superiority at all times, but they must find the challenge exciting or at least compelling. Since American culture has relatively few alternative guidelines for encountering women, it is not surprising that gay males display a variety of somewhat improvised approaches. The assumption that they hate all women simply because they may not want sex with them--or at least prefer men as sexual partners--is a gross over-generalization. If there are no sexual tensions present, gay males can relate to heterosexual women much as the latter in turn relate to each other. In being "one of the girls" there is a kind of equality, but not one that assumes all men and women are really equal. Another form of encounter involves playing mock heterosexual roles. Gay bars are often frequented by heterosexual women who enjoy playing safe but conventional games with men who can be elaborately attentive but always stop short of explicit sexual demands. On the other hand, John Rechy believes in the possibility of "a very special intimacy, respect, and true love" that "acknowledges--not denies --each other's humanity, individuality, and sexual choice."[40]

John Malone argues that particularly in recent years many gay men and "straight" women have formed deep friendships that break through categorically defined barriers to a considerable extent. Gay men are often quite willing to accept women for themselves rather than as representatives of their sex, and they are receptive to the idea that women are intellectually as capable as men. A really successful relationship, however, depends on the ability of both people to accept the male's homosexuality. Relationships with women can become sexual, and here Malone finds problems. Gay men tend to be little different from "straight" men in wanting to be the boss, he contends. Indeed, "the qualities that many gay men value in a woman friend--independence, strength, intelligence--often come to seem threatening in a potential sexual relationship."[41] Thus where sexual involvements are not ruled out, gay men apparently evidence little commitment to breaking through conventional expectations. They seem to feel obliged to play the heterosexual game--indeed they feel women expect them to--but they do not seem to enjoy it. Often they see women as overly demanding, clinging and lacking in self-sufficiency. "Men do not have the cloying needs in a relationship that are so typical of women," says one male in The Spada Report. "Most women that I've met want me to play a role, and are too passive, and expect me to do everything," says another.[42]

The traits that heterosexual males find appealing in women and which flatter their sense of superiority and elicit a certain protectiveness seem only to make gay males uncomfortable and even hostile. Gay men also seem to lack the capacity of heterosexual males not to take feminine role playing at face value. The latter know that dependency is a game and that women can take care of themselves in many ways. Gay men take such dependency more seriously and seem less confident about asserting themselves--though possibly no less determined to do so. One may argue that gay men turn to other men for sex because they fear being dominated by women. It is equally plausible that they shun power games with women along with conventional role playing because they are uncomfortable relating on these terms. Where sex is not included they can often be good friends with women, and on a one-to-one basis break through categorically defined barriers much more successfully than most heterosexuals can with each other. At the same time in larger situations gay men are as likely as "straight" men to reflect an unconscious assumption of male superiority.

Theoretically the same possibilities exist in relationships between "straight" men and gay women whose sexual prefer-

149

ence is known, not disguised. Some men might very well enjoy friendly relations with women in which the need for playing sexual games does not exist. Certainly there are situations in which lesbians are genially treated as "one of the boys" by fellow workers and close friends. This seems a more likely possibility than really accepting them as women who love women. If gay men find it difficult in relationships that have become sexual to rise above their masculine conditioning, it is unlikely that most "straight" men will be more flexible. Thus the only realistic possibilities for egalitarian relationships in this area lie in keeping sex out of them.

"Straight" male/lesbian relationships, however, are more apt to move in a sexual direction than ones involving "straight" women and gay men. Probably in both instances the strongest impetus for sex must come from the heterosexual person. If that person is a woman, there is a greater likelihood that she will prefer an involvement without the complications of sex. Even if this is not the case, her conditioning will usually prompt her to be sensitive to the desires of her companion and to accept a relationship which is not sexual if that is what he wants. If the heterosexual person is a male, his unconsciously sexual way of dealing with all women must be consciously curbed, and few men probably feel it worthwhile to inhibit themselves in this regard. The tendency to move things in a sexual direction will be abetted by the lesbian's greater tendency, because she is a woman, to accommodate him. That the results may very well only confirm her feelings that men are insensitive and domineering does not alter the fact that in parallel situations she is more likely to find herself confronting a person of the opposite sex on explicitly sexual grounds and relating accordingly than is a gay male.

Indeed the likelihood is greater whether the gay person's sexual preference is revealed or not. Because gay women tend less to internalize a categorical definition of themselves as homosexual and to see sexual relationships more in situational terms, heterosexual encounters can be more freely entered into. Martin and Lyon estimate that three-fourths of the gay women they have known have had heterosexual intercourse. "For the majority of these women the experience was good, erotically," they note. "But there was not the emotional involvement which was present in a Lesbian sexual relationship."[43] Such women obviously have a clearly worked out preference regarding sex partners. Experiences with the opposite sex simply confirm such a preference; they are not tests of one's fundamental orientation. That lesbian feminist loyalties may very well undercut such flexibility is a further indication of the encroachment of individualistic patterns upon the vestiges of traditionalism in the lives of many gay women.

The Conflict Between Self and Society--

In James Baldwin's novel <u>Giovanni's Room</u> David is torn between his lover Giovanni and his fiancee Hella. He wants to have children and to be safe "with my manhood unquestioned." Hence the importance of "a woman to be for me a steady ground, like the earth itself, where I could always be renewed." David is the American innocent, oriented toward freedom and away from power. His interest in marriage involves a rejection of a hypomasculine style, for he realizes that "nothing is more unbearable, once one has it, than freedom." This is why he asks Hella to marry him: to give himself "something to be moored to." With Giovanni David only feels shame at having become "so abruptly, so hideously entangled with a boy." The alternative to heterosexual involvements is for him not an idealized asexual world of male friendships, but one in which sexual relations bring only guilt and shame. Thus he can accept neither his homosexuality nor his relationship with Giovanni. He complains that Giovanni wants to be the man and the laborer with David waiting at home as his "little <u>girl</u>." Giovanni answers contemptuously: "If I wanted a little girl, I would be <u>with</u> a little girl."[44]

The hypomasculine style has a strong appeal because it idealizes close and non-competitive relationships among men. Once there is a possibility of sex, however, the spectre of dominance and submission, of loss of manhood, is raised. Although in fact homosexual relations among American males rarely evidence what this spectre conjures up, it continues to fuel general homophobic anxieties. For someone like David this is enough to poison all his relationships--homosexual and heterosexual. It is easy to accept the cultural assumption that sex represents a fall from grace. If this is true, the special world of innocence and freedom that hypomasculine males inhabit cannot accommodate real lovers whether they are women or other men.

Patricia Nell Warren's novel <u>The Front Runner</u> would appear to contradict this assertion. Billy Sive is much more typically hypomasculine than David is. At the same time Billy is quietly but openly and proudly gay. The story is told through the eyes of the older man who eventually becomes his lover. Harlan's very conventional father had taught him to "worship at the altar of manhood," and as a boy he loved competition. His running style makes him a "kicker," someone who runs most of the race with the pack and is not afraid of using his elbows and spikes to gain the lead in the end. As a coach in a small experimental college, he cannot tolerate effeminacy and is repelled by homosexuals who are not totally masculine. His ideal is "an athletic looking guy in his late teens or early twenties."[45] Billy perfectly fits his ideal.

In running style Billy is a "front runner," someone who is

panicked unless he runs at the head of the pack throughout the race. Harlan sees him as "savagely competitive" with a "desperate need to be himself, and to prove that he had some worth as a man and as a human being." One cannot help wondering, however, whether Harlan's conventionally masculine viewpoint does not influence his judgment that Billy is as competitive as he is. When people harass Billy, he "simply tuned them out," and he does not readily reveal himself to other people. He reminds one very much of Phineas in A Separate Peace, for he wants the freedom to determine his own life and yet has great charm and ability to relate to people in unstructured ways. At school "his sunny candor disarmed everyone." The same thing happens when he goes to the Olympic Village in Montreal. Like the Leatherstocking, he is basically tolerant of other people. In contrast to Harlan he respects transvestites and relates easily and comfortably to women though he has no sexual interest in them.[46]

Harlan has "always found women passive, devouring," but "Billy's male intensity met me half-way," he says. He is jealous and fearful of losing Billy and wants a kind of marital arrangement to insure that the two of them will remain together. Not surprisingly, Billy exhibits no jealousy and has no desire to formalize their relationship. In time he consents to a ceremony, which Harlan somewhat inconsistently describes in terms which accord fully with the principles of individualism and equality: "Neither of us was bound to obey, or to be the property of the other. We were two men, male in every sense of the word, and free. Yet in that very freedom we bound ourselves to each other in an equality of giving."[47]

While Warren suggests something of the special concerns in gay relationships which distinguish them from heterosexual ones, her basic intention is to help heal the breach between self and society that gay people must always confront. To do this she adopts a literary formula, going back to Cooper, which meets essentially heterosexual needs. Despite their explicit avowals of homosexuality, Harlan and Billy stand toward one another as Gene stands toward Phineas and Joe Starrett to Shane. Just as in these other books, the hypomasculine male cannot remain indefinitely; Billy is killed in Montreal by a homophobic assassin. The ending of the novel is weak and unconvincing and can only be explained by the conventional loyalties that lie at the heart of the formula which Warren employs. Harlan and Billy both are concerned about having offspring. Some of Billy's sperm is frozen, and after his death a kind-hearted lesbian friend consents to have his baby. The surrender to convention becomes almost complete when she blossoms into a loving and tender mother, who lives with Harlan on an asexual basis. He claims to have learned "a lot of things about the way women can care and give," but he adds categorically that "their caring and giving, and ours, are just two different worlds."[48] He takes another male lover after an appropriate period of mourning, but his essentially conventional masculinity remains intact.

Warren's next novel, The Fancy Dancer, is also based on a strategy of accommodation. Tom, a Roman Catholic priest who is unaware of his homosexual orientation, is courted by and eventually becomes the lover of a part-Indian loner named Vidal. Vidal is typically masculine in his outlook and style. He is tough, independent, disinclined to be exclusively monogamous and an individualist who does not identify himself with his ethnic background. His interest in Tom is strongly sexual from the beginning whereas Tom must learn to care before he experiences such feelings--as in time indeed he does. Tom's style is, in conventional terms, essentially a feminine one. As a priest he is devoted to helping others, and he is very much aware of the weight of the past and the importance of institutions. Thus he is neither the loner nor the individualist that Vidal is. Toward Vidal he remains largely content to react rather than to act. In role-playing terms the match is perfect. Not surprisingly, it is Vidal who sees them both as becoming too dependent on each other. "People don't know how to be emotionally self-sufficient anymore," he insists.[49] Before he had met Tom he had come to terms with his homosexuality on his own, and now he must deal with his life goals on his own as well. By contrast Tom's acceptance of his homosexuality relates to his role as a priest. He takes up a special ministry to gay people and in so doing affirms his commitment to others and to the Church.

Because Warren's books so strongly reflect conventional assumptions about sex-related differences, one can argue that her central characters come across essentially as heterosexual. However potentially acceptable this may make them, the fact remains that gay people are different from "straight" people in many respects. This is a present social and psychological reality which categorization both reflects and reinforces. How and in what ways to take this into account is a challenge for all who are directly involved. The situation is complicated by the fact that gay people can largely control the degree to which society in general as well as specific individuals are aware of them. In this regard they differ both from women and from people of color and perhaps come closest to contemporary Irish-Americans.[50]

Although the Irish are stereotyped in benign ways that homosexuals are not, there exists a reservoir of latent antipathy to them both as an ethnic and as a religious minority. Anxiety about their distinctiveness still lingers as the basis for viewing them in categorical terms. At the same time there is a kind of impatience regarding their differences as if somehow these need not exist. The Irish could be fully assimilated if only they wanted to be. Thus they have strong inducements to assimi-

late and many reasons for feeling they belong within the mainstream and not much support (except on St. Patrick's Day) for
pride in their own distinctiveness. At the same time they are
aware that differences do exist and still matter. They would
have to deny part of themselves to belong fully and to ignore
the fact that most people signify awareness of Irishness in
terms of negative judgments--of the Catholic Church, of politi-
cians, of attitudes within the Irish community toward black
people.

Gay people too are pressured to assimilate because their
homosexuality is seen as a negative attribute which they would
be better off without. They too could be accepted if only they
would choose not to call attention to their differences. If
differences cannot be denied without violating one's integrity,
then one faces the challenge of functioning within society without accepting its hostile judgments. C. A. Tripp feels that it
is quite possible to be loyal to the general conventions of
one's culture and still hold onto a separate identity that sets
one apart in negative ways. "As long as a person fits neatly
into most of the conventionalities of his social milieu, a localized area of alienation (homosexuality, Jewishness, or whatever) not only delivers less than its proportional amount of
hindrance, it often produces drive and even gusto," he argues.[51]

With greater or lesser facility this is what gay people
have long tried to do. In the last decades, however, many of
them have sought to eliminate the split between their private
worlds and the public world which pressures them to change or at
least to remain invisible. Patricia Nell Warren's books are obviously meant as a contribution to this effort, but they only
begin to raise the question of how significant differences and
mainstream values can be reconciled. American cultural experience has provided the basis for several different approaches,
and the recent efforts of various other minorities--particularly
women--have further refined alternatives that can apply as well
to those whose choice of sexual partners is assumed to stamp
them in wholly unique ways.

Overview--

Being gay in America requires learning to live a double
life by disguising one's sexual orientation much of the time.
Gay people of both sexes feel the weight of social opprobrium,
but lesbians must confront as well the limitations of being born
female. Categories based on sexual object choice encourage people with same-sex interests to develop a gay identity by accepting sexual orientation as a crucial--perhaps the crucial--ele-
ment of their identity as human beings. The more society's negative judgments are internalized, the more one's sense of oneself will reflect a lack of self-esteem and self-acceptance. At

154

the same time because sexual orientation can be disguised, gay people have some measure of control over the impact of the larger society upon their lives. Their sense of doubleness makes them much more self-conscious about both their sexual identities and the roles they play than heterosexuals are.

The gay world is the product of social changes that have enabled gay people to associate with like-minded others. Needless to say, sexual object choice along with all that it implies is the key factor bringing them together. The gay male community is structured to facilitate sexual encounters as well as social ones; it has many different aspects that appeal to different people for varying reasons. Everywhere, however, the emphasis is upon independence, freedom and equality for people who function within this world essentially as individuals. By contrast, the lesbian world has long placed a greater stress upon personal as opposed to impersonal relationships and upon social more than sexual encounters.

One of the most striking characteristics of the gay male world is the relative absence of an emphasis upon power. Its commitment to freedom and independence is based on a kind of tacit agreement to keep power concerns out of the sexual realm. Thus there is no counterpart among gay men to the affirmations of male sexual superiority that are so important in the interactions of heterosexual men and women. There is little collectively exercised power either, largely because the gay world is still too loosely organized to control people's lives in such ways. Gay men do exercise some power over the larger society in such areas as fashion and entertainment, but not in ways that threaten heterosexual male superiority. The priority upon freedom is also evidenced in a fairly general commitment to flexible role behavior. For the most part the masculine/feminine dichotomy tends to be blurred, and where this is not the case distinctions are often treated in ways that suggest they are not taken so seriously as in the "straight" world. Such distinctions were at one time strongly emphasized among lesbians, but lesbian feminists nowadays generally reject them in favor of egalitarian relationships.

Gay male couples seek to preserve the freedom and individuality of each partner by emphasizing like-mindedness and equality as the essential elements of cohesion in their relationships. Such bonds are more fragile than those uniting heterosexual couples because neither person has any special power advantages. Conflict strikes at the essence of these relationships and must be resolved in fairly easy and open ways if two people are to remain together. As personal freedom and equality become more important in heterosexual relationships, these too become more fragile. Roles are more flexible among gay male couples than among heterosexual ones. This generalization also

155

applies more to younger lesbian couples than to older ones.

Gay males often form close and comfortable friendships with heterosexual women because they are more willing to accept women as equals than most heterosexual males are. At the same time the former mostly share with the latter both a generalized sense of male superiority and a disposition in relationships that do become sexual to exhibit fairly conventional expectations. The response of gay males is further complicated by the fact that they do not tend to eroticize many of the feminine behaviors that heterosexual males find appealing. They are not comfortable in unequal relationships, and yet they seem to feel obliged to insist on inequality anyway. Egalitarian friendships between heterosexual males and lesbians are equally dependent on ruling sex out of bounds; the problem is that pressures pushing such relationships in a sexual direction are much stronger.

Some writers have experimented with the hypomasculine formula as a device for dealing sympathetically with gay males. Because the formula essentially meets heterosexual needs this is difficult, for it is based on a conviction that sex represents a fall from grace which does not easily allow the hypomasculine male sexual ties of any sort. Such efforts serve to point up the difficulty of closing the gap which separates the gay person from the larger society. Gay people are different; this is a present social and psychological reality which categorization reflects as well as reinforces. They can be accepted if they do not call attention to what makes them different, but the problem remains how to function effectively in a society which stigmatizes one in fundamental ways without accepting such crippling judgments.

PART III

BREAKING DOWN THE BARRIERS

CHAPTER EIGHT

ASSIMILATION VERSUS PLURALISM

A perennial hope of Americans is that the primacy of the individual will remain paramount despite the existence of the forces of "mechanism" in society, to use Charles Horton Cooley's term. In recent decades sex-related role expectations have been criticized as arbitrary impositions that undercut the practice of individualism. Because middle-class heterosexual males remain the keepers of mainstream values, they have generally been ambivalent onlookers as many women and gay people have questioned long-held convictions about their status in society. While Leatherstocking always stressed a commonality behind white and red "gifts," most people do not see female and homosexual "gifts" as potentially irrelevant to the processes of interaction. The categorically defined distinctiveness of women as well as of homosexuals is assumed to be the key to understanding and dealing with them. Because sex-related differences are deemed so important, efforts to reconsider them have the potential of fundamentally challenging assumptions which individualism both upholds and yet also ultimately undercuts.

Minority Consciousness--

For some time now it has been common to refer to women and gay people in minority-group terms. One of the first persons to suggest that women are a minority-group was Helen Mayer Hacker. In 1951 she drew upon Louis Wirth's general definition of a minority as "any group of people who, because of their physical or cultural characteristics, are singled out from the others in the society in which they live for differential and unequal treatment, and who therefore regard themselves as objects of collective discrimination." By definition "minority status carries with it the exclusion from full participation in the life of the society." This definition links categorizing people in negative terms not just with differential but with collectively discriminatory treatment. Those who are not aware of discrimination as well as those who accept differential treatment as proper will "feel no minority-group consciousness, harbor no resentment, and, hence, cannot properly be said to belong in a minority group."[1] Clearly as long as women see themselves in conventionally categorical terms, they will not regard themselves as a minority group but rather as persons who are fundamentally different from men but still free to fulfill themselves as female individuals and as Americans.

With reference to lingering traditional expectations buttressed by heterosexual assumptions, women are not a minority but a sex, whose individual fates are intimately bound up with the lives of specific males of all classes and ethnic and racial backgrounds. Categorizing women in terms of sex, however, creates the basis for a minority-group status by insisting upon their collective separateness and failing to insure their functional equality with men. The negative designation of any cultural category creates the framework for such a status. The widespread disposition to justify categorization, however, is what in time produces a minority-group consciousness. Americans have rarely been content merely to label and then to exclude groupings of people from equal participation in the society. Nature must validate such a practice and the negatively categorized acknowledge their natural limitations. While external controls are not abandoned, people are encouraged to accept willingly a collective identity which ultimately rests on individualistic premises. The more individuals come to see themselves in categorically defined terms, the more they are brought into the mainstream value system. As long as a separate status remains acceptable, the expression of individualism can be contained within categorically articulated structures. A minority-group consciousness evidences the failure of categorization wholly to reconcile people to the limitations that nature has supposedly imposed upon them.

Nancy F. Cott's study of women in New England in the late eighteenth and early nineteenth centuries emphasizes the importance of a sense of collective identity and friendship ties among women as necessary preconditions for protesting their inferior status in American society. The common identification of women with the heart, Cott suggests, implied that "they would find answering sensibilities only among their own sex." While close ties with other women acknowledged the validity of sexual categories, these ties were purely elective and "assumed a new value in women's lives in this era because relations between equals--'peer relationships'--were superceding hierarchical relationships as the desired norms of human interaction." These voluntary forms of interaction "expressed a new individuality on women's part" as well as the "construction of a sex-group identity." Cott sees both the "woman question" and the women's rights movement of the nineteenth century as "predicated on the appearance of women as a discrete class and on the concomitant group-consciousness of sisterhood." Even though only a few women actually challenged sexual categorization and favored going beyond the boundaries of their sphere, "not until they saw themselves thus classed by sex would women join to protest their sexual fate."[2] Since women had no collective sexual fate until modern times, feminism reflected categorical assumptions even as it protested their limitations.

During the last few decades minority-group consciousness has been widely emphasized in many areas of American life. Women and gay people have joined a variety of other groups in calling for freedom from forces that control people's lives and prevent them from fully participating as individuals in society. While there are significant distinctions among minority groups, there are important similarities arising from the way in which cultural categories function in America as models for dealing with all significant collective differences among people. Moreover, the various movements have greatly influenced one another as elements of a wide-spread challenge in this generation to the limits long maintained by categorizing Americans in various ways. This is important not only for the challengers, but also for the challenged. Wherever the applicability of individualistic assumptions can be successfully asserted, the forces of "mechanism" are brought into question.

Assimilation--

The minority-group analogy has suggested to many people a cultural model for dealing with sex-related differences based generally on the possibilities of assimilating individuals into the mainstream of American life. The motto "E pluribus unum" on the Great Seal long ago summed up the general assurance "that this new land would bring unity out of diversity as a matter of course."[3] Viewing ethnicity in such terms suggests a process in which immigrants and their descendents acquire individuality and by so doing become Americans. They cease to think of themselves as part of a series of larger wholes that had characterized life in the old country and come to see themselves as essentially individuals free to rise on their own and responsible for their own lives. Because individualism has always been seen as a defining characteristic of a way of life consciously attained, it follows that all ethnics who are assimilated into the larger society choose to become Americans.

To apply assimilationist principles to women and gay people means emulating conventional masculinity. While June Singer criticizes "some women" for "attempting to be as much like men as it is possible for a woman to be,"[4] the masculine model remains the most complete embodiment of the allegiance American culture pays to individualism. The logic of this connection has long been obvious to those who have questioned conventional sex roles in America. In 1891 a woman writing in Popular Science Monthly noted that generally speaking "when the importance of individuality has been insisted on, the individuality in view is that of man." As far as women are concerned, it is "enough for them if they can be so fortunate as to minister not unworthily to some grand male individuality." Nevertheless, they have been listening to all the talk about individuality and "are applying it to themselves."[5] The fact that the principles of individualism are potentially applicable to everyone is what permits a pattern of thinking that would be inconceivable in societies in which rights and privileges flow from outward social distinctions which are considered unalterable.

Victoria Billings maintains that independence is what women need most in America: "It puts them in control of their lives and gives them the chance to consider a wide range of options, including those outside the typical bounds of their sex role." Equality of opportunity is important, she notes, but women must have the will to take advantage of opportunities available to them. While "men have learned how to meet their needs for security without sacrificing too much individuality or independence," Billings feels, most women remain convinced that security is more important. Obviously this must change. Billings insists that "women should not blindly follow the success patterns that have trapped thousands of men unsuited for the struggle," but still much of her advice regarding work and success agrees perfectly with the strategies aspiring males have long been taught to employ. She cautions against becoming too closely involved with one's co-workers. After all, "men have emotions and prejudices, but they're trained to disguise them." Women are also reminded that economic mobility is part of success. After two years on a job, it is time to reevaluate one's situation.[6] Clearly for Billings women must become part of the world of male achievement by pursuing success and asserting their personal independence.

The classic assimilationist argument on women's behalf remains Betty Friedan's The Feminine Mystique, the manifesto which heralded the advent of contemporary feminism. Friedan attacks "the glorification of women's role" as "a poor substitute for free participation in the world as an individual." The "unique human capacity . . . to live not at the mercy of the world, but as a builder and designer of that world" applies, in Friedan's view, to women as well as men. If women are to free themselves from the limitations of the "feminine mystique" and "take their education and their abilities seriously and put them to use, ultimately they have to compete with men." She feels that "it is better for a woman to compete impersonally in society, as men do, than to compete for dominance in her own home with her husband, compete with her neighbors for empty status, and so smother her son that he cannot compete at all." Friedan has no essential dispute with how masculinity is defined in America. Indeed, one of her strongest arguments against the "feminine mystique" is that women under its spell rear their sons to be overly dependent and hence unmasculine. Not surprisingly in this context, she ominiously refers to "the homosexuality that is spreading like a murky smog over the American scene." Friedan's only objection is that women have been shut out of the world of truly masculine achievement and competition. If a woman is clear about what she wants in life, "she can fulfill a commitment to profession and politics, and to marriage and motherhood with equal seriousness."[7]

Assimilation involves, according to Stephen Steinberg,

"the adoption of significant aspects of the dominant culture, but that does not preclude subtle differences in values and outlook."[8] It does not require that all distinctions be obliterated--only those which undercut the integration process. Friedan assumes that if women compete with men on the same terms that the latter compete with one another, feminine role expectations need not be an impediment. In her opinion women are encouraged to make too much of housework and mothering--tasks that can easily be accomplished when there is an incentive to get them out of the way. Like ethnics women will retain some differences, but these should constitute no essential barrier to assimilation. What matters is not minor differences, but the individualistic values to which men and women both have the right to lay claim.

An assimilationist approach to male homosexuality may very well support categorical assumptions about women. The tactically prudent course is simply to advance one's own special claims to integration into the masculine mainstream. Needless to say, women can do the same thing in reverse with regard to homosexuality, as Friedan makes clear. Wainwright Churchill's cross-cultural study of male homosexuality came out not long after The Feminine Mystique. The author's basic concern is the large number of males whose bisexual interests cause them to be stigmatized as homosexuals. His sympathies do not extend to males who are exclusively homosexual, and he blames their exclusiveness for the minority status which categorization spells out for them in America. Outside Judeo-Christendom there are no homosexual minorities because "homosexuality seldom if ever becomes fetishized into a way of life." There are many men in our society as well "who participate in homosexual relationships sporadically or even regularly who never identify themselves with a homosexual minority and who therefore do not take on the characteristics of a minority."[9] Homosexual interests that are not exclusive are, in Churchill's opinion, part of normal male sexuality and thus should not set men apart. Because he does not question the masculine/feminine dichotomy, he must accept as unequal and inferior not only women but those men whose strongly homosexual interests cause them to be similarly labeled as truly different. Like Friedan he is concerned with assimilating as many people to the conventional masculine standard as possible, not with fundamentally questioning that standard.

Morton Hunt suggests an alternative route to social acceptance. He speaks approvingly of those who "live openly as gays, keeping a certain amount of the manner and style of gayness but basically adopting a straight lifestyle, even as people from another country keep some of their favorite customs while becoming Americans." The acceptance Hunt has in mind is based on as near perfect an approximation of heterosexual marriage patterns as it is possible for gay people to achieve. He obviously dislikes what he terms "queer" gays, who behave in ways that "straight" people find different and therefore hard to accept. By contrast "straight" gays in many important respects resemble "healthy and successful heterosexuals." Hunt's ideal gay couple consists of a successful designer of middle-class homes and an equally successful interior decorator. These two men live together in a wealthy Marin County suburb north of San Francisco. While the two are, according to Hunt, distinctly gay, "their relationship is very much like that of a straight husband and wife of the modern, liberated kind."[10] This is why they can be so close to their heterosexual friends and why these friends find it so easy to like them.

The model Hunt suggests is as likely to work for gay couples in Marin County as it is for black couples in Westchester County although it requires much patience and forbearance on the part of those who must labor to make themselves acceptable to a majority that is likely to remain wary of them for some time to come. While the ultimate goal is the elimination of all important differences, cultural categories remain a crucial element in the process of assimilation. Heterosexuality and masculinity as standards to which everyone is to be assimilated as nearly as possible are reinforced by people's continuing awareness of homosexuality and femininity as important negative reference points. Richard Zoglin suggests that "business appears to be less afraid of homosexuals than it is of overt homosexual behavior."[11] The assimilationist model obviously does not include homosexuals who do not fit easily into a middle-class world. If they cannot or will not conform, they remain "queer," unassimilated and hopefully invisible.

Within the gay world itself one can find many evidences of an apparent movement toward assimilation. Such an approach had been advocated in the 1950's and 1960's by "homophile" leaders. The Mattachine Society, for instance, soon came to be dominated by people who insisted that homosexuals were just like everyone else except for the very private matter of their sexual object choice. In 1953 the Los Angeles group wrote: "Homosexuals are not seeking to overthrow or destroy any of society's existing institutions, laws or mores, but to be assimilated as constructive, valuable, and responsible citizens."[12] In the 1970's as gay liberation itself moved in a civil rights direction, Barry D. Adam argues, the distinction between the "homophile" and activist approaches blurred. The successes of gay liberation, in his opinion, hastened its demise first in creating an improved environment for gay capitalism and second in "the emboldening of the upper middle class and cooptation of the movement by the resurrected homophile approach." He has in mind such figures as Leonard Matlovich and David Kopay, who may not have been welcomed by the military and sports worlds but who nevertheless openly asserted their right and desire to belong to them. Thus "white, middle-class males appear increasingly willing to embrace the assimilationist formula, adopting the symbols of conformity in return for (often vicarious) participation in the privileges of their class and sex."[13]

One of the most interesting developments within the gay world of the 1970's was a marked increase in the emphasis upon a very masculine appearance, what Jack Nichols called "Butcher Than Thou."[14] In 1975 Wayne Sage pointed out that in the previous five years the number of supermasculine bars had increased 40%, "a rate faster than for any other type of gay bar." Sage also noted that "not unlike the straight world's swinging-singles bars, the urban gay scene puts a high premium on youth, good looks, and, in men, masculinity."[15]

Ambiguities of Assimilation--

Like ethnic versions of the assimilationist model, proposals such as Hunt's and Friedan's incorporate both an acknowledgement of categorical differences and the expectation that these differences will increasingly fade into the background as assimilation progresses. One problem is that differences may not fade away completely or quickly enough to satisfy the majority--or at least its most vocal spokespersons. Another problem is that assimilation may be too selective to qualify as a genuine acceptance of majority values. As long as a minority group is considered categorically distinctive, its approximations of dominant patterns will probably strike many within the mainstream as imperfect and therefore unacceptable. Still another and more complicated problem is that the pursuit of opportunity, which is a basic component of the assimilationist model, yields results which often enhance rather than mute differences.

Since the aim of success is not to make all people economically alike, it is collectively as well as individually in the interest of those who are already part of the mainstream to use categorically defined differences to enhance their own competitive positions. Because the criteria for success have not been established by minority groups, it is not surprising that in many ways members of them may have fewer advantages. As Milton Friedman has maintained, the marketplace only "guarantees an individual the freedom to make the most of the resources he happens to own," and these "reflect largely the accidents of birth, inheritance, and prior good or bad fortune."[16] Theoretically competition is supposed to be based on personal merit alone, but it is impossible to separate personal merit entirely from extrinsic advantages. Moreover, because success in this century has become increasingly linked with complex cooperative relationships, an emphasis upon likeness of mind can justify exclusions on the grounds of incompatibility. Writing about incentives in business in 1938, Chester I. Barnard argued "that ra-

165

cial hostility, class antagonism, and national enmities" (and, one might also add, sex-related tensions) can seriously impair cooperativeness. "The most intangible and subtle of incentives" is "the feeling of personal comfort in social relations."[17]

Success thrives on categorical thinking, and any useful social differences can be exploited by all concerned. Where it is not in the economic interest of minority-group members to divest themselves of their distinctiveness there is no reason to suppose that they will. In a book subtitled Corporate Gamesmanship for Women, Betty Lehan Harragan insists that "it would not occur to an ambitious man to downplay an inborn resource, whether it's height, good looks, or family connections." A woman must become elaborately versed in how men operate with the purpose in mind "not to 'join them' but to surpass them." She makes a great mistake by trying to talk to men in their own terms. Instead she should aim to control communication by obliging men to use non-sexist language with which they are unlikely to be very comfortable. Women cannot get rid of the stereotyped assumptions concerning the opposite sex in men's minds. "What they can do is to use the stereotype when it suits their purpose, but only so far as to confound the opponents." It is possible to manipulate men successfully who want to relate to one as a daughter or a mother figure, but Harragan warns with particular reference to sexual games that "not all male sex-stereotypes of women are equally subject to manipulation." Since her purpose is to teach women to be "viable activists in the impersonal master game of corporate politics where the goal is money, success, and independent power,"[18] she has no reason to encourage any form of assimilative behavior which does not contribute to a woman's competitive advantage.

There are, moreover, all sorts of ways in which minority-group contacts may be useful in furthering one's success though the frequent observation is that women and gay people are only beginning to develop this potential. The competitive pursuit of success does not rule out any legitimate advantage a person may have at his or her disposal. Where minority-group membership can be beneficial, it can be exploited. Where it is not, it can be dispensed with insofar as this is realistically possible. Americans' general loyalty to equality of opportunity makes it difficult for mainstream males to reject entirely the demands of women and gay people for a chance to succeed. To the degree to which the result involves assimilation, the primacy of mainstream values is obviously underscored. If loyalty to success and power also leads to exploiting special group advantages, such loyalty cannot be altogether condemned even if the way it is expressed may often be deplored.

Women and openly gay people--like members of ethnic minorities--are frequently criticized both because they are different and presumably unable to compete on established terms and also because there are ways they possibly can take unfair advantage. Thus categorically defined differences easily become part of the competitive process, and this makes them the basis of much potential friction. Jewish- and Japanese-Americans compete well and succeed in large numbers, and this reality has actually enhanced antagonisms. There is no reason to suppose, therefore, that the case is different with women and gay people who seek power and success. There are likely to be many individual and collective examples of attainment and influence. Yet insofar as even relatively minor differences remain conspicuous, cultural categories will seem as valid as ever. Thus the mainstream male majority is likely to conclude that women and homosexuals are unable or unwilling to meet the challenges of assimilation.

The more assimilation is stressed as an ideal appropriate to particular groups of people, the more sensitive many members of the larger society become to characteristics which cannot be deemed irrelevant to the activities that bring people together. Thus there is a fine line on the part of the male majority between complacency and alarm with regard to women and gay men as potential equals in American society. Morton Hunt's willingness to accept fully assimilated homosexuals coexists with an obvious uneasiness regarding those who remain different. It therefore seems likely that for some time assimilationist assumptions regarding sexual minorities will cause males in America to be hypersensitive to the issue of differences in patterns of behavior. They will remain anxiously alert for any indications in the way women and homosexuals speak or act that seem to challenge or undercut their basic assumptions about their own masculinity. Ironically hypersensitivity to differences coexists with a strong vested interest in the perpetuation of such differences and the social groupings which presumably embody them.

As the reactions to campaigns for equal opportunity and civil rights for gay people indicate, the darker side of assimilation is the fearful possibility of minority-group ascendancy. Grant homosexuals equality and soon they will impose their values on increasing numbers of vulnerable young people. Analogous concerns, fears and resentments certainly form the basis for many men's responses to increased power and opportunity for women and thus feed into a long tradition of anxiety about female dominance. Thomas Berger's Regiment of Women takes place in the twenty-first century where women rule and sex roles are totally reversed. Men are trivial and silly while women are brutal and aggressive and use artificial penises to render men sexually subservient. Georgie Cornell is told by a friend that what women seek in anal intercourse is "power. . . . Pure and simple." He tells a psychiatrist that he does not want to be a boss; he just does not want to be bossed. Her response, significantly, is that this is "unrealistic. The human condition is such that, of two sexes, one will dominate."[19]

Not surprisingly there are women whose quest for personal success involves compounding such fears and deploring what they perceive as the eclipse of male supremacy. Natalie Gittelson has entitled her look at modern men _Dominus_, which she informs the reader means in Latin "master--once a title of honor, accorded to men." Gittelson argues that in the early 1970's men wanted to be both fair and just toward women. Only in time did men begin to wonder how they could be men if women were losing their will to be women. Some men therefore became openly hostile, some compulsive seducers, "but perhaps the most grievously wounded were those who responded to man's fall from eminence by disowning _dominus_ entirely." She refers ominously to "weakening our heterosexual foundations, defaming the family and fatherhood," and perverting "the meaning and substance of manhood, as manhood had always been understood." Gittelson finds that businessmen have been fairly accepting of aspiring women, but they have laid down the law: "The price--or the penalty--for success in a man's world was, in effect, to become one."[20] Clearly the world needs unassimilated women who defer to their men, succor them and support their manhood.

When sex and competition in the marketplace are no longer separated, tensions are greatly increased. Heterosexual men are certainly willing to use sex as a competitive weapon against working women and often resent them both because this tactic seems necessary and because they fear sex may be used against them. A more open pursuit of success and power on the part of gay males easily stimulates similar anxieties. A major component of anti-homosexual attitudes is the feeling that essential emotional distancing among males is threatened by sexual possibilities. Sex is too potent a competitive weapon to be given up unless sexual feelings can be ruled altogether illegitimate. Because this is impossible where women are concerned, the alternative of lowering tensions by declaring sex out of bounds on the job scarcely seems feasible to many men.

Especially where other gay men are concerned, the temptation to use sex if some advantage is to be gained may very well increase along with the possibilities of openness and legitimacy. The fact that most homosexual activity presently evidences relatively little destructive competitiveness or much concern for power is probably because it occurs outside the economic realm. If this were no longer true, it hardly seems likely that gay men (or women) would be more scrupulous than "straight" men or women who are devoted to getting ahead in the world. Sex can easily become a weapon as well as a commodity to be marketed as part of the pursuit of success. Common sense may rule it out of bounds in specific situations, but it is not common sense that prompts either its use or the suspicion that others are committed to its use.

Pluralistic Possibilities--

Because inclusion within the cultural mainstream seems to imply terms exclusively laid down by the white heterosexual male majority, misgivings about assimilation on the part of many minority group members themselves are both understandable and inevitable. Reluctance to fulfill the conditions of assimilation has been an important element in the reaffirmations of cultural pluralism among a variety of ethnic minorities in the last twenty years. The idea of cultural pluralism was first advanced in 1915 by Horace M. Kallen. Rather than assimilation, he proposed a "democracy of nationalities" interacting within the same "federal republic." Each group would enjoy spiritual autonomy although Kallen did not seem to think political and economic autonomy ought to be included as well. Philip Gleason has argued that Kallen attributed inborn racial qualities to groups and that his racialism was central to his supposition that ethnic nationalities would perpetuate themselves indefinitely. In the decades following, a diluted form of the idea of cultural pluralism became widely accepted and by the 1950's meant only that diversity was good provided it was not divisive.[21]

During the last two decades almost the opposite conclusion has been advanced by many who have looked to cultural pluralism as a means of enabling people to preserve unique group differences. Their hope, like Kallen's, is that America will thus exhibit a cultural richness and variety much superior to the uniformities that assimilation suggests. Within the feminist and gay rights movements there have been similar thrusts, particularly in attempts to foster group self-awareness and promote various forms of collective action. The influence of the reaffirmations of ethnic identity has been direct and powerful. It therefore seems justifiable to see these sexual minority-group efforts as posing a pluralist alternative to the strategy of assimilation.

Isolated in many respects from one another and socialized, especially in this century, to view themselves mostly in terms of their ties with men, women have been challenged to think in terms of the special bonds that unite them as a sex. Similarly gay people have been challenged to move collectively beyond a way of life that has long been hidden and very loosely organized. Thus many observers have discerned the emergence of sex-related subcultures along with subsocieties and communities. My own preference is to distinguish between subcultures and subsocieties, but the term subculture (or even culture) is frequently used both to refer to collectively held values and to their institutional embodiments. Communities may refer specifically to localized versions of the latter, but the tendency is

169

often to use the term more generally as well and thus to equate community with subculture.

Laud Humphreys and Brian Miller argue that "the history of ethnic minorities, women, and gays has been one of securing a cultural context in which to assuage problems of self worth and identity."[22] Such a context is built of materials that already exist in the form of traditions, institutions and ways of interacting; it is expanded through greater awareness and understanding of others like oneself. One comes to see oneself as part of a larger whole, to take pride in such an awareness, and thereby to emphasize the importance of one's identity as a woman or a gay person. Knowing more of one's collective past--through access to new studies in women's history and gay history--also helps in building a subcultural sense of commonality, and this sense in turn forms a basis for new subsocietal and community institutions and relationships.

John D'Emilio emphasizes the importance of the legacy of the past, for he sees an urban gay subculture as taking shape in the 1940's. The widespread treatment of homosexuality in the media in the 1960's, he argues, involved "the implicit recognition that gay men and women existed in groups with a network of institutions and resources to sustain their social identity." This treatment "strengthened a sense of belonging to a group" even for those who remained in hiding while others gained access to the subculture as a result of what they learned. Until the 1970's, however, the numbers involved were very small. Then as gay liberation pressure brought about a decline in police harassment, "the gay subculture flourished as never before" in major American cities. Gay liberation encouraged individuals to "break out of the ideological prison that confined them to a sexual self-definition." A purely "sexual subculture" was transformed into an "urban community" as "the group life of gay men and women came to encompass not only erotic interaction but also political, religious, and cultural activity."[23]

According to Humphreys and Miller, "the emergence of an institutionally diverse gay culture" means "the movement of covert individuals from peripheral involvement in gay recreational scenes to the building of enriched identities in a highly developed gay cultural context."[24] Humphreys stresses the importance of consciousness raising and of role models "to convey the pride of gay culture." Without the example of those who are openly gay "it is not possible to escape the oppressive self-hatred and impoverishment" that have so long been a part of belonging to a deviant minority in America.[25] A "real gay community," Dennis Altman therefore asserts, consists of a set of institutions "that represent both a sense of shared values and a willingness to assert one's homosexuality as an important part of one's whole life rather than something private and hidden."[26]

170

In The Politics of Homosexuality Toby Marotta describes the philosophy and strategies of those members of the gay liberation movement who were most committed to the building of a gay subsociety. At first these people, whom Marotta terms reformers, were a faction within the Gay Liberation Front. Their aim was to encourage homosexuals to be openly gay "by developing and protecting gay-identified enterprises, by claiming areas frequented by homosexuals as 'gay turf,' by eliminating obstacles to the efflorescence of identifiably gay communities, and by helping homosexuals and heterosexuals alike appreciate the meaning of sexual liberation." Conflicts with others who wanted extensive changes in American society and who were openly critical of many aspects of the gay community highlighted the fact that the reformers simply wanted more and more gay people to share their own positive outlook about themselves and their special world. They withdrew from the Gay Liberation Front to form the Gay Activists Alliance, one of the professed aims of which was "the right to express our own individuality." They did not endorse cultural isolation but rather a form of pluralism in which culturally different communities remained distinct and yet individuals within them still had ties to the larger society.[27]

The most visible parts of the gay subsociety tend to be dominated by gay males, who already had a much more elaborately organized set of alternative institutions than gay women did. The needs of the latter have been and continue to be more quietly and privately met. As Marotta says of parts of Greenwich Village, "the defining ambience of the Village, as of most gay ghettos, is male homosexual; lesbians there as elsewhere cluster together in their own friendship groups, social clubs, and apartment buildings." The gay subsociety thus still reflects the strong emphasis upon sex that has long been true of the gay world. This remains, Marotta argues, a source of tension as far as the larger society is concerned as well as a "source of continued dispute and division between gay men and lesbians themselves."[28]

It makes sense to think of a lesbian subsociety that is separate from that of gay males. The lesbian community in San Francisco developed in the early 1970's, Deborah Goleman Wolf argues, from the activities of women who separated themselves from heterosexual feminists and gay male activists "to develop support groups based on their own specific needs." In terms of long-range goals "the ideal is a community of lesbians with a core of politically oriented lesbian-feminists whose presence will serve to define and articulate the community." There is a strong emphasis upon equality in individual relationships, "whether of friendship or of love," for these are the building blocks of the community. Such relationships "have two components: support, and the development of the potential of each person."[29] If voluntarism is the basis of membership in the lesbian community, mutual supportiveness and a focus on the individual are among its most important values.

In more open and obvious ways in the last two decades a blossoming women's subculture and subsociety can be described. From consciousness-raising groups to all sorts of collectives, from women's studies programs in colleges to women's banks, presses and other business enterprises, from local action groups to national political organizations, many women have built a series of institutional structures all their own and have developed a strong and positive sense of collective identity. Historical scholarship has increasingly revealed the complexity of the tradition upon which this process rests. As Elizabeth Pleck and Nancy Cott have pointed out, "recent scholars have been exploring women's creation of their own subculture, a way of life defined by language, tasks, and values peculiar to women."[30]

Here as well as among gay people the processes seem quite similar to what William Petersen describes with reference to the continual formation of new ethnic groups. Three stages of development are involved, he notes: from category to group to community. A category is a sub-population with no internal coherence. "From such a base, however, an ethnic group can arise" even though "often there is considerable difficulty in defining a nascent group's precise dimensions." Nevertheless, if conditions are favorable, such a group "often develops enough of an institutional structure to be deemed a community."[31]

Categories (along with social groupings) are not coextensive with communities. The former are all-inclusive culturally articulated designations while the latter are voluntary associations. Social groupings provide the actual framework for communities but obviously include many who do not openly identify themselves with like-minded others. A pluralistic emphasis does not challenge the process of categorization, but it does transform people's sense that they are defined in ways over which they have no control into one of being collectively unique in ways which they willingly affirm. To the degree to which one satisfactorily identifies oneself with a voluntary community, society's negative assessments, which form the basis of categorization, are pushed into the background of one's awareness as are those similarly categorized but not forming part of that community.

Being in but not of the World--

A pluralistic alternative to assimilation implies a dual challenge--how to define a meaningful and useful sense of commonality and how to attain stated ends effectively in a society which places a high premium upon individualism. Any attempt to make a substantial positive commitment to one's status as a member of a sexual minority runs into the problem that a sense of community is still diffuse and a supportive milieu is not yet readily accessible to everyone. As time passes more and more people may very well be drawn into active participation in the subsocieties of women and gay people of both sexes. Specific communities, however, are likely to remain confined mostly to certain urban areas with nuclei consisting of a comparatively small number of committed individuals, who are motivated by a positive desire to associate themselves with like-minded others. The growth of gay ghettos in several major American cities is one evidence of this desire. When homosexuality was more fully suppressed and zealously persecuted, ghetto development was inhibited, Martin P. Levine argues, but "with a modicum of tolerance, the process begins."32

There is a distinct possibility that affirmations of separateness on the part of women and gay people may underscore categorical preconceptions in the minds of the heterosexual male majority. This may in turn simply reinforce patterns of subordination and invisibility. Neither women nor gay people need accept categorically based definitions of themselves which ultimately serve the purposes of heterosexual males instead of their own, but it is a complicated challenge for those who would emphasize pluralism to sort out what are positive elements of uniqueness and to avoid what are negative reflections of their socially inferior status. This is true not just in terms of how others see and consequently treat them, but more importantly in terms of how they see themselves. Internalizing categorical conceptions of femininity and homosexuality is an inevitable consequence of being female or gay in America, and such conceptions are the most readily available materials from which to elaborate a sense of separateness.

To be in the world but not of it suggests a balance of priorities best calculated to make a pluralistic alternative work in American society. Viable subsocieties of women and gay people must be made up of individuals able to function within the larger society without losing their sexually based identification with like-minded others. This implies a cautious and skeptical view of that society but not an essentially hostile one. In the latter eventuality pluralism really passes into alienation. Pluralism assumes a degree of social acceptance and an acknowledged right to remain distinctive while still being an active social participant. By contrast, women or gay people who totally oppose mainstream American life and values can easily conclude that as complete a separation from the larger society as possible is the only sensible goal to pursue.

Some feminists have talked in terms of focusing energies and concerns almost exclusively on other women and having little if anything to do with men. Despite speculations regarding the

173

desirability of celibacy or masturbation as alternatives to heterosexual relationships, such a position obviously makes most
sense for those who accept lesbianism. In Lesbian Nation (1973)
Jill Johnston argues that "the lesbian/feminist is the woman who
defines herself independently of the man." Johnston sees the
female as "a separate species" who is taught that "a woman fulfills herself by uniting with her opposite but in reality she
becomes lost to herself in service to a foreign species." The
alternative is "aggressive control of one's own destiny." Women
must remember that "feminists who still sleep with the man are
delivering their most vital energies to the oppressor." By contrast, "the totally woman committed woman, or lesbian, who
shares this consciousness with other women, is the political nu-
cleus of a woman's or lesbian state."[33]

Johnston conceives of lesbianism more in terms of political and programmatic approaches to the realization of radical
feminist aims than as a matter of sexual object choice. Still,
it is impossible to see where an actively heterosexual woman
would fit in though a celibate one might. By the late 1970's,
Sasha Gregory Lewis maintains, some radical lesbians had taken
the logic of separatism to the extreme of advocating "complete
dissociation from men and all male institutions, including most
forms of employment in the mainstream economy." Furthermore,
"those who do not adhere to this separatist formula are ostra-
cized." The quest for political and spiritual correctness ultimately undercuts both the ideals of freedom and autonomy and the
goal of collective lesbian self-determination."[34]

Hostility to mainstream values and the ways of the larger
society can lead to the conclusion that confrontation is inevitable. John Rechy sees himself and others in the gay world whom
he encounters in the "sexual underground" as sexual outlaws.
Motivated by rage at society's persecution of gay people, the
sexual outlaw continues to defy society: "Promiscuity is his
righteous form of revolution." Rechy insists that "where all
sexual boundaries blur, it is at the expense of all sexual experiences." Thus he wants a world in which people who belong to
different sexual groupings will remain separate and at the same
time freely grant everyone the right to express his or her own
separate identity. The sexual outlaw, he insists, "opposes only
the totalitarian imposition of the heterosexual norm on him."
He does not want to substitute homosexual fascism for heterosexual fascism. The goal of revolution for Rechy is the realization of all possibilities. If the revolution were ever won--
and Rechy seems most reluctant to believe in this eventuality--
he admits that he at least would mourn the passing of the sexual
outlaw, who would no longer have a reason for existence.[35]

In a sense Rechy is too preoccupied with the society he
rebels against to be able to formulate any plausible collective

alternative. He is a loner who stands for a way of life totally outside the mainstream value system. His militancy belongs to the 1970's, but his gay world really has been little affected by the forces contributing to the formulation of a gay pluralistic alternative. In his anger and alienation he remains much more profoundly an outsider. He may hope for a world based on a principle of the right to be different, but he recognizes that in America radical differences are unlikely ever to be fully accepted or even tolerated. If either side were to win, the situation would be entirely altered--and so it is almost necessary to postulate a conflict which is never resolved.

Others too feel that the unique qualities of women or gay people can only flourish outside the heterosexual masculine world. Therefore remaining outsiders has special compensations --understanding, insights, whole areas of experience--which are more important than entering the mainstream. Such a stance may be facilitated by the resources of a sexual subsociety, but it does not presuppose them. It seeks to preserve attitudes and behaviors that have long been part of the gay world or the world of women, and thus it has little investment in social changes which may undercut the unique qualities of these worlds. Dan Curzon sees respectability as a real threat to serious gay literature. "If we give up our history as outcasts (our No Names), and become Joe or Jane Citizen," he argues, then "our distinctiveness, our great diversity of temperament and personality will be lost."[36]

How to deal with the larger society is an even more complicated challenge for those who espouse a truly pluralist alternative because their commitment to individualistic self-determination links them so closely with the mainstream value system. Their involvements are more extensive, and yet they are devoted to the proposition that pluralistic loyalties must not be compromised. One solution seems to be collectively exercised power. This adds a new element to the lives of people who have not been accustomed to wielding much power in the larger world on their own behalf. Power generally is seen as the key to ending conditions of inferiority and invisibility. As in the case of blacks and other ethnic minorities, the powerlessness of sexually based minorities seemingly permits the heterosexual male majority to dictate the terms of their existence, and only power can change this reality.

Except in the most direct and physical ways, however, power to be effective must be tied into the "system." As Toby Marotta points out, politically oriented members of the gay liberation movement were concerned with ongoing political institutions and so acted in certain respects as insiders much more than those who simply wanted to affirm their gayness.[37] The desire for power co-opts, and a politically active person may very well become caught up in concerns and commitments that point away from a strong subcultural identification, thus depriving the community of one more effective participant. Ironically the pursuit of minority-group power has an opposite effect as well. The attempt to exercise it even where it is employed, as it has been in recent years in San Francisco, as part of the organized political process often alienates the larger society by making differences seem more threatening than they would otherwise be. Because a pluralistic alternative almost by definition implies reservations about majority values, accommodation is likely to seem difficult from everyone's point of view. To stress power and group pride even as pragmatic devices for dealing with the larger society emphasizes categorically defined differences in ways that inevitably heighten the importance everyone attaches to them.

Gay identity in America rests squarely on an acceptance of a cultural proclivity for categorization. There is a marked preference, Dennis Altman notes, for seeing homosexuality in sociological terms and stressing "the existence of a separate homosexual identity, culture, and life style." This rejects the more European approach of the Freudian psychoanalytic tradition, which emphasizes the connections between homosexuality and heterosexuality and the potential in everyone for both sorts of responses. The viability of a pluralistic approach is undercut even as the affirmation of a separate gay identity gains ground, in Altman's opinion. For "to demand acceptance of real diversity in sexuality, in gender roles, and in family structures--all of which are implied in a full acceptance of homosexuality--is to go far beyond the sort of pluralism that American society recognizes."[38]

As Philip Gleason has pointed out, the contemporary celebration of ethnic pluralism has coincided with a negative evaluation of American identity. Borrowing from Milton Gordon the definition of ethnicity as a sense of peoplehood, Gleason argues that it applies as much to American identity as to subgroups within America though supporters of pluralism generally do not concede this.[39] As a plan of action, therefore, pluralism fails adequately to take into account the larger unities within American culture as well as the importance of shared cultural values within any nation-state. In accepting groupings as givens, it ignores the arbitrary role of categorization in defining both the boundaries of particular groupings and the identities of their members. Moreover, it fails to confront squarely the fact that the basic reason for categorization is that Americans do not deal with differences easily. As Stephen Steinberg points out, "the history of race and ethnicity has been fraught with tension, rivalry, and conflict."[40] So has the history of sex-related differences.

Emphasizing group pride and power and unity has certain anti-individualistic implications that stem from validating sex-related categories. The feminist advocacy of an independent position for women, June Singer argues, "often tends to polarize further the images we have now of the male and the female, and of 'masculinity' and 'femininity.'"[41] Moreover, the logic of group power and solidarity demands acts of loyalty and obedience from supporters which do not always harmonize with the freedom to make up one's own mind and act as one sees fit on important issues. At the same time there is always the possibilility that individuals will feel disposed to behave in all sorts of independent ways. One respondent in The Spada Report insists that "homosexuality has to be regarded as a part of life, not a way of life."[42] In a somewhat similar vein Victoria Billings maintains that the women's movement should not be used as a crutch. It "can't change your life. It's up to you to do something about changing it."[43] Thus in practice subcultural loyalties can be undercut by competing claims and commitments to which each individual often feels at liberty to respond on his or her own terms.

Advocates of ethnic pluralism in America have generally leaned toward voluntary separateness in selective aspects of a person's life and relied essentially on the willing loyalty of individuals to subcultural values and traditions. Michael Walzer suggests that though ethnic groups "are historical communities, they must function as if they were voluntary associations."[44] Because the subsocieties of women and gay people are also voluntary associations (or clusters of voluntary associations), they include only those who wish to belong. In the case of ethnic subsocieties the fact that they must function over time as voluntary associations has meant that members have a fair measure of self-determination as far as group ties are concerned. One need not therefore be surprised at a similar outcome in the case of many women and homosexuals. Pride in being a woman or being gay is both a reaffirmation of sex-related loyalties and yet within an American context also a license to decide for oneself what meaning those loyalties will have in one's life.

How easily people manage voluntary relationships to particular communities and individualistic participation within the larger society will naturally vary. So will the openness of different communities to such dual allegiance. Stephen Steinberg argues that there is a fundamental tension between ethnic pluralism and democracy, and the logic of his argument applies also to sex-related forms of pluralism. In principle American society sanctions the right of people to maintain "their separate cultures and communities, but it also guarantees individual freedoms and specifically proscribes various forms of discrimination." Groups which enjoy social or economic advantages may very well seek to "deprive outsiders of rights and opportunities protected by democratic norms." Any group which feels economically disadvantaged will not support the status quo. Consequently, Steinberg notes, "most disadvantaged minorities have been willing to compromise their ethnicity for the sake of economic security, social acceptance and a sense of participating fully in society instead of living precariously on the periphery."[45]

Both assimilation and pluralism seem plausible partial explanations of processes that are constantly taking place in America. Assimilation does occur though not so uniformly nor so completely as many have suggested. Group differences remain, but not with such immutability as pluralism envisions. What makes it difficult to determine precisely the proportional weight of these two tendencies is the persistence of the categorical thinking that both buttress in different and complex ways --even though each overtly challenges the limitations upon self-determination that categorization sets forth. Because categories are so amorphous and general, they allow for a substantial degree of acculturation while still emphasizing distinctiveness. The more these are willingly accepted as the basis of one's identity, the greater the tension between one's identification with the group and the freedom to move into the larger society as an individual. Thus it is possible to find evidence for assimilation as well as a basis for pluralism depending on one's point of view.

It is impossible for women and gay people to escape the effects of the individualistic value system. If their differences make assimilation a problemmatic alternative to invisibility, as individuals who are also Americans they are likely to find that possibility appealing to varying degrees. At the same time their differences suggest pluralistic alternatives which the belief in the free association of like-minded individuals also endorses even as it regards with suspicion those who remain outside the larger circle of basic agreement within American society. Thus sexual minorities, collectively speaking, are simultaneously outsiders who cannot get fully in and insiders who cannot get fully out. While this may not be true in individual instances, it is a reality which must somehow be taken into account in projecting the ways in which the status of sexually based minorities within American society can conceivably change.

Overview--

Women and gay people can be termed minorities only when they come to see themselves as collectively set apart from the rest of society and denied full participation in it. Both groups have been greatly influenced in the last generation by the stands taken by members of ethnic and racial minorities in America who have called for freedom from forces arbitrarily controlling their lives. Such a comparison suggests a strategy of assimilating members of sexual minorities into the mainstream of American life as self-determining individuals. This stance accepts the masculine value system as the standard to be emulated by women and gay people who wish to move out of their minority-group status. The long-held assumption that individualistic values on some basic level apply to everyone justifies this strategy for its advocates. At the same time sex-related cultural categories are not rejected because they continue to serve as positive or negative referents. Assimilation does not presuppose that all differences be done away with, but any that impede integration must be eliminated. Only those women and gay people who appear to lead middle-class male-identified lives are favorably looked upon by advocates of assimilation. A concrete example of emulating mainstream masculinity can be found in the cult of machismo which flourished among gay men in the 1970's.

The persistence of any important sex-related differences obviously constitutes a basic difficulty from the perspective of assimilation. Ironically the pursuit of opportunity--which is a key element of the assimilationist model--can actually enhance the premium placed upon differences. In some situations it may be in the interest of minority-group members to take advantage of their uniqueness while in others mainstream males may profit from playing up distinctions. Thus categorically based differences become part of the competitive process and thereby increase sex-related tensions. Heterosexual males are likely to remain hypersensitive to differences they regard as significant and critical of women and gay people for not fitting into their world even as they seek to preserve the sexual status quo. At a deeper level many may actually fear that the tables will be turned and men will be subordinated to women and homosexuals.

Advocates of ethnic pluralism offer an alternative model for sexual minorities. Just as some observers have called attention to the viability of ethnic communities, so others have described the emergence of subcultures and subsocieties of women and gay people. Women have built a variety of separate institutions and have increasingly developed a collective sense of identity and an awareness of a unique past. Some gay people have advocated a form of pluralism in which sex-related communities remain distinct at the same time that individuals within them are free to participate in the larger society in ways of their own choosing. Although one can identify a gay subsociety that includes members of both sexes, in many respects it makes sense to talk of a separate lesbian subsociety. Sexual subsocieties are broken down into specific communities mostly concentrated in urban areas and strongly influenced by the activities of a relatively small number of committed participants. A pluralistic emphasis transforms women's and gay people's sense of being identified in ways over which they have no control into one of being unique in ways they willingly affirm.

While affirmations of pluralism are rooted in categorically based assumptions, women and gay people face the challenge of avoiding negative attitudes or behaviors rooted in the inequities which still define their lives. Viable subsocieties must be made up of people who can function relatively easily within the larger society without losing their sense of subcultural uniqueness and involvement. A pluralistic stance differs therefore from an alienated one, which may be manifested by withdrawal, confrontation or an attempt to preserve what has long been seen as unique. Collectively exercised power has been an important goal of sexual pluralists. However, power can co-opt those who seek to exercise it, or alternatively it can enhance the anxieties of members of the majority. Pluralism accepts social groupings as givens and in so doing ignores the arbitrariness of categorization and the difficulty most Americans have in dealing with fundamental differences among people. Emphasizing the importance of the group can undercut the freedom of choice of individual members. In practice, however, sexual subsocieties must function as voluntary associations, and this means that individuals can decide for themselves the ways they wish to identify with like-minded others and the ways they do not. While neither assimilation nor pluralism seems a wholly feasible possibility as far as sexual minorities are concerned, each appeals to conflicting desires most people have to be free to be part of mainstream American life and to affirm very deeply rooted sex-related identities.

CHAPTER NINE

TRANSFORMING SEX-RELATED CATEGORIES

Individualistic values have generally been presumed to apply to all Americans only within limits that cultural categories dictate. The process by which members of negatively categorized groupings move into the mainstream is slow and complicated. As long as differences remain, there is the possibility that they will be seen and experienced as barriers to full acceptance. Certainly the indications at present are that we are living in a time when many women and gay people are moving increasingly into the mainstream, but the process does not apply equally to everyone nor is it irreversible. At the turn of the century many women were filled with similar hopes, which were subsequently dashed. Trends are always difficult to predict, and the staying power of categorical assumptions should never be discounted.

Non-categorical versus Categorical Differences--

That the individual ought not to be at the mercy of social and economic forces beyond his control remains one of the oldest and most deeply held principles of individualism in America. Liberals and conservatives both agree that class differentiation is tolerable only when individuals are free to change their status if they want to. Americans view economic and social class structures in essentially instrumental terms. These are external to the self and are valued mainly for the benefits they afford. Someone may identify himself in large measure with his job or profession. But just as Puritans were once cautioned to love their callings with "weaned affections," so are contemporary Americans advised against an overidentification that may hamper advancement, lock one into an obsolete line of work, or impede one's adjustment to retirement. Each person's relationship, moreover, to economic and social class structures is always assumed to be a changing one--partly as a result of his own mobility, partly because the structures themselves are not considered fixed. Thus Americans are not readily disposed to think in class terms because these structures lack both the immutability and the intrinsic value that make them loom so large in many traditional societies.

If economic and class differences are anxiously dwelt upon, there is a greater tendency to view them in categorical terms. In most people's minds the category of "the poor" functions essentially to differentiate and label the disadvantaged rather than to describe a social class and its structural relationships with other social classes. C. Wright Mills' book The Power Elite is a warning that the rich and powerful share a collective identity that differentiates them in invidious ways from the mainstream of American life. Thus there is a noticeable tendency on Mills' part to think in categorical terms. Even though there is no completely stable upper class with a fixed membership, an upper class still exists, he argues, with the power to shape members' attitudes and create a sense of special interests. Each trusts the other because of social origin and formal education, and continued association furthers this trust. Hence the ability to act together as business, government and military elites.[1] Social critics have long emphasized the structural and institutional bases of entrenched wealth and long-term poverty, but for the most part Americans have resisted categorizing the rich or the poor. We do not believe that the poor should always be with us.

Ann Douglas observes that in the mid-nineteenth century and since popular American literature has been dedicated "to the effort of substituting moral, sexual, generational, and even geographical definitions for economic and class-determined ones."[2] Indeed Americans are as reluctant to endow purely economic distinctions with some kind of larger importance as they are disposed to dwell upon the existence of social groupings based on regional, religious, ethnic, racial or sexual differences. In contrast to economic and social class differences, one's relationship to the structures of differentiation in these areas is not purely an instrumental one. They have not been seen as external to the self but rather as closely linked to one's identity, and so presumably one expresses one's individuality through them.

While cultural categories are rooted in perceived differences that seem significant to the larger society, it is that society which is responsible for the stereotyping that circumscribes people's lives and greatly influences their sense of themselves. The level of concern about particular differences affects how strongly they are seen to set people off from the majority. Among regional stereotypes southerners have been more vividly and negatively categorized than easterners or mid-westerners. The same thing is true of Catholics, Jews and fringe Protestant groups as opposed to mainline Protestants such as Methodists and Presbyterians. Categories pertaining to people of color, like those pertaining to women and gay people, remain much more rigid than those relating to white ethnics. The contemporary disposition to categorize all Caucasians as essentially alike would have shocked many Americans at the turn of the century when differences among Nordic, Mediterranean and Slavic types seemed manifestly obvious. What has happened in this instance is at least one example of the mutability of categories as cultural symbols in a fluid and changing society. Those who are labeled in racial or sexual terms continue to be thought of largely in abstract and stereotyped ways and dealt with accordingly. The prevailing attitude toward native Americans has been to categorize them as one wholly separate people rather than to see them as many culturally distinct peoples. It is assumed that those within each racial and sexual grouping want to identify themselves with others of their kind though in fact they are not considered free to do otherwise. Their freedom is their willing acceptance of their distinctive identities.

George Fredrickson and Dale Knobel have predicted that prejudice toward blacks "will survive so long as the black community remains an involuntary racial group rather than a voluntary ethnic community."[3] Different values and behaviors play a role in setting racial and sexual minorities apart from the larger society and making comfortable interactions across categorical lines difficult. Still, prejudice by its very nature feeds on easy generalizations and refuses to permit members of social groupings to be seen as individuals. Thus it often does not matter whether someone who is black or female, for instance, actually rejects mainstream values. Mutuality has often been presumed not to exist merely because categorically defined differences seem obvious.

Both women and gay people still largely perceive themselves and are perceived and treated by many of those around them and by American society in general in stereotyped ways which markedly affect their lives and their sense of themselves. Members of any social grouping experience the world in special ways which define them no matter what their personal wishes may be. It is not within a person's power always to control others' responses nor to leave behind entirely years of socialization. Thus while women and gay people may consciously seek to define themselves in ways that meet their own purposes, they must deal with all the internal and external effects of belonging to social groupings not of their own choosing.

There are variations from grouping to grouping and from person to person in the freedom to act individualistically within relevant frameworks. Ultimately, however, categorization itself implies limitations which individualism calls into question. In 1950 David Riesman defended the unrestricted freedom to form ties not confined by ethnicity or sex. He condemned the post-World War II effort to "re-privatize women by re-defining their role in some comfortably domestic and traditional way." His ideal of autonomy was opposed to all efforts to lock people up in special categories. He called for greater freedom of choice in friendships and criticized ethnic veto group leaders for seeking to confine a person's sociability to his own particular group. This may be called "cultural pluralism," Riesman argued, "though for the individual it operates as a monolith" by restricting him to a single culture.[4]

As long, however, as cultural categories are accepted as valid blueprints for social practice, they are fairly impervious to individualistic assaults. As part of the "natural" order of things, categorical differences are to be distinguished not only from arbitrary and unacceptable class designations, but also from all sorts of voluntary group differences, which the belief in free association encourages. As long as the latter seem compatible with the basic principles of American identity, they pose no problems from the point of view of the majority and thus there is no disposition to categorize. Neither is there much of a disposition to categorize deviate behavior that can be dealt with on an individual basis. Only when, collectively considered, there seems to be a general social "problem," does categorization occur. Because categories represent a non-traditional means of interpreting important cultural differences, their validity is only undercut when people come to see at least certain elements of them as externalized imperatives that can be treated in instrumental ways. By indirectly reinforcing categorical thinking both assimilation and pluralism fail in many respects to do this. An alternative is to challenge categories themselves more systematically than either of these two approaches requires.

Women in Two Worlds--

If the limitations of women's gender role are no longer accepted as necessary consequences of their identities as sexually categorized beings, then it becomes possible to deal more flexibly with the social expectations that pertain to their sex. Because role requirements cannot be completely dissociated from identity, flexibility must be limited to actions which do not call a person's womanhood into question. Protesting against role restrictions points mainly to the importance of greater freedom to do new things, and it does not oblige one to reject whatever seems part of one's identity as a woman. Hence the appeal of resolving the tension between the desire for more behavioral freedom and categorically based loyalties by developing a facility in moving back and forth between one's special sphere and the larger society. There are greater or lesser problems depending upon one's sense of how divergent the values of and experiences within the two spheres are. Nevertheless, large numbers of women for the past two decades--and smaller numbers for even longer--have sought to fulfill the requirements of femininity while at the same time moving out into the masculine mainstream.

In their study, The Managerial Woman, Margaret Hennig and Anne Jardim candidly discuss the problems women face when they seek to succeed in a world that in most respects is alien to all that they as women have been conditioned to accept. The authors suggest the analogy of a person who is going to a foreign country for an extended stay. Having good maps and guides and knowing the rules and being able to play by them are essential to getting along well. If women can learn to play by men's rules, they will know what they must downplay so as not to be seen as foreign to the "system." At the same time they must learn to live with the reality that residues of differences will undoubtedly remain. "A woman may always be anxious over the potential conflict between being a high achiever and a successful woman." She has to decide whether she really wants to succeed by competing with men "in a system they understand better and on terms with which they are far more comfortable and much more familiar."[5]

Hennig and Jardim have no expectation that women can or should abandon all the gender-related attitudes and values they have spent most of their previous lives learning. Still, in the short run the business world will not change very much, and women must adapt themselves to things as they are. Though alarmists may fear that ambitious women are likely to lose their femininity, the pursuit of success does not usually have this effect. In the case of men it tends to increase anxiety about masculinity and thus to enhance allegiance to its imperatives. In parallel situations a woman is likely to feel similar pressures as far as femininity is concerned. Success does not allow her to be conventionally feminine in every respect, but there is no reason why she cannot be as feminine as possible in whatever ways she feels she can be. In the long run Hennig and Jardim hope that women will exert a modifying influence on the masculine value system. They would like to see family responsibilities brought more into line with work demands, paternity leaves and provision made for people who do not want to follow vertical career paths.[6] Clearly this implies a downplaying of the more aggressive and competitive aspects of the business world and an upgrading of concerns associated with the female sphere. In proportion as women can influence the larger world, the tensions between woman's sphere and that world will obviously lessen. For the present, however, women will have to continue to cultivate the skills to function effectively in both worlds.

Achievement-oriented women remain under considerable pressure to fulfill the categorically based expectations of the men in their lives. Mirra Komarovsky has argued that "symmetrical marital roles" and due importance to "the paternal role in child rearing" might prove appealing to many parents if these are "accepted as an honored cultural alternative." Still, she admits that "high-powered, exceptionally creative personalities, male or female, ambitious to reach peak positions, will choose a single-minded dedication to their careers. Such personalities may decide to remain childless or to find mates willing to play complementary roles." Whether such mates are on the average likely to be women she insists is still an open question.[7] Certainly there continue to be all kinds of social pressures on women to fit their careers around those of their men. Thus women who seek success and power in careers and professions, whether they choose to remain unattached or not, must still bear special burdens. They will have to operate in a man's world without the benefits usually of someone's playing a wifely role for them, and they will feel substantial pressure to remain feminine at the same time.

Betty Friedan's The Second Stage directly addresses this dilemma. It rejects the assimilationist approach of The Feminine Mystique in favor of one which grants women an equal influence over the shape of the society of the future. She argues that the first stage of feminism in the 1960's and 70's had merely applied male defined values "to protest our oppression, exploitation and exclusion from man's world," and in her opinion feminists had denied the "personhood of women" in the process. Every woman has both the "need for power, identity, status and security through her own work or action in society" and "the need for love and identity, status, security and generation through marriage, children, home, the family." Recognizing both needs should eliminate the polarization of women into feminist and anti-feminist camps and thus forge anew the bonds of sisterhood uniting all women as a social grouping. Feminism infused with the special qualities of thought long exemplified by women "is an expression of individualism, human autonomy, personal freedom," Friedan insists. While she is committed to forms of sharing between men and women in both the work and home spheres, still she expects both sexes to express their individuality in terms that honor categorically defined differences between them. Indeed, "the more authentically a woman, or a man, is free to know, and become, herself or himself, the more surely, uniquely, she is herself, he is himself. The second stage is not unisex."[8] In preserving the masculine/feminine dichotomy, the second stage is committed to rejecting the idea of a unisexual cultural category that stresses the fundamental alikeness of all men and women.

While this strategy accepts the validity of sex-related categories, it does challenge the role limitations imposed on women. Claiming a degree of self-determination not provided for by accepted definitions of femininity is an important step in asserting the individual's freedom to move beyond rather than simply within the social framework that categorization sets forth. Since it remains important to affirm loyalty to femininity as a general proposition, the challenge is a conservative one. Still, sex-role expectations are externalized to some degree and so can be dealt with at least in part in instrumental terms. An additional step--which women such as Friedan do not take--in further externalizing role limitations is to argue that women are treated as a caste. Carol Andreas uses the concept of caste to emphasize "how social roles are determined by birth rather than by achievement." Because Americans have always con-

sidered caste designations as arbitrary and therefore anti-individualistic, Andreas can insist with regard to the status of women that "no society can claim to be free so long as an individual's social and occupational role remains largely determined by
an accident of birth."[9]

Gay People in the Larger World--

Early in 1982 there was a rash of movies involving gay
characters. Making Love explores how Zack Elliot comes to terms
with homosexual inclinations which surface after eight years of
an ideal marriage. For a very long time "he'd repressed his
feelings, tried to bury them deep inside his work and his marriage," but they burst forth when he falls in love with Bart
McGuire, a loner completely at home in the gay world of the bars
and one-night stands. What enables Zack to resolve his divided
loyalties is his unquestioning acceptance of the heterosexual/
homosexual dichotomy and his complete devotion to the ideal of
an exclusive love between two people. Once he fully acknowledges his attraction to other men, he has no choice but to sever
his ties with his wife Claire. Whether homosexuality is inborn
or acquired, he tells her, "there's something in me that needs
to be with a man." He realizes that were he content with sex
alone, he would not have to make a choice, but "he wanted the
love, the companionship, the closeness he'd shared with Claire,
only now he wanted it from a man." Zack's choice of sexual
partners may be unconventional, but his view of gay love is
identical with his concept of heterosexual love. Not surprisingly, he is scornful of the gay world and of impersonal sex and
believes that there are other gay people like himself who want
"the caring and the sharing" of "equals."[10]

Just as his acceptance of being gay does not presuppose a
rejection of conventionally monogamous values, neither does it
require a rejection of masculinity: "A man is a person who acts
responsibly and who takes responsibility for his own actions.
It's my responsibility to stop denying what I am and what I
need."[11] When Bart refuses to commit himself to a close relationship, Zack recovers quickly and moves to New York where he
leads a life that is remarkably similar to the lives of typically upper middle-class heterosexual men. His career blossoms,
and he eventually finds another lover. From a dramatic point of
view Zack's resolution of his conflicting feelings seems much
too easy, but it follows logically from his acceptance of the
validity of categorizing everyone in terms of sexual orientation. He does not choose to be gay. All that he can choose is
to accept his sexual drives and to be open and honest about
them. In a very real sense he has the best of both worlds, for
he can be unashamedly gay without having to limit his participation in the larger society.

Rebecca Nahas and Myra Turley describe a different way in which some gay men function within the larger society while still insisting on the importance of their homosexual identities. Unlike Zack these men do not rule out close ties with women--even sexual ones. In order to make this approach work, however, they must reject the ideal of a lifetime monogamous commitment. They can then form what Nahas and Turley call "new couple" unions, which allow them "to integrate love relationships with women into their lives without denying their primarily homosexual orientation." The cultural categories of homosexuality and heterosexuality are not repudiated and still apply but in flexible ways to these people's lives. Instead of adopting a conventionally heterosexual style of life like Zack's in "integrating into the straight world as gay men," these men "bring with them the easygoing, flexible style of the gay scene at its best--a way of living which women seeking freedom from traditional social and sexual roles find especially appealing."[12]

While Zack's immersion in the gay subculture is very limited and that of the men just described is unclear, the insistence on affirming one's sexual orientation at the same time that one participates fully in the larger society comes fairly close to expressing the aims and goals of the gay liberation movement as it passed beyond its initial preoccupations. Gay liberationists had been highly critical of the assimilationist goals of the earlier homophile organizations. Although these organizations were important in creating many of the conditions that made gay liberation possible, they had not encouraged homosexuals, Toby Marotta remarks, "to consider how they differed from heterosexuals and to develop the sense of having a distinctive place in society to protect and promote." Nevertheless, when the National Gay Task Force was organized in 1973, its leaders took a more tolerant view of homophile aims. Synthesizing assimilationist and pluralistic approaches, they sought "for homosexuals the right to be treated equitably and, without having to be wholly acculturated, to be integrated."[13]

In a subsequent work Marotta spells out in greater detail the meaning of sexual liberation for him as he sees it exemplified in the lives of some of his classmates of the Harvard Class of 1967. One must deal with the world openly as a gay person, he insists, for "labels are necessary to help members of minority groups develop pride in their distinctive characteristics." Positively affirming homosexuality in categorical terms makes it possible for gay men simultaneously to affirm masculinity in categorical terms as well. One of Marotta's interviewees suggests that the "supermacho" look among gay men today signifies that they "are more comfortable with the thought that they are, after all, men, and that they can be just as masculine as any other men." On the one hand Marotta maintains that "the familial, fraternal, civic, and occupational parts" of gay people's lives "are very much like everyone else's." On the other hand, he notes, "we have learned to approach sex, sex roles, intimacy, love, and relationships in very non-traditional ways, and this sets us apart as gay men."[14] Marotta's essential support for mainstream American values and his belief that these are changing in ways that will facilitate the acceptance of gay people as a politically significant minority make him optimistic about the future. Categorically defined differences will not disappear, but they will not prevent gay people as individuals from fully participating in the American Dream even though they will remain culturally distinctive and collectively identifiable.

Dennis Altman argues that present-day gay identity and culture are built "on existing male/female differences" to a degree earlier advocates of liberation failed entirely to foresee. He is by no means happy with the kinds of separation that this implies, nor is he so certain as many that one can have the best of both worlds as long as gay and "straight" people differ radically in fundamental values. He however describes a process of coming together in which gay people alter the values of the majority by pioneering ways of living that are appropriate for everyone in an advanced technological society. Altman believes that despite gay separatism, "the recognition of group identity allows minorities to influence the broader culture." Thus America "is becoming homosexualized in the sense that more people are behaving in the way traditionally ascribed to homosexuals, and that lesbians and gay men are exploring models for living everyday life that are relevant to everyone." In stressing growing similarities in how Americans approach sex and sexual relationships, Altman is suggesting that the freedom to move beyond the confines dictated by cultural categories rests on a general sense that these have largely ceased to imply vital differences among people. He is not entirely optimistic about the future, but he is certain that "in the long run it would be nice to hope that we can escape the limitations on individual potential and diversity that all categories impose."[15]

Essentially the strategies for escaping both the symbolic and practical limitations of being gay stress two approaches. One can minimize conflict in one's personal relationships to the homosexual and heterosexual worlds by emphasizing a categorical identification with members of one's own sex as Zack and Marotta do. Of necessity this widens the breach between men and women as gay people of both sexes come to identify themselves primarily in terms of gender rather than sexual orientation. The second approach emphasizes the role of social change in creating conditions that downgrade the importance of categorically defined differences. Both Altman and "new couples" point to similar styles of life regardless of sexual orientation that make labels only abstractly relevant to people's lives. Because neither approach seeks to abolish categorical distinctions, however, the individual continues to live in two worlds. If this seems easier for gay people than for women, it is because categorical differences based on sex affect most people's lives more directly and pervasively than those based on sexual object choice.

Men and Women Together--

American men's reactions to changes in women's roles are complicated by the fact that conceptions of femininity have tended to lag far behind increasingly complex forms of interaction with women.[16] Mirra Komarovsky has observed, in the case of a group of seniors in an Ivy League college in 1969-70, a much greater degree of openness with women friends than with male buddies, siblings or parents.[17] Anthony Pietropinto and Jacqueline Simenauer insist that it is wrong to see the average American male as interested only in his own sexual gratification and unconcerned with affection or tenderness. He "apparently feels isolated and lonely enough in the competitive world outside without conducting his sex life under similar conditions of alienation."[18]

The paradox, according to Komarovsky, is that "the ideological support for the belief in sharp sex-role differentiation in marriage has weakened, but the belief itself has not been relinquished." There is a "raised male expectation of enjoying an emotional and intellectual companionship with women" along with the "deeply rooted norm that the husband should be the superior achiever in the occupational world and the wife, the primary child rearer."[19] Emotional and intellectual companionship suggests interaction of individuals who are essentially equals. However, men have long sought willing emotional support from women, and the predisposition of most conventional males is to continue to insist on sensitivity to their needs. Then outward changes in women's roles and styles of life can at least be accepted and sometimes even approved.

The purpose in part of Pietropinto and Simenauer's study of 4000 males of all age groups, geographical areas and social strata is to "help women to communicate properly with men, to express feelings in a noncritical way, and to avoid the things that trigger off unconscious threats in men's minds." If women expect men to accept important changes in the female role, the authors clearly imply, women themselves will have to be especially sensitive and supportive. One respondent notes that due to women's liberation modern women "make good wives and mothers, definitely, because they are more capable, more qualified, and have more knowhow." Still, another worries that women are becoming too independent and need to "reassure the men that while they, the women, demand and need their wants, the women have not forgotten the men's needs."[20]

190

Because American men have long wanted their women to be both independent and yielding, the conception of independence can be expanded to include more individualistic sorts of behavior as long as there is a satisfying amount of yielding. Perhaps this position is best summed up by one male's view of his ideal woman. His basic requirement is that she "be a woman of strength, able to deal with the real world, successful at getting what she wants, but without being a competitive, driven type or a 'ball breaker,' the way some women are getting to be." Rather, "no matter how successful she'd become, I'd want her to retain that softness, vulnerability and emotional quality."[21] Pietropinto and Simenauer explain that the reason so many men say they prefer sexually aggressive women is that they assume that "such a woman must be totally committed to them, through marriage or other compact." Accordingly, one man talks of his fantasies of a woman who is "beautiful--sensuous, intelligent and thought a lot more of my needs than her own."[22] Commenting on "the ambivalent feelings of contemporary men," Donald H. Bell concludes that "we want women who will take care of us and women who will stand on their own feet, women who are lovers, women who are achievers, and women who are mothers."[23]

Pietropinto and Simenauer ultimately posit a lofty ideal of equality, freedom and individuality for both men and women erected upon a foundation of conventional feminine supportiveness. They look to "the love and friendship of a concerned female companion" to free a man "from some of the old masculine-feminine conventions that prescribe and restrict his behavior. Together, they may find not different identities as man and woman, but a common identity as human." These authors thus expect that men will change in important ways which will bring the two sexes closer together, but the rhetoric of a common humanity notwithstanding, important gender-role differences are still endorsed. Because women can be trusted to continue to subordinate their individuality to men's, their rights and claims to individualism can be confidently and safely honored. "The more choices women have and the more freedom to make those choices," we are told, "the more individual they will become--and the more likeable."[24] If increasingly individualistic women still ultimately honor the male's superior claims to individuality, categorical assumptions about women will have been modified but not fundamentally rejected.

Mirra Komarovsky notes what seem to her many inconsistencies in men's attitudes toward women. At least among the college seniors she interviewed, she finds an acknowledgement of "the right of an able woman to a career of her choice" and "admiration for women who measure up in terms of the dominant values of our society" along with "the lure but also the threat that such women present." Also there is "the deeply internalized norm of male occupational superiority pitted against the principle of equal opportunity irrespective of sex." Komarovsky argues that these seniors still measured themselves against the traditional ideal of masculinity though they questioned some elements. This ideal included some qualities previously defined as feminine such as "patience, sensitivity, and artistic appreciation." However, the latter "had not so much replaced as augmented the familiar manly profile." Komarovsky makes this important point in another way by noting that while one-third of the traits attributed to the ideal man fell within the feminine cluster, "this is not to obscure another of our findings that the ideal man for these seniors was still an 'assertive,' 'strong,' 'courageous,' 'aggressive' and 'masculine' man."[25]

Thus many men as well as women seem to feel increasingly free to add to their behaviors traits once restricted to the opposite sex. Pietropinto and Simenauer argue that whereas a generation ago a man might have found oral sex with himself in a recumbant position "threateningly passive and feminine," today most men "feel they are entitled to a pleasant respite from constantly proving their prowess."[26] Just as women should be free to add some masculine behaviors to their feminine ones, so in the opposite proportion ought men to be similarly free. One woman insists: "I wanted a man who was sensitive and in touch, but in addition to, not instead of the other."[27] Here we are not talking about some conception of a blending of opposites, but simply of a willingness to find attractive traits associated with the opposite sex so long as a person's basic masculinity or femininity is beyond question. Openness to more flexible role behaviors in both sexes coexists with a firm commitment to the importance of sex-related cultural categories.

Anne Steinmann and David J. Fox's book, The Male Dilemma, is based on extensive interviews with both men and women which challenge categorical assumptions in an apparently more direct way. The authors sought to determine how both sexes see themselves and how they think they are perceived by the opposite sex. Their research revealed that men "are a lot more active, free, independent, and aggressive than they think women want them to be." In point of fact women said that their ideal was "a strong, aggressive, and self-assertive man." They further told the authors "that men wanted a woman more passive and family-oriented than they, the women, wanted to be."[28] Clearly both sexes reflect a conflict between their own individualistic desires and their assumption that family responsibilities call for a submerging of self-assertiveness. Both have masculinized (individualistic) self-images and at the same time erroneously assume the opposite sex has feminized expectations regarding them.

The answer for Steinman and Fox is not, however, for each sex simply to agree on a shared masculine value system. Rather they insist that while the two sexes are indeed different, differences should be no barrier to greatly expanded role flexibility. They argue that women will perhaps always be more internally oriented than men and men more externally oriented than women, but "sensitivity, compassion, understanding are important in men's lives" just as "independence, achievement, and activity" are in women's. Each affirmation of gender-role flexibility is accompanied by the reassurance that categorical differences between the sexes are not ultimately being challenged. Within the educational system "child, adolescent or adult should not be barred from any activity because of sex." Naturally there will "always be differences--physical, social and psychological--between men and women, and between boys and girls." But at home, in school and in society young people "can be given a wider range of acceptable alternatives and greater freedom in choosing the kind of lives they will lead." Such freedom does not, however, point to the emergence of a single sex-related cultural category or "unisex world," which the authors consider "relatively pallid and unexciting in comparison to a duosex world."[29]

The affirmation of categorical differences assures men that it is possible to retain their masculinity and women their femininity at the same time that they are encouraged to be more individualistic in their choices and behaviors than they have been allowed to be in the past. While the two sexes are different because of biology, "viewed as complete human beings, men and women are much more similar than it is generally assumed," Steinman and Fox insist, and so they should help each other achieve the goals of "a secure individual identity, and a loving companionable relationship."[30] Whereas once men had depended upon women's supplementary role to enable them to participate vicariously in behaviors they could not allow in themselves, now many are apparently adding these traits to their own behavioral styles--but still in large measure as supplements which do not fundamentally challenge categorical distinctions between the sexes. Women in turn may augment their femininity in parallel ways instead of living vicariously through their men.

Minority Consciousness among Males--

In a psychological sense it is certainly possible for some heterosexual males to regard themselves as a minority group or at least to exhibit a minority-group consciousness. On one level this occurs when male--particularly white male--supremacy is challenged and many men come to see themselves as a beleaguered sex. On another level, a relatively small number of males have become openly critical of the fact that categorically defined expectations stress a fairly narrow set of values and behaviors and exclude everything else. Stuart Carter insists that "men are as much victims of socially imposed standards as are women, possibly more so."[31] George Leonard has suggested that one reason masculinity may have become so restrictive for many males is the emphasis upon competition in modern society. One must agree to do exactly what one's competitors do--only a little faster or better.[32] Donald Sabo and Ross Runfola feel that "competition has lost its functional effectiveness in both personal and social life." Consequently male liberationists seek to understand the oppression that results from being socialized "into destructive sex roles that limit their opportunities for emotional expression and interpersonal fulfillment."[33]

Individualism has long been associated with freedom from supposedly arbitrary social impositions. One may thus argue that if the masculine role is overly restrictive of a person's freedom to be self-determining and independent, men need to reassert their individuality and free themselves from what they find uncomfortable and limiting about it. Such an attitude challenges the conventional disposition to view masculinity exclusively in categorical terms. To be acceptably masculine seems to critics to involve conformity at least in behavioral terms to externally imposed demands rather than simply fulfillment of one's inner potential as a male.

Burt Avedon argues that though men think they are free, in fact they "are enslaved by a mystique of masculinity." Thus they need to abandon, "if not for oneself at least for others, the notion that one has to adhere to the stereotype of manhood." They must learn to live in a world in which men will be freer to choose a variety of styles for themselves, and so "we will see a tremendous increase in male sensitivity" as long, but only as long, as American society remains affluent. Apparently behavioral flexibility is a luxury which hard times do not allow. Affirmations of sensitivity are likely to be complicated by an uneasy awareness that these may undercut masculinity. They can, however, be tolerated if basic manliness is reaffirmed in unmistakable ways. Thus Avedon argues that despite growing similarities between the sexes, "during our lifetimes at least, our culture will continue to mandate that men behave in special ways." Among American men "the need to feel manhood will no doubt continue. The need to prove it to ourselves or anyone else may not."[34] Masculinity for Avedon remains closely linked to male identity, but the freedom to be less conventional means that outward behaviors no longer should be taken as sure indications of a man's loyalty (or disloyalty) to his sex.

Similarly in Tenderness Is Strength Harold C. Lyon, Jr. insists that he is not "advocating total egalitarianism or indiscriminate interchangeability of roles between men and women." On the basis of this assertion that sexual categories still matter he can then maintain that "the rare and beautiful man is the one whose strength shines through his tenderness."

Tenderness does not mean, however, "that men cannot still be naturally aggressive." While "military camaraderie, athletic fellowship, or the macho affection of hunting and fishing buddies" are "all genuine expressions of tenderness," the tenderness Lyon maintains that he was able to achieve with a very close friend carried them both beyond the confines of conventional masculinity but remained safely within the boundaries of heterosexual normality. The relationship "was entirely free of the rigid roles that had been conditioned in us," but the reader is reassured that "there was nothing of a homosexual nature about this expression of love between us." Lyon insists that it is vital for men who are critical of the masculine role to link up with "other tender people in mutual support groups," for "tender males are definitely a minority."[35] Voluntary ties with like-minded others provide personal support for Lyon in moving beyond the limits of masculinity, but at the same time he gives his cause credibility by reaffirming his loyalty to all other males as a social grouping.

A conscious disenchantment with many aspects of the masculine role may prompt an embrace of feminine values which does not cancel out basic masculine loyalties or encourage women to feel equally free to move beyond the confines of their role. Early advocates of men's liberation equated the feminine realm with everything that was worthwhile and the masculine realm with all that must be rejected. In a pamphlet issued by a men's consciousness group in 1971 entitled Unbecoming Men, one writer argues that "women's qualities--responsiveness to others, sensitivity, compassion, patience, subtlety, intuitive conceptualizing, etc.--are exactly the ones our future utopian society will foster and flourish on; while the male qualities--self-interest, competitiveness, aggressiveness, force, rigid thinking, etc.-- are precisely our enemies and are what we are struggling to eliminate." While women represent the values men must aim for, the writer argues that men have to deal with their own sexism; they cannot expect women to show them the way. The concluding article triumphantly affirms that these men had learned, through their encounter group experience, "to become more whole, more human, and less male."[36]

Despite the commitment to male self-help there was initially an enormous dependence on women for moral guidance that bordered on nineteenth-century gallantry. This approach of course represented only a small minority of American males. If the majority had not given up their commitment to masculinity, neither had the minority--as they often confessed. Thus it is not difficult to understand why an initial and unqualified sense that liberation and the cultivation of feminine values are identical would give way to a more pragmatic stance calculated to appeal to a much larger number of men, who may have wanted to go beyond the narrow confines of conventional masculinity but who were not prepared to "unbecome" men in the process.

In a short book subtitled Out of the Tough-Guy Trap into a Better Marriage, Clayton Barbeau depicts a new frontier to challenge modern American males to move beyond categorically defined confines but in recognizably masculine and individualistic ways. In a time when the old frontiers are gone "there still remains for each man the frontier of his own consciousness, the wilderness of his own feelings." Each man must reject the "macho" images of the advertisers and "wrestle with his own redefinition of his manliness and assert his own dignity as a person." While "the basic gender differences between men and women remain," men must accept women not as members of "a different species" but as "fellow human beings involved in the common task of civilizing the world."[37] King David Boyer, Jr. argues that a new avenue toward masculinity is emerging which is "concerned with the way the man manages his life, with the way he conducts himself as a human being" in everything he does. Boyer cautions that "this route to masculinity-individuality is not the easy one." Clearly it hints at nothing unmasculine, for "it involves thinking, evaluating and reevaluating, rather than the blind adherence to standards of role behavior."[38]

Joseph Pleck's book, The Myth of Masculinity, offers a systematic critique of the Male Sex Role Identity paradigm, which he sees as the product of forty years of work on the part of professionals in many fields to underwrite conventional sex roles. The basic feature of the paradigm is the assumption that "sex roles develop from within, rather than being arbitrarily imposed from without." The MSRI paradigm has the effect of preventing "individuals who violate the traditional role for their sex from challenging it; instead, they feel personally inadequate and insecure." As an alternative approach Pleck describes the Sex Role Strain paradigm, which he sees emerging from the breakdown of the MSRI paradigm. The newer paradigm clearly provides a rationale for pragmatic changes and role flexibility. It concentrates on "the implications of sex-typed traits for social approval and situational adaptation." SRS researchers study stereotypes, by which they mean perceptions of what each sex actually is like. They are more interested in absolute stereotypes (traits that characterize one sex, whether sex-differentiating or not) than in relative stereotypes (categorical traits which clearly differentiate the sexes). Their accumulation of data "that women and men have both masculine and feminine traits and are more similar than different" is actually changing present stereotypes.[39]

From the SRS perspective sex roles are seen as external impositions which fit individual lives only imperfectly. Because there are enormous personality variations among individuals, "no matter what the normative sex role patterns are, inevitably some will not fit them."[40] By emphasizing the belief that sex roles are arbitrary social impositions, the SRS paradigm defines them in essentially traditional terms as formal behavioral expectations like those of social class. Thus modern assumptions justify an individualistic and instrumental approach to them. The various protests against sex-role restrictions we have considered are consequently attempts to distinguish the behavioral elements from the other aspects of sex-related cultural categories. Behavioral limitations are challenged, but all else is left intact. There remains in fact a strong loyalty to sexual categorization, for that loyalty is linked to a sense of male identity. One is not free, therefore, to act as if masculinity and heterosexuality were entirely matters of social convention which one should feel free to accept or reject on wholly individualistic grounds.

Donald H. Bell insists upon the importance for men today to "broaden our repertoire of possible behaviors." Uncertainties about what is expected allow "us to become what might be termed 'self-created' individuals, people who are no longer defined merely by the images of the past, but who are increasingly able to develop our own beliefs and modes of action." This does not necessarily mean, he cautions, "that eventually we might live in a world in which meaningful distinctions between the sexes no longer prevail." Indeed he is "convinced that for the foreseeable future we will not live in a world which is constructed along 'unisex' lines--a world which does not seek to differentiate between men and women."[41] The freedom to do what one chooses to do is not the same as the freedom to be whatever one chooses to be. The behavioral flexibility which the former implies can be assimilated to the mainstream interpretation of masculine individuality only on condition that men willingly affirm their categorically defined identities.

Gaining Maneuvering Room--

As more women enter increasingly into the mainstream, a lessening of the polarization of the sexes seems a logical although by no means uniform outcome. The observation has frequently been made that present-day realities call for more balance. Indeed one of the greatest sources of anxiety for those who still believe in nineteenth-century style "old individualism" is that masculinity has been seriously undercut by the processes of modern American society. The threat seems less severe to those who are less devoted to the myth of the masculine past, but both sides agree on the impact of contemporary life in weakening the masculine/feminine dichotomy. David Riesman's conception of "other-direction" points away from the excessively masculine preoccupation of "inner-direction" to a more "feminine" emphasis upon sensitivity to other people. "Other-directed" males are less success-oriented and less power-oriented than "inner-directed" ones. Indeed, "the other-directed man simply does not seek power; perhaps, rather, he avoids and evades it."[42]

The emphasis on success and power has a direct bearing on the polarization of the sexes. Both success and power underscore the importance of hierarchical relationships and point away from all forms of equality other than equality of opportunity. One need not posit the disappearance of masculine concerns with success and power to argue that any muting of the emphasis upon them is likely to reduce the emphasis upon sexual polarization. The importance of categorical differences of all sorts is sharpened by the pursuit of opportunity as people seek to underscore and take advantage of whatever will aggrandize their own positions. The masculine success ethic has long been buttressed in Americans' minds by the belief in women's selflessness and lack of ambition. If some men feel freer to adopt traits of behavior long characterized as feminine, it may very well be because a lessened commitment to success makes it possible for them to incorporate a tension that once may not have been possible--which was why it had to be externalized.

Mirra Komarovsky says she was surprised by the skepticism about psychological sex differences expressed by the seniors she studied "and by the considerable convergence in the ideals of masculinity and femininity." Thus she argues that "it becomes increasingly difficult to view such American values as freedom of choice, fair play, full development of one's potential, and achievement, as exclusively male privileges."[43] A major thrust of the ferment of the last several decades has been to affirm the right of individuals to be self-determining. It follows logically, therefore, that sex-related differences--like race, ethnicity or age--ought not to be the basis for arbitrary limits on what people can do with their lives. One has the right not to be treated disadvantageously as part of an undifferentiated social grouping because this subjects one unfairly to forces beyond one's control.

The mainstream American interpretation of individualism asserts that individuals have rights of self-determination as against the claims of their various social roles and institutional involvements. Society is seen as an elaborate edifice, but in contrast to traditional conceptions the individual stands apart to some degree from the various social structures with which he or she must inevitably deal. One does not ignore them or seek to abolish them, but one refuses at the same time to be wholly bound by them. Categorically defined social identities and expectations and their supporting social structures are not strictly speaking arbitrary impositions. Only as elements of them come to be seen in this light can these be challenged in the name of individualistic self-determination. Most Americans would agree that on some very deep level they are moved by the idea that they are not the prisoners of their social fates. Mainstream culture does not deny the reality of a person's social fate--of the impact of forces which one cannot wholly control--but it does assert in the name of individualism the capacity to free oneself largely from the tyranny of circumstances.

The effects of individualistic assumptions continuously operate upon culturally elaborated differences in American life. Regional and local ties and institutions may define a person's social reality and values in a great many special ways. An individualistic stance does not require that one repudiate all local and regional loyalties--only that one be free to choose how and in what ways one applies them to one's life. In general Americans are not prompted very strongly to categorize regional and local differences as long as they feel there is no conflict between them and the practice of individualism. The reason southerners have been seen in more explicitly categorical terms than other Americans is because the unique ethos of the South has seemed to both outsiders and insiders to preclude relating to the basic elements of a southern identity in voluntaristic terms. Much power over the individual has been attributed to certain traditional values, community and family ties, and regional loyalties. The fact that the South has more recently come to signify Sun Belt opportunities and the good life for many newcomers suggests that the conflict between a southern identity and an American identity has been considerably reduced.

In theory each person has long been considered free to join any Protestant church he chooses because voluntary religious differences are compatible with the assertion of individualism--but only within certain limits. If the larger society feels that acceptable limits have been transgressed, negative categorizing inevitably results. Apparently voluntary commitments may be seen on careful examination to reflect personal (often authoritarian) needs over which the individual has little control or to be the result of subtle forms of manipulation which belie freedom of choice. From the individual's point of view there is likely to be little sense of being limited or controlled so long as he identifies with particular religious tenets and yet feels free to participate in the larger society as much as he wishes. The greater the sense of conflict between group identification and the values of the larger society, the greater the tendency over time for individual members to question a religious identification or societal restrictions limiting freedom of choice. In the former instance they are prompted to assert their freedom to reject beliefs or practices that prevent them from interacting comfortably with the larger society. In the latter instance they are likely to insist that their religious identification is freely chosen and is thus compatible with mainstream values.

Roman Catholic commitments have generally seemed to other Americans to be categorically significant because they are felt to be so closely tied to people's identities and patterns of behavior at variance with mainstream expectations. The question as to how Catholicism related to the emphasis upon individualism, religious voluntarism and American identity did not become really significant until the immigration of great numbers of Irish Catholics in the middle decades of the nineteenth century "brought religious and ethnic considerations into the discussion of what it meant to be an American."[44] One can mark the movement of American Catholics into the mainstream and the ease with which they were accepted in part by the willingness of both Catholics and non-Catholics to view the Church as simply one of many religious organizations competing for the voluntary allegiance of their members.

Behind the freedom granted individuals to deal with categorically defined distinctions in increasingly instrumental terms is the sense on the part of the larger society that such distinctions are less important than they were once deemed to be. This allows a growing emphasis upon the commonalities that in theory unite all Americans as individuals. Because racial exclusiveness runs counter to the defining principles of American nationality, Philip Gleason has argued, "the official commitment to those principles has worked historically to overcome exclusions and to make the practical boundaries of American identity more congruent with its theoretical universalism."[45] Mandatory desegregation of public schools and affirmative action programs aim not to undercut the practice of individualism, but to enable members of racial minorities to act as individuals and so make their own way in society. Thus Michael Walzer has observed that the impact of the state's dealing with groups has been basically individualistic. The chief purpose of quotas, he argues, "is to give opportunities to individuals, not a voice to groups."[46]

Michele Wallace's book, Black Macho and the Myth of the Super-Woman, clearly sets forth an individualistic approach to being black. Wallace is highly critical of the late 1960's cult of black machismo, which she sees an an attempt to glorify a life of oppression forced on black people by white society. For her there is nothing appealing or enriching about ghetto life, and she distinguishes its inherent violence from other aspects of the black experience--music, language, ways of cooking and dressing--which in her opinion "came out of an understanding and acceptance on the part of black people of themselves as a unique culture within America, a culture which had a right to exist and to continue to exist." Her relationship to the black experience is thus a voluntaristic one, for she clearly feels free to pick and choose what she likes. At the same time Wallace emphasizes the importance of affirming one's identity as a black person.

200

She rejects the alternative of assimilation because this means "the cultural annihilation of black people." Instead she opts for the struggle "for a decent existence for all black people and the continuation of their cultural and racial identity," and she insists that "pursuing money, economic independence, does not mean that one has to become white."[47] This acceptance of core American values obviously does not assume that black people will be pursuing a totally separate existence.

Wallace's position suggests that the weight of racial prejudice and discrimination is most likely to be lifted as key elements of categorically defined differences become increasingly matters of choice which do not set individuals off from the larger society in invidious ways. Stephen Steinberg argues that "there has been a collapse of the caste system that once relegated blacks almost without exception to the economic periphery." Thus one can reasonably "expect that reductions in economic inequalities between whites and blacks will be accompanied by a waning of prejudice, as occurred with Irish, Jews, Japanese, and others who have risen in the class system."[48] Fredrickson and Knobel cautiously note a trend "in the direction of according to Americans of various Asian ancestries a status roughly equivalent to that of white 'ethnics.'" If this trend continues, they feel "it will provide strong evidence that racism is a situational and historically determined phenomenon and not the result of some innate 'consciousness of kind.'"[49] Arguably the same logic applies to sexism.

Cultural categories arise in response to specific historical conditions, change over time, and even fade in importance in many instances. All aspects are potentially mutable, but the least so are the symbolic significance attached to the designations themselves and the individual identities that develop as a consequence. Because America has a long history of racist and sexist thinking which has assumed innate differences, full acceptance of such negatively categorized people still seems enormously difficult. Thus for the foreseeable future it is likely that sex-related categories will continue to seem to most Americans both viable and useful. Categorization blurs the concepts of sex, sexual identity, physical distinctiveness, sexual object choice and sex roles. At the same time the increasing tendency to see sex roles in instrumental terms weakens the link with sex-related forms of identity and threatens to undermine the importance of these identities themselves. Hence the need for affirming one's identity as a male or a female, a heterosexual or a homosexual, even as one claims more and more freedom to define the behavioral implications of these identities. Insofar as approaches to sex-role flexibility operate within mainstream assumptions, therefore, their purpose will not be to abolish distinctions but rather to seek ways to provide individuals maneuvering room within and beyond them.

Mary E. Hotvedt and William Paul are optimistic about escaping the limitations of sexual categorization without denying its validity. Hotvedt argues that among gay men and women respectively "there is the same emphasis on sensitivity plus masculinity, and on self-assuredness plus womanliness, that is prized by many heterosexuals these days." Because both gay and "straight" people are rejecting simplified role assumptions, "we see similarities that foster a sense of belonging--and variations, which imply a sense of options in creating social relationships."[50] Paul feels that "it is possible that the larger common similarities between heterosexuals and Gay men and Lesbians will emerge so as to make these group distinctions less salient." This would make the minority status of gay people similar to "that of Catholics: people with a positive group identity, yet well integrated on the basis of individual characteristics shared with the majority."[51] Clyde W. Franklin seems to have something similar in mind regarding men and women when he talks of the humanist man's commitment to sex-role equality. Changing cognitions, feelings and behaviors are leading to "a society where men and women are equally valued and where each participates equally according to individual predilections."[52]

Just as great numbers of Americans have come to believe that one's religious, ethnic or racial identification should not limit one's chances and opportunities within society, so many have come to feel that the same logic applies to sex-related behaviors and expectations. Individuals should be free to make as much or as little of these as they choose. Such freedom in America has not resulted in the disappearance of ethnic, racial or religious (cultural and social) differences, and there is no reason to suppose that sex-related differences will altogether disappear either. Masculinity and femininity, as well as homosexuality and heterosexuality, may become less sharply differentiated, but the other half of the coin of equality of opportunity and freedom of choice has always been the assumption that these take place within a context of basic agreement and general social stability. That is why the individual can be granted the freedom to relate to social structures--including sexual ones--voluntaristically. If one is able to use them to accomplish one's own ends, one has a vested interest in preserving their cultural significance as well as their social utility--however qualified one's support might be.

Overview--

Americans are not particularly disposed to think in class terms even though they are aware of economic and social class differences. The reason is that the individual's relationship to class structures is defined instrumentally, thus stressing his ability to change his status if he chooses. By contrast distinctions based on such factors as ethnicity, race and sex

202

are not seen in instrumental terms. Rather these are viewed as closely linked with personal identity; one therefore expresses one's individuality through them. Race and sex differences are assumed to influence individuals in ways over which they have little control. Certainly stereotyped conceptions of women and gay people do have a powerful effect on their lives and their self-conceptions. Cultural categories themselves imply limitations, but as long as they are seen as simply descriptive of "natural" differences, they are not experienced as limitations. They will only be called into question when at least to some degree they are viewed as externally imposed restrictions which can be dealt with instrumentally.

In the case of women gender-role flexibility requires that such roles no longer be seen as innately predetermined. At the same time, many women have favored a strategy that involves the fulfillment of feminine expectations (thereby validating their identities as women) at the same time that it stresses individual freedom and self-determination. Those dedicated to the pursuit of success in the larger world are likely to feel a strong need to see themselves and to be seen as feminine in as many ways as possible. Because women feel pressure to be effective both within their own sphere and within the larger world, sexual categories are affirmed even as role limitations are being rejected. Externalizing sex-role expectations thus enables many women to move beyond categorically defined barriers.

Gay males have also sought to formulate strategies for functioning effectively within the larger society while continuing to affirm their homosexual identities. Such strategies represent a synthesis of assimilationist and pluralist positions. One strategy involves identifying themselves with all other males. A second stresses behavioral changes within the larger society that minimize differences between "straight" and gay people. Nevertheless, gay people must continue to function in two different worlds.

Cultural definitions of masculinity and femininity have not changed as rapidly as sex-related behaviors. While intimacy between men and women has increased, each sex continues to have fairly conventional expectations of the other. Men who feel their own needs are being satisfied tend to be more supportive of changes in women's role behavior. Many want their women to be conventionally feminine as well as independent and achievement-oriented. In their own lives men feel more free to adopt behavioral traits once considered exclusively feminine. Both sexes seem to favor greater role flexibility so long as a person's masculinity or femininity is not in question. While sexual differences thus remain important, they are not considered barriers to more freedom as far as role expectations are concerned. A greater range of behaviors indicates that men and women are giving up the tendency to live vicariously through members of the opposite sex.

A minority of males has emphasized the restrictive, externally imposed quality of masculine role expectations. While early advocates of men's liberation stressed emulating the values associated with women, a larger number of men have favored a greater role flexibility that does not seem to them to undercut their masculinity. Their behavioral assumptions accord with the Sex Role Strain paradigm, which Joseph Pleck sees as replacing the MSRI paradigm. The newer paradigm provides a rationale for pragmatic role changes and role flexibility. Sex roles are thus conceived in outward and traditional terms distinct from other elements of sex-related cultural categories.

The lessening of the polarization of masculinity and femininity in the twentieth century and the protests against arbitrary sex-role limitations must be placed in a larger context of other categorically defined limits upon self-determination. In the case of regionally and religiously defined differences it seems fairly easy in most instances to acknowledge an individual's right to determine for himself the role region or religion will play in his life. This position also involves a sense that such differences are no longer vitally important. Clearly such an accommodation is much more difficult in the case of racial and sex-related differences, but granting individuals a greater degree of self-determination seems possible. Categorization blurs the concepts of sex, sexual identity, physical differences, sexual object choice and sex-role expectations. Treating roles in instrumental terms still threatens many people's sexual identities. Hence the importance of affirming masculinity and femininity, as well as heterosexuality and homosexuality, even as individuals seek more maneuvering room within and beyond sexual categories.

CHAPTER TEN

REPUDIATING SEX-RELATED CATEGORIES

Americans have no familial or social destiny in the sense that people in traditional societies do. What we have are many destinies which are a consequence of the fact that we all belong to social groupings not of our own choosing. Men and women, gays and "straights," have been expected to fulfill their sexual destinies by developing the personal identities and accepting the outward forms of sexual differentiation that embody categorical assumptions. More recently many have sought to deal more individualistically with these destinies by remaining loyal to deeper categorical meanings but not consenting to be wholly bound by the roles that are still tied to them. Other Americans, however, have found sex-related categories much less authentic. This has prompted an exploration of the possibilities of more systematically repudiating them by reinterpreting what is implied in dichotomizing people in terms of sex and sexual object choice. Not surprisingly, many have been disposed to question some elements and not others. Nevertheless, all have ventured beyond the assertion that while men and women (and/or homosexuals and heterosexuals) should be free from external constraints on their behavioral options, in fundamental and unchangeable ways they are "naturally" opposites of one another.

The Ideal of Liberation--

Though it is impossible to establish a precise point of demarcation, approaches to change can pass beyond the boundaries of the mainstream--where individual freedom and categorical expectations uneasily coexist--into an ideal world of much greater personal freedom and self-determination essentially beyond sex-related categories. Myron Brenton's The American Male, which appeared in the mid-1960's, is an important precursor of the men's liberation movement. Brenton is opposed to seeing men and women in terms of categories rather than as unique individuals, for "human beings have an enormous range of possibilities in terms of traits and in the ability to play roles of all kinds." The problem is that "these possibilities are severely foreshortened by the process of sex differentiation too rigidly applied and by masculinity and femininity too narrowly defined." Someone who can accept himself and his sex comfortably is able to "conform to sex-role demands when conformity is in accord with his personality or does no violence to it and to reject the rest without feeling threatened." If Brenton's ideal society comes to pass, categorical differences between the sexes will not have been altogether repudiated, but he does call for a "psychic kind of primitiveness" that enables a person "to go beyond stereotypes and to distinguish people--whether in terms of sex, race, age, occupation, or whatever--as individuals." Individualism cannot now "be what it was in the nineteenth or eighteenth century," but it is not "irretrievably lost." American males can therefore choose to accept "the ultimate masculine challenge" to do "away with stereotypes, guidelines, and life plans."[1] Brenton can be seen as a borderline figure in his attempt to define masculinity in more flexible terms which still project a familiar image of self-reliance, individualism and independence. At the same time his unequivocal devotion to individualism prompts him in some respects to reject gender-based categories altogether.

Warren Farrell's The Liberated Man (1974) defines the basic goal of men's liberation as getting "beyond masculinity." Men need to be encouraged to develop "enough internal security so that both women and men can attain the psychological freedom to control their own lives." Everyone should be free of categorical limitations, free to act as a self-determining individual, for "human liberation means opening options at an early enough age so that the environment is not used to impose certain values on girls and others on boys--except the value of openness."[2] Mark Gerzon's A Choice of Heroes (1982) juxtaposes five conventional masculine archetypes--each of which "requires the denial of the feminine"--against a parallel series of emerging archetypes. The latter suggest "new men, who not only differ from past archetypes, but who also differ among themselves." An emphasis upon individual differences among males is balanced by an acknowledgement of categorical differences between the two sexes. Unlike the Expert, the Colleague "is open to learning from women precisely because they are different from him." Nevertheless, Gerzon finally insists that all five new archetypes are similar in that "the human qualities they symbolize transcend sexual identity," not simply sex-role expectations. Rather than being "for men only," like the old archetypes, "they are, in fact, emerging humanities."[3]

Among gay males as well one finds evidence of a struggle to get beyond categorically defined limitations. In The Gay Mystique (1972) Peter Fisher advocates an instrumental approach to homosexual categorization. He favors seeing "sexuality as a mode of self-expression, rather than self-definition." He predicts that "the rigid distinction between heterosexual and homosexual behavior" will in time "probably vanish" as "people of all sexual orientations feel free to enjoy their full range of sexuality." Fisher insists that "gay people are questioning the very nature of gender, without refusing to acknowledge its existence, as some of the more radical feminists do today." They are increasingly basing their identities "on a radical freedom and individuality, a refusal to be defined by others, a deep commitment to self-determination."[4] At the time Fisher was writing radicals within the Gay Liberation Front were labeling existing forms of gay male behavior "unliberated." Toby Marotta describes these critics as not having a strong and positive sense of identification with the gay community. He says that they had been greatly influenced by radical lesbians, who very much disapproved of gay men's "bald pursuit of sex." This reinforced the feeling "that liberation required abandoning traditional gay male patterns." One expression of this position labeled all of the long-practiced ways of the gay world "exploitative institutions designed to keep gay men in the roles given to them by a male heterosexual system."[5]

In a sexually egalitarian society, Esther Peterson once remarked, "no one is forced into a predetermined role on account of sex," and "men and women have the option to plan and pattern their lives as they themselves choose."[6] Such a position can--and for Peterson did--lend itself to a fairly mainstream interpretation. If, however, equality is really taken seriously, the categorical differences that have underscored inequality must also be questioned. Elizabeth Janeway has labeled as very exciting "the idea of a truly equal relationship, a relationship free of the formal, built-in social inequity constant to most male-female attitudes in our society."[7] In the mid-1970's Mary Ryan argued that "there are no incontrovertible biological determinants of the functions of the sexes" beyond the roles directly related to sexual intercourse and procreation. The hope which infuses Womanhood in America is that sex differences will be confined to reproductive biology, "and thus release men and women to develop and exercise the individuality that typifies humanity rather than sex."[8]

The emphasis upon a common humanity shared by people who are seen as free individuals clearly challenges the validity of collectively distinguishing all men from all women. "We need a vision of what it would mean to be a society comprised not of feminine and masculine creatures, but of humans," Janet Saltzman Chafetz proclaims. In such a society "men and women will increasingly come together as independent human beings who truly love and respect one another's individuality." The learned behavioral, temperamental, emotional, intellectual and attitudinal characteristics that males and females display in our society are what constitute gender roles, she maintains. These "socially or culturally defined expectations that individuals in a given situation are expected to fulfill" include more than simply the customary outward behaviors that either traditional or conventional assumptions emphasize. Chafetz is critical of the stress upon "a radical dichotomy of human types, despite both the many differences between individuals of the same sex and the many similarities between people of 'opposite' sexes." The "self-definition" as well as "certain behaviors" people are encouraged to assume may not fit their "natural proclivities" and express only half their human potential. Her hope by contrast is for "a society of humans whose lives are based on achieved

rather than ascribed characteristics." Men and women as individuals would be free to structure their lives in terms of "a
set of humanistic and socially conscious values that embraces
the best of both traditional masculinity and traditional femininity." Masculinity and femininity thus remain for Chafetz
conceptually viable standards even though they would not be categorically restrictive as they now are. At the same time it is
also important for her that "natural" (and presumably immutable)
differences be clearly distinguished from the culturally based
distinctions that are subject to reformulation: "It is only when
we sort things out and separate sex from gender role that the
latter can change without affecting the functioning of the
former."9

The Dimensions of Androgyny--

    Challenging sex-related categories calls for new cultural
symbols that would clarify the meaning of no longer collectively
distinguishing men from women and restricting them to sexually
determined behavioral roles, outlooks and even identities. The
term liberation has been one such symbol that was widely used in
the 1970's to capture the meaning of transcending categorically
defined masculine and feminine spheres. Androgyny has been
another. "I believe," Carolyn Heilbrun says, "that our future
salvation lies in a movement away from sexual polarization and
the prison of gender toward a world in which individual roles
and modes of personal behavior can be freely chosen." What she
favors is a dedication to androgyny, which suggests "a full
range of experience open to individuals," or in other words, "a
spectrum upon which human beings choose their places without regard to propriety or custom."10 June Singer argues that "we
need to think of ourselves no longer as exclusively 'masculine'
or exclusively 'feminine' but rather as whole beings in whom the
opposite qualities are ever-present."11

    As an ideal for men in America androgyny means to its male
proponents freedom from conventional masculine restrictions and
openness to a range of feelings and responses hitherto limited
to women. Jack Nichols argues for the importance of men's getting in touch with their feelings both because this allows them
to share with women access to intuition and also because feelings are what prompt a man "to break out of constricting frameworks." Indeed "without them a powerful bulwark of individualism is missing." There is agreement as well that certain aspects of masculinity which American society has long accepted,
particularly the exercise of power and the competitive pursuit
of success, cannot be retained. For advocates of liberation the
freedom to determine one's own life must not be compromised by
the limitations on all concerned that power and success entail.
Nichols rejects the drive for success because "it is anti-individualistic, and for the purpose of winning it would wipe out or

ignore all unique characteristics that do not seem relevant to the contest at hand."[12] "Freedom," Jack Sawyer insists, "requires that there not be dominance and submission, but that all individuals be free to determine their own lives as equals." Success in the popular imagination, he notes, requires dominance over other males in the occupational sphere and over women in the social sphere. However, "it is not really possible for two persons to have a free relation when one holds the balance of power over the other."[13] "Androgyny," says Marc Fasteau, "would end men's preoccupation with dominance and control" in sexual relations with women. The latter in turn would claim "the all-important freedom to express and act on their own desires."[14]

Liberation therefore means freedom for both sexes from conventional sexually based limitations upon their actions, values and sense of themselves. Androgyny as an ideal, obviously, does not imply a wholesale blending of masculinity and femininity as the terms are presently understood. It rejects male dominance and self-interested opportunism as well as female submissiveness and invisible supportiveness. Because it is expressed within a categorically defined context, mainstream individualism stresses the separateness of each person rather than the uniqueness. To theorists of liberation expressing one's own uniqueness is the fundamental reason for rejecting the assumption that all individuals included within a given social grouping are basically alike. "Androgyny is the encouragement of every human being to be as individual as a snowflake," Warren Farrell insists. "It is not unisex. It is multi-individuality."[15]

Andrea S. Hayman is so concerned about the fostering of individual uniqueness that she rejects the term androgyny because it suggests unisex to her. "Men's and women's liberation," she argues, "need not necessarily lead to the same androgynous behavior by men and women. Rather, all persons can develop individually without the limitations of a sex stereotype."[16] Similarly Rebecca, Hefner and Oleshansky see androgyny as a sex-role stereotype potentially as binding as those of masculinity and femininity. Instead they favor "sex-role transcendence," a freedom from all sex-role norms.[17] If people are not to be categorized in sexually dichotomous terms, neither should they be categorized in unisexual ways. Even those who endorse androgyny do not do so in categorical terms. All critics of conventional sex roles agree in opposing the idea of a single unisexual or androgynous cultural category. In contrast to mainstream critics like Betty Friedan, however, advocates of liberation insist on the individual uniqueness of each man and woman rather than the collective distinctiveness of each sex.

Many special characteristics which set one individual off from another in America are the consequence of belonging to different social groupings. In a society in which categorically

209

defined differences have no meaning each individual would presumably be free to be his or her own unique self. At the same time the range of variations under such circumstances would be limited in many respects even though no two people would be exactly alike. The kinds of variety that exist in traditional societies where there are obvious differences between nobility and commons, great wealth and abject poverty, or in our own society between whites and people of color, one ethnic group and another, men and women, would be gone. Thus uniqueness among individuals must not be equated with familiar forms of social variety. Should categorically based distinctions lose their symbolic importance, an emphasis upon a common humanity would undoubtedly be augmented. If people no longer thought in categorical terms, such an emphasis would not however suggest, as it easily does today, an undifferentiated alikeness of all human beings in the same sense as all males are conventionally assumed to be alike or all blacks.

Because the uniqueness of each person in a liberated society would not coexist with many of the varieties of categorically reinforced distinctiveness we are presently accustomed to, individuals would have little incentive and few resources to differ markedly from one another. Like power, differences of many sorts really demand social supports rooted in institutional forms and structures without which they cannot be easily sustained. Where differences do not matter much because they have little or no vitality as cultural symbols, there is less of a tendency to cultivate them and much less general awareness of them. Variations which have only an individual import simply do not stand out in the ways that collective differences fraught with cultural and social meaning do. This is obviously true in the case of racial differences among young children who are not yet conditioned to their cultural significance. Such youngsters may be conscious of variations in skin color but will lack any real incentive to make something of them. People would not be motivated to attach symbolic weight--particularly in invidious ways--to all sorts of collective differences which are presently emphasized. There would be fundamental equality as well in a liberated society, for the cultural assumptions and social structures that make some people the categorical unequals of others would also be absent.

What would happen if categorically defined barriers were abolished is very well illustrated by attitudes toward homosexuality. As a historically recent cultural formulation which does not take into account the range of human variation, the homosexual-heterosexual dichotomy would have no place in a liberated society. June Singer argues that the categories of homosexual, heterosexual or bisexual, "when used as labels, fix an idea in mind that need not be fixed but can be extremely fluid." A homosexual object choice may be a perfectly natural way of expressing one's sexuality "in the context of androgyny." Ideally, "if human beings are released, or can release themselves, from the boundaries of sex and gender, there can be a far wider reaching-out in love to people as people on the basis of individual needs and desires."[18] Marc Fasteau sees the "extreme version of the male stereotype" as leading to excessive masculinity or to a complete rejection of a conventional masculine status in the form of exclusive homosexuality. However, "an androgynous society, which would not teach the association of maleness, constant dominance, and aggressive sex, would make both compulsions less likely." At the same time, "homosexual activity may become for larger numbers of men than at present an accepted, if occasional and subsidiary part of life."[19] Presumably everyone would be open to the possibility of same-sex as well as opposite-sex feelings and experiences or at least in no way anxious about such a range of behaviors in others.

The distinction between homosexual and heterosexual experiences and relationships would no longer be culturally significant. Homosexuality as well as heterosexuality would cease to be collectively meaningful symbols, and thus the terms would undoubtedly be dropped from the language. This does not mean, however, that people would necessarily cease to distinguish between homosexual and heterosexual acts or develop individual preferences--only that same-sex interests or relationships would not make someone a "homosexual." One would simply be a person with certain feelings that would not be seen as setting one significantly apart. Each individual would remain unique and free and yet conscious of no culturally prescribed barrier separating one grouping of people from another in terms of sexual object choice.

Just as the repudiation of cultural categories would not necessarily eliminate the conceptual distinction between homosexual and heterosexual acts, neither would it obliterate all distinctions between men and women. If the sexes were no longer thought of in collective terms, however, people would be much more aware of individual differences and also of commonalities that have nothing to do with sex. Generalizations would be understood only as statistical abstractions, not as evidence of categorical alikeness or of dichotomous distinctions. Neither would there be an unwillingness to recognize the existential realities of human reproduction. Indeed a liberated society would be challenged to be sensitive to these realities without making them the basis of cultural categories that prescribe the boundaries of people's lives.

What are valid sex-related differences and how to take account of them without endorsing categorizing remains a difficult task, however, in a context in which dichotomizing has for so long been accepted. Linda E. Olds argues that "men and women

211

both have been imprisoned by their bondage to artificial dualities and characteristics that are projected at a cultural level and falsely deemed male or female." What is demonstrably cultural can be altered she assumes, but at the same time she is concerned with what cannot or should not be altered. She insists that "androgyny is not likely of any necessity to alter choice of sexual partner or one's identification with one's bodily gender or sex," thus freeing androgyny as a cultural symbol from any necessary homosexual or transsexual taint. Indeed "it is every bit as likely to free men and women up to enjoy their own conventional sexual identity as a man or a woman." We are also told that "androgynous women are very affirmative in their enjoyment of being women." On a more grandly symbolic level, moreover, Olds' book, Fully Human: How Everyone Can Integrate the Benefits of Masculine and Feminine Sex Roles, is dedicated "to the preservation of both the metaphorically masculine and feminine realms of behaviors, values and inner orientations."[20]

Olds' concern throughout her work is to persuade the reader that there is no necessary link between biological maleness and masculine values or femaleness and feminine values. In terms of present realities, she contends, "men and women can be conditioned into either the masculine or feminine realm of dominant values," as evidenced by masculine-identified feminists of a decade ago. Olds admits that the concepts of masculinity and femininity "keep us dangerously close to assuming they bear some intrinsic relationship to maleness and femaleness." While the terms are still meaningful to most people, everyone needs to realize that "the 'masculine' and the 'feminine' are realms within each individual, male and female." Thus "once they have both been given full expression and integration, it is no longer necessary to retain these labels as clues or guides."[21] The terms themselves as cultural symbols will disappear once men and women as individuals have fully incorporated the meaning of androgyny into their lives.

In Gender: An Ethnomethodological Approach Suzanne J. Kessler and Wendy McKenna propose a much more thoroughgoing critique of sexual categorization. They point out that "the grounds for questioning existing dichotomous gender roles do not question the existence of two genders." Their book does in fact question "the dichotomous nature of gender, itself," by "questioning dichotomous criteria for gender attributions" (deciding whether someone is female or male). They are not convinced "that in all cultures people have always attributed gender according to the male/female dichotomy, although it is clear that all ethnographers have taken that for granted." They suggest, for instance, that the berdache in many cultures may have been treated as outside the male/female framework. In at least some preindustrial cultures gender attribution has been based on gender role "just as in our culture genitals are seen as the basis." Their observation, it seems to me, not only supports a distinction regarding sex-related differences between premodern and modern societies but also suggests in part why men and women in earlier times were not thought of in categorical terms. The outward emphasis upon roles was not a rigidly or unchangingly dichotomous one, as evidenced by wives who conducted their deceased husbands' businesses and little boys who were dressed like girls. The absolute conviction that everyone must forever belong to one of two genders results in dichotomizing form as much as behavior: "As a result we end up with two genders, at least as different physically as they have been traditionally thought to be behaviorally." The authors even question what they see as the assumption of the advocates of androgyny "that there are real masculine and feminine traits which can be combined."[22]

Kessler and McKenna therefore conclude that "as long as the categories 'female' and 'male' present themselves to people in everyday life as external, objective, dichotomous, physical facts, there will be scientific and naive searches for differences, and differences will be found." These are inevitably the basis for discrimination and oppression, they contend. Thus "unless and until gender, in all of its manifestations including the physical, is seen as a social construction, action that will radically change our incorrigible propositions cannot occur." The authors accept the characteristically American assumption that what is culturally determined can be challenged and then symbolically reformulated. They differ in arguing that virtually in their entirety gender-based categories are cultural artifacts. The only biological element is related to reproduction. They insist, however, that male and female cannot be totally equated with "sperm carrier" and "egg carrier." Biological imperatives require only the union of the latter, and "because the reproductive dichotomy would not be constituted as a lifetime dichotomy, it would not be an essential characteristic of people." Gender attribution and the resulting assigning of the labels male and female are not the same things as "gender differentiation." The latter involves recognizing reproductive differences only.[23] Beyond these nothing else is "naturally" determined. Thus sexual categories have no intrinsic validity nor presumably any cultural or social justification once this is recognized.

Philip Slater insists that "a viable society needs a great variety of contradictory human responses." Variety may be achieved through distinctive groups that limit people in different ways. "On the other hand, if a society is to function with uniform participants, each one must be individually complex and comprehensive in his or her available responses." Slater terms the latter alternative "utopian," and he does not endorse it as advocates of liberation do.[24] Still, they would certainly agree with the distinction he makes between a society in which variety is based on collective differences among people (whether in class and status terms as in traditional societies or categorical terms as in our own) and one in which it is based on individual differences. In present-day America individualism must operate within the limits that cultural categories mandate. In a liberated society there would be no such limits.

Liberation and Social Unity--

In his study, Women and Equality, William H. Chafe argues that equality as a norm must, to gain acceptance in America, provide "ample room for individual self-expression and fulfillment." At the same time self-expression must occur within limits which insure similar opportunities for everyone. The problem is that the goal of equality is inconsistent with the "ethos of individualism and libertarianism." The former presupposes willingness to work within a collective structure while individualism assumes "acting on one's own desires as a first priority, with collective interests as a secondary concern." Nevertheless, in typically liberationist terms Chafe says that in a truly egalitarian society men and women will "learn to view each other as individuals, separate and independent of each other, each with the right to self-determination and fulfillment."[25]

Advocates of liberation are convinced that a sense of oneself as a free and unique being is not incompatible with an emphasis upon interdependence and common purpose. They favor voluntarism as the basis for all relationships in society, and they are much more confident than mainstream individualists that self and society can be harmonized. June Singer distinguishes between the individual (good) and the individualist (bad). She sees emerging "a preference for cooperation rather than competition, for a team approach to problems rather than a strictly individualistic approach" as well as "for emphasizing sexuality and relationship over and above power and violence."[26]

Stressing voluntary cooperative involvements, Jack Nichols sees the values of the new sexuality as "cooperation, spontaneity, passivity (openness), sharing, sensitivity, trust, and freedom." He strongly endorses personal relationships based on free consent. "Dependency creates resentment for both partners in a relationship," he insists. Breaking the "dependency habit" clearly requires that men and women "stand on their own" as equals rather than as categorically opposite beings. Nichols distinguishes between what he calls "relationships" and "coupling." "A relationship allows one to be oneself, to go anywhere freely, to see anyone affectionately, and to speak openly and honestly about any matter." This kind of tie fulfills basic criteria of individualism and voluntarism because each person retains his or her freedom and self-determination--separateness --while freely consenting to a close involvement. Not surprisingly, "coupling"--the conventional male-female bond--"is destructive of individual strength and initiative, and in its shadow individuality withers." Nichols is not in favor of rearing children to depend on conventional structures--"familial, ethnic, religious or political"--because such involuntary social constructions "are presently crumbling before the mighty onrush of a new and different world civilization."[27]

Marc Fasteau maintains that America's success myths highlight the "lonely independent efforts" of the individual male. Androgyny, by contrast, "would recognize, along with the uniqueness of human beings, their need for and dependence on others." He praises "traditional individualism" for fostering "respect for civil liberties and the recognition of at least the potential dignity and worth of every person." These legacies need not be discarded though one no longer accepts "this ideology as a psychodynamic engine of progress today." Fasteau rejects the idea that we should be totally free and "independent of everything but the drive to achieve." This has created a nation of lonely men who seek "impersonal substitutes for personal connection" instead of fostering an outlook "which honors the relatedness of human beings."[28]

At the end of the nineteenth century Charlotte Perkins Gilman similarly linked feminist goals with voluntaristic forms of social interaction. "The basic condition of human life is union; the organic social relation, the interchange of functional service," she argued. She was highly critical of the effects of "individualism with sex-advantage" which prompted men to sacrifice public good for personal gain in supporting their families. At the same time she noted with approval that "the progress of social organization has produced a corresponding degree of individualization." As individual consciousness grows, she believed, so does social consciousness: "We have grown to care for one another." Social progress in her opinion has made possible a higher form of marriage between "class equals," who share equally in the world's work, and whose relationship no longer prevents women from forming close friendships with members of both sexes. For both young and old "enforced association on family lines" needs to give way to "free association on social lines." Gilman considered herself a socialist and took for granted the desire and willingness of everyone to participate voluntarily in the common life around him or her. Her ideal society was held together not by forms and structures based on differences in status and power, but by voluntary consent. "'Love,'" she maintained, "is merely the first condition of social existence. It is cohesion, working among us as the constituent particles of society."[29]

I have argued previously that there are two largely separate traditions of American individualism, one stemming from the orthodox Calvinist emphasis on the equality of the elect before God and the other from the more secular emphasis upon human sufficiency and achievement. Each sees the individual as having a fundamental validity apart from the social context in which he or she functions. From the former come, in secularized form, the ideals of hypomasculinity, equality and of community based on personal freedom and like-mindedness. The latter emphasizes the importance of cultural categories as well as equality of opportunity and success and the fluid and impersonal social hierarches which make achievement possible. Advocates of liberation and androgyny reject the mainstream tradition (which some specifically equate with individualism as opposed to individuality) in favor of the former one.

The ideal of freedom, individual fulfillment and harmonious interaction with like-minded others can be seen as an expression of an unfulfilled desire at the heart of the individualistic value system. In religious terms it is a millennial or paradisiacal hope; in contemporary sex-related terms it implies liberation from categorically defined cultural expectations and related social structures. In Eros and Civilization Herbert Marcuse argues that "imagination envisions the reconciliation of the individual with the whole." Everyone would cooperate "for the free development and fulfillment of individual needs." Thus "men would really exist as individuals, each shaping his own life." As part of the process of liberation Marcuse sees the resexualization of the body, now no longer just an instrument of labor, "a decline of genital supremacy," a new understanding of same-sex relationships, and "a disintegration of the institutions in which the private interpersonal relations have been organized, particularly the monogamic and patriarchal family."[30]

In The Dialectic of Sex Shulamith Firestone takes Marcuse a step beyond the liberation of mankind from the tyranny of toil to the liberation of women from "the tyranny of their reproductive biology." She calls as well for "the full self-determination, including economic independence, of both women and children" and "the total integration of women and children into all aspects of the larger society." In such an ideal world "all relationships would be based on love alone, uncorrupted by objective dependencies and the resulting class inequalities." Modern technology is what has made possible freedom from toil and from childbearing, for "we have the knowledge to create a paradise on earth anew."[31]

The ideal of sexual liberation is a logical extension of the emphasis upon the individual in modern Western culture. In America particularly it represents a challenge both to traditional values and to cultural categories, which have functioned

216

in many respects as symbolic alternatives to hierarchical ideals. Liberation insists that it is possible to transcend these forces of "mechanism" to achieve a society based entirely on individual freedom and voluntary commitment. The fact that it does not for its advocates imply anarchy and social disintegration is the result of essentially "feminine" assumptions. The "masculine" component of the ideal of androgyny is autonomy and a strong sense of individuality. The "feminine" component is an equally strong sense of unstructured human involvement. Two rather different books emphasize the fact that women in America are custodians of sociability just as men are custodians of individuality. Thus men must learn the lessons of interrelatedness without losing touch with their individuality while women must learn to be more self-determining without relinquishing any of their sensitivity to others.

In _Toward a New Psychology of Women_ Jean Baker Miller questions "the very nature" of "the whole dichotomization of the essentials of human experience," the "attempt to divide ourselves so that we force men to center around themselves and women to center around 'the other.'" Women's "greater recognition of the essential cooperative nature of human existence" makes them important agents of social change, for everyone must come to understand that "individual development proceeds only by means of affiliation." What Miller is clearly suggesting is that the lesson of human connectedness needs to be stressed much more than the lesson of autonomy. While women want independence rather than dependence, she goes on, they do not want what men presently understand by this term. Rather they desire the conditions that will permit "feeling effective and free along with feeling intense connections with other people." To realize these ideals women "will have to acquire economic, political, and social power and authority." By power, however, Miller means "the capacity to implement," not "the ability to advance oneself and, simultaneously, to control, limit, and if possible, destroy the power of others." Thus she rejects power as I (being a male, she might very well argue) have previously defined the term. The characteristics that permit women to act as agents of liberation, Miller admits, "are the very characteristics that are specifically dysfunctional for success in the world as it is." Nevertheless, she adds, they may "be the important ones for making the world different."[32]

Nancy Chodorow's _The Reproduction of Mothering_ seeks to explain in psychoanalytic terms why men and women develop the differences in perspective upon which Miller bases her argument. Mothers are much more likely, Chodorow argues, to push sons out of the preoedipal relationship than daughters, who consequently "come to define and experience themselves as continuous with others." By contrast "boys come to define themselves as more separate and distinct." Thus "the basic feminine sense of self is connected to the world, the basic masculine sense of self is separate." Chodorow points out that there are two fundamentally different conceptions of human nature in terms of which psychoanalysts operate--"whether human connection and sociality or human isolation and self-centeredness are more in need of psychological and social explanation." In contrast to mainstream individualistic assumptions, her own view is that human connectedness can simply be taken for granted, for it derives from the infant's initial closeness with its mother. Boys must learn to be separate. They "are taught to be masculine more consciously than girls are taught to be feminine." A boy therefore "represses those qualities he takes to be feminine inside himself, and rejects and devalues women and whatever he considers to be feminine in the social world."[33]

If men find it all too "natural" to be individualistic, women must always struggle with individuation. The basic problem, Chodorow concludes, is that primary child care falls almost exclusively to the mother. If children were dependent on both sexes from the outset, boys and girls equally would come to "establish an individuated sense of self in relation to both." Men's needs to keep women in secondary and powerless positions would be greatly reduced, and women would be helped "to develop the autonomy which too much embeddedness in relationship has often taken from them." Moreover, good primary relationships would provide a foundation for nurturance and love for everyone, "and women would retain these even as men would gain them."[34] The result of what Chodorow proposes would be to undercut the psychological and also cultural bases of support for specifically sex-related attitudes, values, approaches and forms of behavior. It seems logical to suppose, furthermore, that sexual identity itself would be less critically important than it presently is.

Like Miller, Chodorow assumes that women are more in touch with the most essential elements of liberation. Given the realities of male and female socialization in America, it is not difficult to see why emphasizing individualistic self-determination in conjunction with empathy and concerned involvement with others is less of a challenge to long-held conceptions of femininity than of masculinity. It many ways the androgynous ideal is not too different from the ideal of the American Girl, whose claims have in theory if not in fact been long recognized. Thus the ideal of the liberated society bears a much stronger evidence of women's influence than the approaches I dealt with in the last two chapters. There women were called upon to accommodate themselves to or at most to help modify a society essentially structured along masculine lines. Here they can participate in the creation of a new society, and the males (both gay and "straight") who support them have been more than willing to acknowledge that men have a good deal more to learn from women than women from men.

Linda E. Olds feels that "in the journey toward wholeness in contemporary culture and personality development, the realm of the metaphorical feminine stands out as the dimension most in need of exploration and affirmation." This would involve "a re-valuation of interpersonal sensitivity, holistic perception, the values of relatedness, responsiveness, and love." The feminine dimension, she insists, is not woman's special province "however much it has been assigned, allowed, or left by default to her as her special province and area of training." While Olds is cri-tical of the feminists of the early 70's for emulating too ex-clusively masculine values, she is equally concerned that the subsequent "wave of feminine revivalism . . . threatens to err in the opposite direction."[35] As a proposed cultural symbol em-bodying stringent reservations about mainstream American values, androgyny has evidenced a decided tilt toward the metaphorical feminine. Because the dominant culture has long incorporated femininity as the polar opposite of masculinity, such a tilt can function both symbolically and practically not as a genuine al-ternative but as a contemporary affirmation of woman's sphere and the uniqueness of those who uphold its special values.

As long as both sexes focus on the ideal society of the future, potential differences in perspective arising out of dif-ferences in early socialization are not likely to seem too im-portant. Male supporters may in the long run, however, prove to be less willing or able to abandon their commitments to conven-tional masculinity than they have said they are. The fact that masculinity is much more deeply internalized than femininity makes it harder for men to detach themselves from sex-related attitudinal and behavioral imperatives. It is possible, there-fore, that the androgynous ideal might come to seem an impossi-bility to those who remain free at any time to take advantage of their still privileged status within American society.

The Dark Side of Liberation--

The ideal of liberation takes for granted both the indi-viduality of each person and the possibility of repudiating sex-related categories. One does not constantly have to establish one's individuality by asserting one's relative freedom to move in and out of social forms and structures, which are both neces-sary and a threat to freedom at the same time. There is greater room for a certain passivity--which in part is why many meta-phorically feminine qualities are appealing--and little sense of the conflict between self and society because involvements with others are not seen in institutional terms. If one assumes, as Chodorow does, that human beings are basically social and that sociability goes back to the early infant-parent bond, which need never be wholly shattered, then liberation simply means in-

219

tegrating this feeling of human connectedness with a sense of
one's own individuality. If, however, one takes the opposite
position, liberation becomes a paradisiacal wish and thus an in-
finitely more problemmatical attempt to recapture the lost intimacy of infancy. From this perspective such a wish is simultaneously enormously appealing and equally terrifying, for it cannot be reconciled with each person's individuality. If realized, it annihilates individuality, and thus it is ultimately a
death wish.

Dorothy Dinnerstein's The Mermaid and the Minotaur, like
Chodorow's book, is an argument against exclusive parenting by
women. The meaning of liberation, nevertheless, is more opaque
because the ultimate aloneness of the individual makes gender-
related values and practices both inauthentic and very formidable indeed to transcend. Female responsibility for early child
care and education, Dinnerstein argues, "seems to have been
built into our history since forms of life now identifiable as
incipiently human first emerged." Because of her exclusive role
in parenting, woman "will be seen as naturally fit to nurture
other people's individuality." Yet at the same time she will
also be seen as "the one who beckons her loved ones back from
selfhood, who wants to engulf, dissolve, drown, suffocate them
as autonomous persons." All of us, men as well as women, fear
the kind of power we feel our mothers have exercised over us.
Such power "is far too potent and dangerous a force to be allowed free sway in adult life." As critical as she is of the
male-dominated world, Dinnerstein nevertheless is sympathetic
with its basic thrust as "our ongoing struggle to carve out, and
fence around, a realm for the exercise of sober self-reliance."[36]

Once men and women act equally as parents, women as a
"category of persons" will no longer be "temptingly available as
a focus for our most stubborn childhood wish--the wish to be
free and at the same time to be taken care of." Thus all of us
--males and females--"would be forced at the beginning, before
our spirit was broken, to outgrow that wish and face the ultimate necessity to take care of ourselves." Our present gender
arrangement, by contrast, "has helped us keep unintegrated the
two sides of our ambivalence about becoming adults, about em-
bracing the freedom and responsibility and loneliness of our actual condition." Whatever gender comes to mean in the course of
liberation, it "will no longer be dominated by girls' continuity, and boys' discontinuity, with the adults who initiate us
into the human condition." Moreover, we have the "liberty to
reject what is oppressive and maiming in our prevailing male-
female arrangements."[37] Dinnerstein tends to generalize as part
of the human condition attitudes and assumptions that are largely culture-bound. This, however, makes the task of repudiating
sex-related categories even more formidable. It gives them a
kind of timeless importance in contrast to seeing them as his-

torically recent and parochial cultural arrangements. Also individuality is taken less for granted than it is for Chodorow and many other advocates of liberation. If it must be strenuously established, it will have to be more actively guarded. The fact that Dinnerstein's perspective is more fully grounded in mainstream assumptions does not diminish the appeal of liberation for her, but it does complicate the process of realization.

A second general problem relating to liberation derives from the fact that if its advocates assume that outward social constraints can be fairly readily opposed, they do not presume that inward constraints can be so easily dealt with. There is a greater tendency within this tradition of individualism than within the dominant tradition to stress inwardness and inner freedom. The result is that cultural values can be even more deeply internalized and voluntary assent to them much harder to resist. As far as the goals of liberation are concerned, repudiating sex-related categories is ultimately a matter of desire or will. One may be held back because one's very identity as a sexual being simply will not allow one to do otherwise.

It must not be forgotten that this tradition of individualism ultimately goes back to the Puritans' ideal of freedom as self-denial and willing conformity to God's decrees. Sacvan Bercovitch suggests that "the militancy they hoped would abase the self released all the energies of the self, both constructive and destructive."[38] Despair and passionate self-assertion were both reactions to feeling bound by a recalcitrant will which stood in the way of the ideal of sainthood. Similarly today a belief in the ideal of androgyny and sexual liberation can give way to a feeling of hopelessness and powerlessness before forces that one cannot escape and which cannot be defeated or even beaten back in any type of outward combat. This can lead to a compelling desire for power and the capacity to dominate one's world that liberation explicitly condemns and reality inevitably thwarts.

Marilyn French's central character in The Women's Room--Mira--is a person who does not feel that she belongs to society as it presently exists. At the same time she comes to the despairing conclusion that there is no possibility of fundamentally altering the dynamics of power and sexual politics. Unlike the advocates of liberation and androgyny, Mira remains throughout the novel fascinated--even obsessed--with power. "The sheer naked power" of the great waves along the Maine coast is for her "a symbol of what life is all about." When she becomes seriously interested in a young man, she sees "her choice clearly as being between sex and independence," for "sex meant surrender to the male." Men's power and women's submissiveness are monumental realities for Mira, and one cannot help being struck by her sense of powerlessness where men are concerned. She comes to dread sex with her husband Norm and to feel "violated and used and willess." Power and dependence are not incompatible, and yet Mira seems totally lacking in any of the conventional feminine skills that enable women to achieve at least some measure of power to effect their own ends. At the same time she also wants something which power can never really give--independence. In the last years of her marriage "it was just the feeling of freedom she craved." Listening to Mira tell about married life, her friend Val finds "one long training in humiliation, an education in suppressing self." She feels that Mira's periodic efforts to glorify the woman's role admit a (categorically defined) "identity among all women, which implies lack of individuality."39

Several times during the course of the novel Mira articulates a vision of spontaneous involvement with other people which is unstructured and thus compatible with her desire for independence and control over her own life. She particularly remembers a very special party as "an image of complete human harmony and love." Mira's relationship with Ben initially promises the same kind of reconciliation of independence and relatedness, "intimacy and spontaneity, security and freedom." Yet she also desires a joint publicly recognized identity as a consequence of which "women, anyway--lose the other one, the private one." In time Mira realizes that Ben "only loved her when her desires were the same as his."40 In the end she cannot accept conventional relationships because these are based inevitably upon dominance for men and submission for women. At the same time she cannot believe in the long-term possibility of free and voluntary modes of relating though she very much wants to. Mira's most intense relationships are initially based on a powerful feeling of identification with each man and a willingness to surrender her will to his followed by anger and self-assertion that each man is totally unprepared for. Conventional males are likely to find her puzzling and exasperating and, like both Norm and Ben, turn with apparent relief to more accommodating females. Ironically, if the latter do not regard men as the enemy, it is probably because their sense of their own power is greater than Mira's and their commitment to freedom and self-determination less.

Given the rather dismal picture of heterosexual relationships that French presents, one would expect a more positive view of a lesbian alternative than one finds. Isolde comes across as a very supportive, understanding and appealing character in many respects. Yet she finds herself playing the woman's role toward other women, who apparently accommodate themselves with ease to temporary positions of dominance. "She was the woman for everyone; she played the woman to women's men," Isolde recognizes. "And suffered the way women suffered from men." Because she cannot bear the thought of sex with a man, "a normal life, husband, kids, house, all that, what is considered the good life, the right life, the fulfilling life--that's always been out of the question for me," she maintains. Consequently she has learned to take what she can get, "joy on the wing or something like that."[41] Lesbianism for her is not a choice or even an alternative way of expressing herself toward others--but her fate, just as Mira's particular form of heterosexuality is her fate. And neither can escape the issue of dominance and submission--nor the inward pressures which compel a woman to assume the submissive role most of the time.

From the late 1960's through much of the 1970's liberation and androgyny were fervently advanced as cultural ideals which would be increasingly realized as more and more people came to believe in them and act upon them. Mira finds herself in a world where these expectations have not been realized and her own faith in them has greatly diminished. Her situation is not unique, for in the last few years many people have come to feel that the possibility of repudiating sex-related categories is more open to question than it once was. Social constraints such as economic discrimination and institutionalized racism and sexism highlight the power of society to keep people in line and to limit the range of truly individualized choices. And many seem to have lost their commitment to the ideals of liberation. Because these ideals are so deeply rooted in the individualistic value system, however, they cannot be dismissed as merely ephemeral expressions which have now passed from the scene. Their appeal for many persists even though it is equally clear that current realities within American life must also be confronted.

Overview--

More radical approaches than those we have considered so far have challenged in varying degrees the validity of sex-related categories themselves. Most have assumed that while there are unalterable "natural" differences between men and women, gender differences are culturally based and therefore subject to reformulation. The alternative to categorically defined distinctions is an emphasis upon a common humanity shared by all individuals regardless of sex or sexual object choice. The terms liberation and androgyny symbolize this alternative.

For both sexes liberation suggests freedom from categorically prescribed limitations on a person's acts, values and sense of self. For men specifically these goals involve a repudiation of the emphasis upon power and success that are so important to conventional masculinity. An insistence upon the uniqueness of each individual is basic to the liberationist point of view. Hence the metaphor of the snowflake. Nevertheless, the range of individual differences in a liberated society would not seem large to anyone accustomed to the kinds of social variety that have distinguished past and present societies. Individual differences would not stand out in the way that culturally significant collective differences now do. The uniqueness of each individual would be balanced by an emphasis upon a shared humanity; the latter, however, does not imply an undifferentiated alikeness as categorization presently does. Another important aspect of a liberated society would be an emphasis upon human equality. The institutional structures and values that now enforce inequality would no longer exist.

In a liberated society same-sex interests and acts would not set an individual apart by making him or her a "homosexual." Such a term would be meaningless though people would still distinguish between homosexual and heterosexual acts and certainly develop personal preferences. All distinctions between men and women would not be obliterated though they would be blurred by the emphasis upon individual uniqueness and shared traits and values that are not sex-specific. A liberated society would be challenged to take sex-related differences into account without resorting to categorizing. Strategies range from arguing that conventionally dichotomous attributes apply to both sexes to questioning all elements of dichotomizing sex and gender, including physical differences and whether so-called masculine and feminine traits even exist.

Advocates of liberation also stress interdependence, idealizing a society of free individuals voluntarily united by ties of like-mindedness. They therefore exemplify the secondary tradition of individualism in America and self-consciously reject the dominant tradition, which some associate with individualism as opposed to individuality. In androgynous terms the masculine component of the ideal of liberation is a commitment to individuality. The feminine component is a commitment to unstructured relatedness to other people. Thus men must learn to cultivate relatedness and women individuality without losing the qualities long deemed appropriate to their sex. If such wholeness is to be achieved, present-day child-rearing practices must be altered. The effect would be to undercut the psychological and cultural bases of support for categorically defined sex-related attitudes, values and behaviors. It would appear, furthermore, that much less importance would be attached to sexual identity than is presently the case. The ideal of a liberated society strongly reflects the importance attached to the metaphorical feminine. While men as well as women have championed this ideal, there are grounds for questioning the long-term commitment of many of the former.

There is a dark side to the ideal of liberation that reflects an ambivalent commitment to mainstream as well as liberationist perspectives and values. From the former vantage point liberation may seem to represent a paradisiacal wish that threa-

224

tens individuality in the same way that the all-powerful mother threatens the young child seeking to establish a sense of a unique self. Categories seem less culture-bound and thus more formidable to oppose--and they tend also to be highly internalized, thus leaving the individual with little will to resist. In varying degrees one is likely to feel disillusioned and powerless. Nowadays many people are skeptical about the ideal of liberation, but its appeal must not be dismissed because it reflects an important aspect of the individualistic value system.

CHAPTER ELEVEN

CONFRONTING AN UNLIBERATED WORLD

While it is possible to criticize actual and proposed sex-related changes in America from a traditional viewpoint, it is not surprising that almost all critics operate in terms of categorical assumptions. Their intention is to vindicate conventional patterns of behavior, and yet mainstream values both permit and accommodate themselves to sex-role change. Because the proponents of liberation advocate a much more thorough-going form of change, they serve more readily as targets for criticism than those who are willing to accept existing sex-related categories. The feelings and attitudes that lie behind the calls for liberation are not new to the American scene. Sometimes they have been more strongly espoused than at other times, but they have always posed a potential challenge to the role limitations, sexual inequality and invisibility that mainstream culture has mandated. Longings have usually been counterbalanced, however, by awareness of everyday realities, for the connection between mainstream values and liberationist ideals is a complex one.

Critiques of Sexual Liberation--

Conservative critics strenuously insist that there are innate differences between the sexes which can never be overcome, though much social havoc may result from the attempt to do so. They invoke "nature" rather than tradition as the justification for sex-related categories and thus concede what Americans generally assume--that all cultural symbols and related social arrangements are subject to reformulation if people collectively wish to alter them. Only as part of the "natural" order of things can sex-related categories be unassailably upheld. In a 1980 article in Commentary Michael Levin adamantly asserts that because sex-role differentiation occurs in all societies, "it is evidently an innate feature of human beings that they will train their male and female offspring differently." He therefore scoffs at the idea that there is some kind of "humanness" apart from one's male or female essence, for "we come into the world not as bits of prime matter but as males or females."[1]

In a book entitled The Inevitability of Patriarchy Steven Goldberg defends sexual inequality on the grounds that "the hormonal renders the social inevitable." Men are innately more aggressive than women, and their aggressive advantage "will be given freest play" in a society "in which social mobility is relatively free of traditional barriers to advancement." Goldberg concedes that there are differences among men as among women, but statistical generalizations are both possible and valid as bases for social policy. "The behavioral manifestations of sexual biological differences are, to be sure, quantitatively and statistically not qualitatively and absolutely, different for the two sexes," he admits. However, "any statistically important innate sexual differences will result in socialization based on stereotype." Goldberg's endorsement of categorization at the same time that he endorses the capitalistic value system buttresses a thesis which provides a rationale for success and for social distinctions which favor the successful. As a member of a social grouping rather than as a unique individual, each man proceeds on his own and yet shares the same goals as all other American men. In Goldberg's opinion a woman can, if she is determined, become a social rebel, but "she can never hope to live in a society that does not attach feminine expectations to women."[2]

Nina Lee Colwill has pointed out that there would be no need for statistics "if all males differed from all females on the traits, abilities, and behaviors that we have come to call sex differences." Clearly statistics are necessary "in order to be able to speak of sex differences, because on nearly every known behavior, the sexes overlap."[3] Thomas F. Pettigrew argues that "by classifying incoming information within our categories, we render the world meaningful." The danger, however, is that "this process typically leads us to overestimate the similarity among items <u>within</u> categories and the differences between items <u>across</u> categories."[4]

Mainstream individualists like Goldberg find the categories and related stereotypes that impress them both obvious and "natural." Advocates of liberation and androgyny prefer not to think in categorical terms even though they would not deny the present reality of sex-related categories. Sandra and Daryl Bem insist that individuality and self-fulfillment for each woman are not possible "as long as a woman's socialization does not nurture her uniqueness, but treats her only as a member of a group on the basis of some assumed <u>average</u> characteristic."[5] If individualism prompts one to deal with reality in very general or very personal terms, categorical thinking represents one tendency and androgynous thinking the other. In neither case is sex-role behavior seen in terms of culturally sanctioned and contextually appropriate forms of social interaction.

Goldberg fears that the dictates of "nature" are being ignored, and this prompts him to insist that "nurture must conform to the limits set by nature."[6] For him "nature" functions as a metaphor for social policy by prescribing the maintenance of individual as well as collective male power. He certainly does not assume that men are the victims of "natural" forces beyond their control even though in their aggressiveness they act as they must. Passive acquiescence to the dictates of "nature" in theory becomes in practice active self-assertion within categorically appropriate confines.

Goldberg is convinced that "the vast majority of women" would not "want to deny the biological basis of the enormous powers inherent in women's roles as directors of societies' emotional resources."[7] His conventional celebration of femininity is a familiar effort to persuade women to fulfill their destiny as categorically distinctive beings. That their power may be lesser in some respects and different from men's does not mean to Goldberg that they lack power or the acknowledged right to use it. Liberation really is not a matter of power but of equality, freedom and self-determination. Women whose primary aim is power are correct to be skeptical of liberationist aspects of feminism. Effective power is inherently conservative because it rests of necessity on established forms and structures even though it may seek to modify and in time even extensively alter them.

In her book, The Power of the Positive Woman, Phyllis Schlafly speaks approvingly of Goldberg's thesis and strenuously upholds the proposition that the sexes are basically dichotomous. The Positive Woman "wants to be treated like a woman, and she knows that her chance for success in a man's world is increased by requiring men to treat her like a woman." The fact that men possess a physical advantage over women does not doom the weaker sex "to a life of servility and subservience." On the contrary, knowing how to take advantage of men's sexual needs gives the Positive Woman "a complementary advantage which is at least as great--and, in the hands of a skillful woman, far greater."[8] "Nature" has not rendered her helpless at all, for femininity provides a framework within which the resourceful woman can maneuver to gain her individual ends and wield personal power.

Someone who is "looking for security--emotional, social, financial"--will naturally turn to marriage and motherhood, which "are the most reliable security the world can offer." In Schlafly's opinion it is obviously in such a person's interest to oppose the Equal Rights Amendment because it "would bring a drastic reduction in the rights of the wife." The Positive Woman can move beyond the home to combine marriage with a career. Such a task is not easy, "but it is possible for an ingenious and hard-working woman." Schlafly is a pragmatic conservative. If a woman has nothing practical and useful to gain from relinquishing feminine privileges, Schlafly sees no reason why she should have to. Her pragmatism extends as well to profitting from many improvements in the status of women for which feminists and their supporters are responsible. The result of changes in equal opportunity laws, we are told, is "that the Positive Woman in America today faces a future in which her educational and employment options are unlimited."[9]

Like Goldberg, Schlafly insists that "it is on its women that a civilization depends." The Positive Woman eagerly accepts this responsibility. "If her influence is limited to her immediate family, she knows that, after all, nothing is more important than building the morals and integrity of the family unit." Despite such conventional sentiments, it is quite clear that activities beyond the home are what really interest Schlafly. The public arena is where she seeks to exercise her considerable influence and power, for "no national problem is too immense for American women." As a national housekeeper in the tradition of nineteenth-century social feminism, Schlafly knows how to take advantage of her femininity in order to "control her own destiny, to reach new heights of achievement, and to motivate and influence others."[10]

One of the most sophisticated early critiques of the women's liberation movement, Midge Decter's The New Chastity, has much to say about the social reality that the author finds behind the protests for change. Still, in the final analysis her thesis rests--as do those of Schlafly and Goldberg--on a set of abstract categorical propositions about "nature" and the human condition. Decter denies that women's liberation really represents a demand for equal rights or a yearning for freedom from oppression. Rather it reflects "the difficulties women are experiencing with the rights and freedoms they already enjoy." As a result of increased sexual freedom they "have lost the sense of their peculiar womanly power to control the terms of the relations between themselves and men." Consequently women's liberation seeks to spell out a rationale for avoiding willing and cooperative involvements with men.[11]

It is Decter's contention that rather than a freer society that permits women "a larger and wider variety of opportunity," what radical women really want is a society "in which the very terms 'freedom' and 'opportunity' will be redefined so as to conform with their desires." The morality and culture of liberation would seem to suggest a new sweetness and gentleness, she maintains, but this is "the sweetness of children not yet thrust into that adult world of begetting and striving where the aggressions that create conflict have also been a necessary condition for the sustenance of life on earth."[12] What she sees, therefore, is an example of paradisiacal longing, which ultimately stands as a testament of unwillingness to deal with the world as it is. By contrast the dominant tradition of American individualism, she implies, at least is realistic enough to take account of the fact that men and women are ambitious and self-interested, that power is a basic reality of human existence, that society by definition restricts the individual's freedom to do what he or she pleases, and that the categorical differences between the sexes are immutable.

Decter is highly critical of what she sees as the intent of women's liberation "to create a world, or a culture, in which either literally or to all intents and purposes there would be no men and no women." Thus she finds "no more radical nor desperately nihilistic statement to issue forth from the lips of humans than that there are no necessary differences between the sexes." Her argument is not sociological but theoretical--a categorical invocation of "nature," "for such differences both issue in and do in themselves constitute the most fundamental principle of the continuation of life on earth."[13] Even the most radical proponent of change would concede the reality of reproductive differences. The disagreement centers around the cultural symbolism attached to these differences and the social implementation of conventional beliefs and assumptions. Critics such as Decter acknowledge this in the anxiety they betray that the laws of "nature" are less obvious and less obligatory than their arguments would suppose. Hence the need to help "nature" out by supporting social policies aimed at insuring "natural" behavior. John Stuart Mill long ago pointed out the basic inconsistency and hence prescriptive bias of such an approach. "The anxiety of mankind to interfere in behalf of nature," he argued, "for fear lest nature should not succeed in effecting its purpose, is an altogether unnecessary solicitude."[14]

Peter N. Stearns' book, Be a Man!, presents a very useful contrast to the positions of conservative critics like Goldberg, Schlafly and Decter. Stearns too is skeptical of efforts to transcend sexual barriers, but he does not base his analysis on categorical assumptions. "Nature" is not for him the guarantor of sex-related differences because "there is relatively little about man that is biologically determined, though that 'little' is vitally important." Thus "what form the definition of male identity takes depends far more on cultural than on biological factors; moreover, it changes substantially over time." Stearns does not, however, make the characteristic American assumption that all cultural symbols and their consequent social forms and structures can readily or should be reformulated to enhance individual freedom and self-determination. "Saying that a trait is a product of culture must not lead to the assumption that we can easily get rid of it," he cautions.[15]

Stearns' study is concerned with Western Europe as well as the United States, and he is explicit in voicing a preference for European practices over American ones. One does not find there "the extremes of gender tension characteristic of the United States" during the 1970's. Not surprisingly for him "American patterns are not necessarily the most desirable." Obviously he does not share the individualistic assumptions of either the critics or the advocates of sexual liberation. He does not ignore individual action or responsibility, but his focus is society and not the individual. Thus his sympathetic treatment

231

of European life--with its denser and less individualistically oriented social structure--leads to an analysis which has clearly traditional overtones and no categorical ones. Stearns sees gender as an important external structure for providing a means of personal identity. "Gender," he argues, "for all its insensitivity to individual variation, may serve as a useful personal baseline, when community and family structures are too relaxed to provide norms of their own." The androgynous movement, he remarks, is largely American, and it ignores the fact that gender is a serviceable social artifice.[16]

In Stearns' analysis the individual uses gender in an instrumental way to play a part in society. Hence gender roles, as he sees them, closely resemble actors' roles in a play as they do in traditional societies. In most contexts on this side of the Atlantic the word role has a similar meaning though the individual is assumed to be much freer to determine the roles he or she plays in life. Sex roles in America are atypical because they are ascribed and hence do not involve the freedom of choice of most other roles. In this regard they fit Stearns' usage. However, since they are so closely linked with identity and the physical self, they are very different from actors' roles.

Stearns foresees greater and greater equalization of economic roles in the West but without a significant disappearance of ascribed gender characteristics. Society still needs "the vigor that comes from sanctioned gender diversity." Indeed, work "can benefit from the application of different gender styles." Stearns is not locked into defending a definition of masculinity which is immutable because the laws of biology are presumably fixed and unchanging; his more or less traditional assumptions allow for organic change. He is pleased to note that more and more men are seeking "the return to a greater array of male roles, a more diverse male balance," than has existed since the advent of capitalism. Within the family he calls for "a reassertion of a paternal style" that will lessen generational tension, assure more social and personal continuity, and "reduce the atomized approach to achievement outside the home."[17]

Despite agreement about the importance of gender differences and the imprudence of those who question them, mainstream critics of liberation are loyal to individualistic assumptions which loosen the connection between the self and society as Stearns is not. Their commitment to the values of a culture in which people pride themselves on their freedom from tradition means that they cannot stress as he does the significance of history as a guarantor of sex-related differences. Finally, they are unwilling to dismiss, as he dismisses, the very existence of sexual categories grounded in the dictates of "nature."

Ideals and Social Reality--

How fully the ideal of sexual equality, androgyny and liberation can be translated into social reality on any large scale remains an open question. In Him/Her/Self Peter Filene says his initial purpose was "to learn how men and women might go beyond 'masculine' and 'feminine' into roles that exclude as little as possible of their personalities." He had completed the book, however, "with a chastened understanding of how difficult this ideal has been and still is" though he retains "a belief in the (difficult) possibility of people living more fully as themselves." That the New Left leadership of the 1960's turned to street fighting and bombs, Filene argues, evidenced the fact that "the classic impulse of 'proving masculinity' had always been there beneath the androgynous behavior." It is his firm belief, moreover, that "men will not liberate themselves until they revalue the culturally entrenched meanings of achievement and success." It is his skepticism about the willingness of American men to change that prompts him to place his ultimate reliance on women to "push them--in rage or in love--toward the hope of becoming persons together."[18]

In her book Gyn/Ecology Mary Daly rejects the ideal Filene postulates along with the term androgyny itself. "Experience proved that this word," she maintains, "which we now recognize as expressing pseudowholeness in its combination of distorted gender descriptions, failed and betrayed our thought." To propagate the idea that men too are feminine simply "distracts attention from the fact that femininity is a man-made construct, having essentially nothing to do with femaleness." For a woman to get in touch with her basic (and therefore "natural") femaleness she must be "woman-identified, having rejected false loyalties to men on all levels," not just on a sexual level. Daly uses the term Lesbian for such a woman. Thus the goal of women everywhere must be to strive for sisterhood by "developing ways of moving into different cognitive space, even when we are caught in male-controlled physical space." Although Daly dissociates herself from the proponents of androgyny and rejects the desirability of women's having anything to do with men no matter what their attitudes and values might be, her approach is similarly individualistic in its affirmation of freedom, selfhood and voluntarism. She insists that "male bonding/comradeship requires the stunting of individuality" whereas "female-identified bonding is based upon the highly individualized strength of Self-accepting Hags." Without models, roles or institutionalized relationships to fall back upon, "Lesbians/Spinsters find in our authentic likeness to each other the opportunity to exhibit and develop genuine differences."[19] Unlike the proponents of androgyny, Daly is firmly committed to the "natural" collective distinctiveness of women, though in emphasizing individual differences she departs from mainstream categorical thinking. She does not look forward to a transformation of all of society, but she remains hopeful about the possibilities open to those

233

who want to withdraw into their own special world.

Alexandra G. Kaplan and Mary Anne Sedney's textbook, Psychology and Sex Roles: an Androgynous Perspective, represents an ultimately skeptical judgment of the more immediate prospects of androgyny. Partly the authors reflect the more practical and less idealistic mood of the present. Partly their point of view stems from a greater emphasis upon changes in social forms and structures than is the case for many advocates of androgyny. They define androgyny for their purposes as "the combined presence of socially valued, stereotypic, feminine and masculine characteristics." The combination of traits may follow a dualistic model based on "the separate coexistence of feminine and masculine characteristics." In this case a person is likely to reflect different traits at different times, for masculinity and femininity still remain categorically distinct from one another. The authors, however, prefer a hybrid model in which "masculinity and femininity become fully integrated, or blended." The androgynous person, they argue, "should be able to react according to what she or he feels is most appropriate for the situation, rather than according to the way a man or a woman is 'supposed' to react."[20]

There are potentially negative repercussions stemming from having feminine and masculine characteristics, Kaplan and Sedney concede. First is "the increased possibility of conflict, both within the self and between self and society." Also there is the problem of ambiguity, for "greater complexity of perceptions and response style" may often go "against the cultural grain." The authors' picture of a truly androgynous society is described as a "fantasy," as "dreaming," and as "unrealistic"; however appealing, "such a society is not around the corner." "Without change in the broader spheres of society, individual change is problematic," they insist, but they do not counsel everyone to abandon the pursuit of androgyny. Because of its current disadvantages, people are advised to find alternative social structures within which to function or "be ready to face the continuing clash between androgyny and the prevailing social values."[21]

Christopher Lasch's The Culture of Narcissism is a much more pessimistic appraisal of the contemporary scene as well as of the ideal of androgyny. His book "describes a way of life that is dying--the culture of competitive individualism, which in its decadence has carried the logic of individualism to the extreme of a war of all against all, the pursuit of happiness to the dead end of a narcissistic preoccupation with the self." While he does not advocate a return to the past, he clearly believes relationships between the sexes were formerly better managed in America than they are today. Once polite conventions "surrounded essentially exploitive relationships with a network of reciprocal obligations, which if nothing else made exploitation easier to bear." Now democracy and feminism have stripped away such conventions, laying bare once hidden sexual antagonisms. "The abolition of sexual tensions is an unworthy goal in any case," Lasch believes; "the point is to live with them more gracefully than we have lived with them in the past." The persistence of traditional elements in the relationship of men and women institutionalized an antagonism that Lasch sees as part of the nature of things, for men's resentment of women is too irrational, he feels, to be easily appeased or presumably ever eradicated.[22] Now individualistic assumptions would seem to govern the interactions of men and women without check, and Lasch has too many reservations about contemporary individualism not to be dismayed by such a reality.

Marvin Harris's hope in America Now is for a return to a society "more in accord with the vision of freedom and affluence on which past generations of Americans were nourished." In the course of his analysis he notes that "gay liberation accompanied women's liberation because each movement represents a different facet of the collapse of the marital and procreative imperative and the male-dominated breadwinner family." He is not explicitly critical of either movement, but he does make clear his desire for a national consensus unmarred by the special points of view of these and other separate interest groups. The task of his book "is to reassert the primacy of rational endeavor and objective knowledge in the struggle to save and renew the American dream." Otherwise, Harris warns, "the alternative is to stand by helplessly as special interest groups tear the United States apart in the name of their 'separate realities,' or to wait until one of them grows strong enough to force its own irrational and subjective brand of reality on all the rest."[23]

Because America remains an individualistic as well as a heterosexual male-dominated society, women and gay people are unlikely to reconcile themselves to their lot as Lasch would like. Moreover, they will doubtless continue to be more concerned with their separate realities than Harris would prefer. In Reinventing Womanhood Carolyn Heilbrun rejects the alternative of becoming an honorary man for women seeking to succeed in such a society. This involves "neither admiring nor bonding with other women, offering no encouragement to those who might come after them, preserving the socially required 'femininity,' but sacrificing their womanhood." Rather as outsiders women should "bond among themselves, offering each other comradeship, encouragement, protection, support." Heilbrun sees woman's most persistent problem as how "to discover for herself an identity not limited by custom or defined by attachment to some man." The answer she sees is for women to "learn to appropriate for their own use the examples of human autonomy and self-fulfillment displayed to us by the male world." This is possible because "ultimately, there are no male models, there are only mod-

235

els of selfhood from which woman chooses to learn." Moreover, "women must want to be where the power is, but they must want to be there as women, and in large numbers."[24] Asserting their individuality and self-determination as far as identity is concerned and at the same time bonding with other women constitute a prescription for operating more or less androgynously in the world as it exists today. It is not clear, however, just how such collective action is likely to change things.

By contrast two other works express considerable optimism that women's participation in the world of work will ultimately have an important transforming effect not just on them but on society as a whole and on the cultural meaning of gender differences. In The Two-Paycheck Marriage Caroline Bird finds much more evidence of individualism in dual-career marriages, where both partners are more self-reliant and less dependent for their self-esteem on their spouses. Thus "the happiest marriages," she insists, "are those in which husband and wife are equal--in other words, the one[s] where power is not an issue" as it is where there is an "imbalance of achievement." We are moving into "a world of individuals rather than families in which men and women will earn and spend in much the same way." In such a world individuals will be linked together by freely chosen voluntary ties. Family members will therefore relate better to one another "because they will depend on each other primarily as friends."[25]

In a world of individuals the differences between men and women will diminish as both sexes increasingly share similar experiences, and so "women will become more like men than men will become like women." Bird thus confidently asserts that "femininity" is simply "an artifact of powerlessness that will never be missed." Somewhat contradictorily she also believes that "money, power or prestige" will not be transcendent because other values associated with women will have a greater influence than has been true in the past. She suggests that while "women have always wanted work that allowed for life off the job," in time "men, too, will have a choice over the investment they wish to make in their work." Thus we can look forward to a different and exciting world in which "the economy of the future will be based on individuals who are growing and changing on timetables that have nothing to do with their sex."[26] Androgynous possibilities based partly on certain metaphorically feminine values can therefore be expected to develop necessarily out of the economic realities of modern capitalism.

Elizabeth Nickles' The Coming Matriarchy: How Women Will Gain the Balance of Power represents a similar blurring of the lines between mainstream and liberationist approaches. Without in any way repudiating the values of capitalism Nickles anticipates a society that will be androgynous in many respects though she insists that "sexual differences will never disappear." "As stereotypes ease, each sex will explore gender attributes that were previously inhibited," she predicts. What gives women the advantage over men, in Nickles' view, is that they exhibit a different and in terms of present realities a more appropriate beta style of leadership in which power "is exercised for the good of the group rather than an individual." This will result in important changes for society by bringing "a greater recognition of the quality of life." Nickles insists that what she means by the coming matriarchy "is not a matter of simple role-reversal, but of role diversification, offering each sex a broader spectrum of options and opportunities." The society she describes exhibits many of the ideals of liberation. Child care will be a sexually shared responsibility--which is why there will "be a decline in sexual stereotyping, with both men and women perceived as sharing role attributes." Moreover, Nickles anticipates a "letup of emphasis on profit and productivity as ends in themselves" that "will open the door for new lifestyles in which leisure has a social value as great as work does today."[27]

Society and Sexual Liberation--

If assessments of present and future realities offer rather ambiguous assurances about the likelihood of sexual liberation, still it is important to recognize that it exists both as an ideal and as a potentiality inherent within the individualistic value system. The emphasis upon the pursuit of opportunity and the importance attached to categorizing people have long restricted the ultimate implications of individualism to limited and often indirect literary forms of expression. Thus one would expect a fuller manifestation only if success and categorization were to lose much of their appeal to large numbers of Americans. In speculating about the future, therefore, one must speak in hypothetical terms--about what might result from certain cultural and social changes rather than what necessarily will be. Whether one anticipates a future of greater leisure and economic abundance or a time of more austerity and simpler lives, the emphasis upon competitiveness and success may very well diminish in importance. If this were to take place, a necessary condition would exist for the realization of the ideals of sexual liberation.

Americans still find assigning people to social groupings the most convenient way of dealing with sex-related differences. Unlike traditional societies ours is fundamentally concerned not with outward sex-role conformity, with insuring that people simply act in ways appropriate to their sex and sexual interests, but rather with insisting on the reality of a common identity among all who are similarly categorized. Whereas traditional role expectations are unabashedly prescriptive, catego-

237

ries are assumed to be essentially descriptive. Nevertheless, people accept categories not just because they find them descriptively accurate but because they believe in their rightness. They make the world easier to understand and to deal with. As cultural symbols they are a useful means of thinking about other people in ways that justify distinctions within an individualistic and egalitarian context. It is ironic that categorical differences of all sorts have been so strenuously insisted upon not by a people that finds human equality inconceivable, but by one that accepts it as a fundamental value.

Personal identity is a crucial aspect of individuality, and in the modern world each person's identity is closely linked with such important factors as sex, race, ethnicity, nationality and religion. Nevertheless, the pattern within American history has been to enhance the role of personal choice within these frameworks. This is why the argument in favor of more sex-role flexibility has such a strong appeal when it is couched in minority-group terms. The difficulty of this position lies in separating behavioral expectations from the deeper elements of gender and gender identity. Proponents of liberation in effect assume that this cannot really be done. Still, challenging sex-related differences on many levels including sexual identity is bound to make a great many people uneasy. Such uneasiness is evidence of the fact that no new cultural symbols have effectively superceded those based on categorization. This will remain the case so long as the spectrum of views concerning how sex-related differences ought to be interpreted persists.

There seems to be a growing consensus as to the importance of increased role flexibility. For many, however, affirming the other aspects of categorically defined differences is a necessary condition of sex-role freedom--whether in terms of celebrating sisterhood and gay pride or stressing the importance of sexual differentiation along the lines of appearance and one's sense of self. Those who question sex-related differences more systematically still are not in agreement about how far to go. The extreme position is that there should be no culturally emphasized differences except those strictly dictated by reproductive biology--and even this may be unnecessary some day. Behind the desire for placing virtually no premium upon any collective sex-related differences among people is the belief that such distinctions are inevitably invidious ones. Thus it follows that a society of free and equal individuals cannot stress group differences over which people have no control. Less extreme views continue to hold that distinctions are still valid on some levels, but categorization is not. Whether the former is possible without the latter has yet to be determined.

Only a willingness to follow the logic of individualism to its ultimate conclusion will induce Americans to think in other than categorical terms. This requires that they recognize that while categories seem useful and persuasive cultural prescriptions, ignoring individual variations distorts reality more than it describes it. On the one hand, change would involve a genuine acceptance of the uniqueness of each person and the right to define oneself and to live one's life without arbitrary limitations on one's choices and opportunities. It would have to be beyond dispute that neither society in general nor groups of people in particular have the right to circumscribe individuals' lives solely on the basis of sex or sexual object choice any more than on the basis of race or religion. On the other hand, it would involve an acceptance of a common humanity that obliterates the boundaries that cultural categories mandate. In the process Americans would have to learn to be increasingly sensitive to each other's unique differences and to recognize that a person cannot expect to be treated as an individual if he or she consents to be defined solely in terms of one or more dominant stereotypes.

The process of transcending sex-related differences increasingly involves interactions among people that make categorical distinctions irrelevant. While formal modes of interaction can work for different groupings of people, more informal and open kinds of interaction require a sense of commonality--an ability to go beyond what distinguishes one person from another to what is shared. Conventional forms of interaction between men and women thrive on customary sexual differences. Real communication and understanding do not. As John Stuart Mill long ago noted, "intimate society between people radically dissimilar to one another, is an idle dream. Unlikeness may attract, but it is likeness which retains."[28]

Cultural categories can slowly lose their validity in people's minds and their effect on values and institutions before they essentially disappear. Even in specific ways society can refuse to apply them as a basis of social policy. A few years ago the United States Supreme Court struck down a provision in a retirement fund which required higher contributions from women on the grounds that they as a group live longer than men. The American Association of University Professors in an amicus curiae brief argued that the basic purpose of Title VII of the 1964 Civil Rights Act is "to afford individuals equal treatment . . . without regard to group characteristics."[29] The status and roles of American women are significantly--if too slowly-- changing. As women participate more in the larger world, they may very well change that world and how they are perceived by it in ways that undermine in many respects the credibility of categorical distinctions.

In terms of changing attitudes what I am suggesting generally parallels with reference to sex what David Hackett Fischer advocates with reference to age. He comes out in favor of "a world in which the deep eternal differences between age and youth are recognized and respected without being organized into a system of social inequality." To this end "we must learn to think of elderly people as individuals, rather than as a homogeneous group," and "seek to enlarge their autonomy and independence." Fischer calls only for obliterating categorical distinctions based on age, not for denying the impact of the aging process itself. In terms of present realities "there are social and cultural limits upon the aged which can be removed."[30] This will only be possible if we cease to think of them as indistinguishable members of a stereotyped social grouping.

Categorizing people in terms of age or sex or race is a comparatively recent historical phenomenon. Recognizing this fact undercuts claims to timeless natural validity which are crucial if categories are to retain their credibility in Americans' minds. Inequalities and prejudices have existed in other historical contexts, but abolishing the categories which have sustained inequalities in America will not bring back the practices of traditional societies, particularly with regard to women. If they cannot be seen as categorically distinctive and heterosexually available, our society has no really effective means at its disposal for continuing to subordinate them. Categorization does not actually create differences though it endows them with special cultural significance and determines their social implementation in important respects. If transcending sex-related differences seems a more likely possibility now than in the past, it is because these differences have become less significant than they once were.

In the case of homosexuality, prejudice existed long before there was categorization, but it appears that the hostility of the historical traditions of Western civilization and of Christianity has been too casually assumed. In his brilliant study of gay people in pre-modern Europe John Boswell argues that there was no general prejudice against them among early Christians. "Many prominent and respected Christians--some canonized--were involved in relationships which would almost certainly be considered homosexual in cultures hostile to same-sex eroticism," he maintains. He cautiously offers the generalization that "homosexuality is usually tolerated and often idealized in highly urban societies." At worst it is seen as harmless. Then in terms which modern advocates of liberation would doubtless endorse, he goes on to state that "at best, it is seen as an expression of precisely that sort of spiritual loyalty, independent of the constraints of blood relation, which creates and maintains municipalities and civilizations, a more intense form of the love and devotion which should exist between citizens regardless of biological accident or particulars of kinship."[31]

The unity that Boswell describes is based entirely on voluntary ties, and it represents the opposite of what traditional societies conceive as the basis of social unity. Individualism in America implies a social stance and a certain set of values which facilitate voluntary involvements of all sorts leading finally to a shared American identity. Understood in liberationist terms it does not mean, as its critics have often charged, that everyone is likely to become a free-floating atom without any group ties or traces of influences beyond the scope of personal whim--only that there be self-determination with respect to group ties and individual control over such influences. Insofar as free choice exists the potentiality of liberation is approximated. This criterion can be fairly easily applied to the American Home Economic Association's new definition of the family. It is "two or more persons who share resources, share responsibility for decisions, share values and goals, and have commitments to one another over time." Moreover, "it is this network of sharing and commitments that most accurately describes the family unity, regardless of blood, legal ties, adoption or marriage."[32]

Voluntary ties may be based on factors such as blood which are not strictly matters of personal choice. Outward pressures as well as internalized categorical ones must not, however, figure in. For these ties to be truly voluntary ones there must be freedom of choice here too. Michael Novak argues that a basic principle of pluralism in America is that "individuals are free to make as much, or as little, of their ethnic belonging as they choose." This does not, however, mean that we are not influenced by social factors over which we have no control, Novak insists, but he discerns as well as endorses the development among Americans of what he calls a "pluralistic personality." Having a unique historical range and liberty, it is not "rootless," nor is it parochial and isolated. Instead it represents "a capacity to enter into multiple perspectives."[33]

Sex and sexual object choice may also be the basis for voluntary ties, for it is difficult to believe that sex-related differences in some form will not persist. As long as these lie outside the range of individual choice, however, there will continue to be tension between individualistic values and categorically defined ones. Transforming the essential elements of sex-related differences from ascriptive into voluntary ones would allow people in limited collective ways to emphasize aspects of their sexuality along with like-minded others without constituting a basis for prejudice and discrimination. At the same time it hardly seems likely that the differences that would emerge voluntarily would necessarily validate presently familiar dichotomous views of gender and sexual object choice. As yet, however, pluralism functions too much within the confines of categorically based inequalities to serve as a clear model of what truly free sex-related associations might be like.

The mainstream proclivity for seeing sex-related differences in categorical terms, coupled with the tendency to conceive of the individual as in some sense separate from society, encourages an overemphasis upon supposedly "natural" determinants of identity and behavior. Thus the search for the biological causes of homosexuality continues despite the failure of each new theory to withstand careful scrutiny. This whole approach too cavalierly ignores the enormous biosocial complexity of all aspects of sexual behavior. If we tend perhaps too easily to think that culturally based differences can be altered without difficulty, we are too prone to suppose that "natural" ones are immutable. Moreover, we are overly naive in our faith that we know what "nature" is and can easily isolate its influences. Each person's capabilities and endowments are far too complex to be subsumed under the labels male and female, gay and "straight." In the final analysis taking account of individual variations is what individualism is all about.

Still, there is an ambiguity within the tradition of American individualism upon which the liberation movements draw. It is certainly possible to argue that each person is a unique product of his biosocial heritage and that society should honor this uniqueness without coming to the conclusion that one can transcend that heritage in any way. Shane says he is what he is and this cannot be changed. Ultimately we are all subject to some kind of overarching necessity, this line of argument would suggest, and to accept ourselves is to accept the fact that we cannot be otherwise than what we are. Shane's statement clearly assumes, however, that change is a matter of will or desire. Awareness of alternatives is a necessary prerequisite to any desire to transcend one's fate--and that can only come from experience, involvement with other people, and an understanding of oneself and one's culture and society. Though all of us participate in culture and in nature, we are separate too. We act as well as react, and we have the capacity--even if we often fail to exercise it--to choose among alternatives. "Among the myriad of potentialities with which every individual is born," Roger J. Williams has pointed out, "there still are an infinite number of possibilities of development" as long as the "ability to order one's own life exists."[34] Individual possibilities are not unlimited, but they can be no more varied than cultural dictates now permit.

The Individual and Sexual Liberation--

Certainly it is possible to be drawn to the ideal of liberation and still remain committed in many ways to the sexual values and related categories of mainstream American culture. In The New Male Herb Goldberg insists that it is important to avoid being swallowed up in one's role because "role expectations and demands are static, while human emotions are not." For him "authentic liberation means assertion, freeing up, breaking through gender barriers and refusing to continue playing self-denying and self-destructive games." He calls for "an end to the all-consuming obsession with success" and celebrates the ideal of buddyship as a means of reducing and softening "the defensive, guarded, detached and competitive posture most men have toward each other."[35] Although the title of Goldberg's book is The New Male, most of his comments actually focus on the old male and what is wrong with him. The influence of the conventional masculine value system persists--which is why so much passion is expended on condemning it.

The basic presupposition of advocates of liberation is that sex roles and related social structures are secondary and to have any validity they must reflect the inner self and its needs and desires. One ought not to base one's identity upon preexisting gender expectations nor even to approach these instrumentally and selectively. Because people are all so different, roles must reflect such variety, and this is only possible if one proceeds from the individual outwards. Roles per se are not rejected, but to be authentic they must emerge as self-determined by-products of human interaction.

Those committed to liberation tend to be more concerned with altered modes of consciousness and related cultural reformulations than with restructuring institutions. In this respect they differ from those whose approach is more programmatic. The distinction is not of course absolute in all instances--particularly with regard to equal parenting--but the different approaches have different implications in people's lives. In the latter case, structural changes in social arrangements have first priority. In the former, external change has less significance. One may therefore begin with one's own life. While the ultimate hope is to participate as extensively as possible in a system of shared values, the individualistic emphasis upon likeness of mind as the basis for defining interaction makes it possible for someone to posit fairly limited forms of liberation. Thus transcending sex-related categories may be thought of in terms of how a person or a few like-minded people can achieve some degree of personal liberation in an as yet unliberated world.

I am not referring to a rebellious stance but rather to an autonomous one, and this surely deserves to be seen as a manifestation of individualism. As examples of what I am talking about I will confine myself to two writers, both women in whose lives lesbian attachments figure strongly. Being doubly alienated from the world of masculine power, lesbians cannot pass themselves off as part of it the way gay males can, nor can they

easily act as the supposedly willing supporters of men whose
protection they expect to receive in return. They must be independent in many respects, and yet as women they have been socialized to think in terms of relatedness. These preconditions
do not of course insure any special consciousness, but they are
important starting points for a few whose art depicts autonomous
possibilities. Seymour Kleinberg notes that lesbian writers
usually "examine their themes in the social and psychological
context of ordinary life far more than men, who are more moral-
istic, and who often see gay life as tragically alienated."[36]

Rita Mae Brown's Rubyfruit Jungle is the story of a young
woman whose independence, self-reliance and passion to lead her
own life on her own terms clearly suggest her dedication to individualism. Molly Bolt refuses to accept conventional distinctions based on sex or race. In Florida she ignores racial etiquette and will not stay "away from people because they look
different." She comes to see herself as very much the loner because her aspirations are so completely outside the normal female orbit. Rather than conventional marriage, she says, "I
wanted to go my own way." Hopefully she will also "find some
love here and there," but if the choice is "the now and forever
kind with chains around your vagina and a short circuit in your
brain," she would "rather be alone." She accepts her lesbian
feelings without guilt because being "queer" hurts no one and
feels good. At the same time she rejects labels and simply insists, "I'm me. That's all I am and all I want to be."[37] All
in all, she has no patience with arbitrarily defined cultural
categories nor with the way others try specifically to limit her
actions and dictate her sense of herself.

Nevertheless, she is well aware of social reality, and she
is often willing to fulfill conventional expectations wherever
they suit her purposes. She knows enough from the beginning to
keep her lesbian relationships private and makes a point in high
school of dating the right boys because "they were a conveni-
ence, something you had to wear when you went to school functions, like a bra." College is her ticket "out of the boon-
docks," and despite formidable obstacles she manages to complete
her studies in New York. Along the way she refuses to let a
rich older woman take her in: "It has nothing to do with morality, it has to do with me," she insists. In the end she is
still struggling against the limitations imposed on her in part
because she is a lesbian but mostly because she is a woman. One
admires her spirit and courage, but her basic dilemma stems from
her effort to break out of socially imposed limitations by emulating masculine achievement. As a lesbian she refuses "to look
and act like an imitation man,"[38] and yet like Mira in The Women's Room on a deeper level Molly is male-identified. Like
Mira too she cannot reconcile her desire for success and power
with her commitment to be her own person. She is unable to shut

the world out, and yet she cannot successfully function on its terms either.

Brown's next novel, Six of One, chronicles the lives of several rather unique women who in a small-town setting manage to transcend all sorts of conventional restrictions and still lead full lives surrounded by supportive friends. The moral center of this special world is Cora, whose simplicity and insight are especially important to her aristocratic friend Celeste Chalfonte. Cora believes that "people are like snowflakes. No two alike." Thus she manages always to see others as both unique and her equals. Celeste is witty and cool, yet "she needed to be included in humanity. Cora included her as an equal." Celeste's independent income and her social position allow her and her lover Ramelle to live openly and quietly together without having to battle for the freedom to be lesbian. Two of Celeste's closest friends are heterosexual, and yet the difference in sexual orientation hardly matters except at times to Cora's conventional daughter Louise. Louise is a caricature of mindless femininity and she is constantly scandalized by her unconventional sister Julia, whose egalitarian relationship with her husband Louise is totally unable to understand. They are "pals" and this mystifies Louise, "who devoutly believed men and women were incapable of understanding one another."[39]

Concerns for success and power are not present in the lives of the major characters we are meant to admire. Celeste lives comfortably without having to trouble herself about money while Cora and Julia are content to live simply. It is out of a fundamental contentment based on independence and freedom that the central characters encounter one another as friends and equals. The barriers of class, sex, sexual orientation and race fall easily and naturally when the circumstances are right. Sexual orientation and monogamy as restrictive conventions collapse when Ramelle has an affair with Celeste's brother Curtis. She does not feel guilty because "love multiplies." Celeste and Curtis are unique persons and to compare the beauty of one with that of the other is "an impossible task and a silly one at that." She remains with Celeste though she has Curtis's baby, and both relationships retain their validities. Celeste realizes that the impact Ramelle has had on her life is especially significant in imparting to it an androgynous balance. Independence and self-reliance come easily for her and she is contemptuous of failure. From Ramelle she has learned that "there is an inner life, a life deeper than intellect." Though Celeste speaks out in favor of votes for women, she cannot be described as an activist.[40] Indeed all of the positive characters in the story focus on the quality of their own lives and not on changes in the world around them.

In The Autobiography of Alice B. Toklas Gertrude Stein

spells out the balance she had achieved for herself. Like Celeste she was in fact able to live independently on her own income, and the milieu (Paris) she chose offered none of the obstacles to a lesbian relationship that living in America would have. Stein describes herself as "completely and entirely american." At the same time it is clearly important for her to work out her own relationship with America from a distance. She says she enjoys living in a country surrounded by people who know no English so that she can be "all alone with english and myself." In part she can do this because she is struck by "the disembodied abstract quality of the american character."[41] Since a common identity for Americans lies more in the area of shared beliefs in certain abstract values--in a certain likeness of mind--than in customs and behaviors that have been sanctified by time and tradition, Stein can be as American in France as in America.

However much Stein focused on her own thoughts and her own life, her ties with important artists, writers and intellectuals are well known. So is her influence on a number of American writers, and surely this is due to her ability to help them without imposing her own conceptions. She says she "sticks strictly to general principles, the way of seeing what the writer chooses to see, and the relation between that vision and the way it goes down." This absence of the need to dominate others is clearly what enabled her to relate on terms which honored the uniqueness of each other person. During World War I she drove her car for a war organization and never lacked help when she could not cope with mechanical problems of various sorts. "The important thing, she insists, is that you must have deep down as the deepest thing in you a sense of equality. Then anybody will do anything for you."[42]

Stein was certainly unique, and her style of life in many ways defied convention. At the same time one must acknowledge the links she makes between her sense of herself as an American on the one hand and her commitment to basic equality and her ability to cut through conventional distinctions on the other. She comes across, as indeed she wishes to, not as a woman or as a pseudo-man, but as an American and at the same time as just a person. In so doing she draws upon a long tradition of embodying the meaning of the American experience in the image of the self, which Sacvan Bercovitch argues involves "an essentially symbolic interaction of perceiver and fact."[43] In a way, of course, individualism is at bottom an affirmation of the belief that as Americans we are all just persons.

At the same time each of us continues to be defined in many ways by forces over which we have limited control at best. Personally transcending sex-related categories is more easily imagined than accomplished, and doubtless few are presently able

to shed completely the effects of their cultural and social in-
heritances and conditioning. Nor is there any reason to suppose
that in all respects they would want to even if they could. If
certain aspects are affirmed, however, this can be done in ways
that one chooses for oneself and not on terms laid down by the
larger society. One of the basic elements of the individualistic value system is the personal right of each of us to come to
terms with the world around us in our own special ways. An individualistic culture such as ours does not make it easy for
someone who would like to remain very different. It does not
afford the resources of cultures which place less emphasis upon
likeness of mind, and in the long run it undercuts the desire to
be different as well. Individualism does, however, offer an alternative possibility. Not always nor in every respect, but at
times and in special ways, toward one another it is both possible and very worthwhile just to be persons.

Overview--

        Conservative critics of sex-related changes in American
life and culture strenuously insist that conventional distinctions are "natural" and therefore unalterable. Implicitly they
concede that if these were cultural in origin, they would be al-
terable. In truth, however, their arguments treat "nature" as a
metaphor for approved social policy. Hence it is acceptable to
intervene in order to insure that "nature's" true ends are realized. In contrast to proponents of liberation they stress power
rather than personal freedom. Neither side disputes the reality
of reproductive differences. The disagreement centers upon the
cultural symbolism attached to such differences and the social
consequences that are assumed to follow. It is instructive to
compare these critics with someone whose skepticism about liberation stems from a marked sympathy with many traditional European values. One finds no reference to categorical differences
based on the laws of "nature." Gender is seen as a useful social artifice, a set of externalized behavioral propositions
that are dictated by cultural assumptions. In contrast to Americans, however, there is an insistence that culturally prescribed practices are not easily gotten rid of and should not be.

        Exactly what the social implications of changes in sex-re-
lated values are remains open to a wide variety of interpretations. Some people have rejected or at least questioned the
meaning of androgyny while others continue to believe in its implementation. Some have become fairly dubious about effective
participation in the larger society and have recommended associ-
ating mostly with like-minded others. Such bonding can, however, also serve as a basis for moving into that society. Those
who are most optimistic about the future expect increased participation by women in the world of work to bring about changes
that point in the direction of liberation. Pessimists express

concern about a society fragmented into groups stressing their own limited realities or insist that Americans must simply learn to live with sexual tensions that can never be resolved.

In dealing with the social possibilities of liberation one must speak in hypothetical terms. Any substantial changes must involve fairly widespread questioning of the success ethic in America and the value of categorical thinking. The latter is complicated because categories remain credible cultural symbols for explaining distinctions in an egalitarian and individualistic context. Moreover, no new symbols of equal vitality have yet taken their place. Because it is difficult to separate behavior from other elements of gender and gender identity, any questioning of role restrictions has an impact on all aspects of categorization. An important element of change would be the general commitment to implementing the longstanding belief in freedom and equality for all Americans. This would mean that a society of free and equal individuals cannot stress collective differences over which individuals have no control. One beginning is to support policies that create situations which render categorical distinctions irrelevant. Social and cultural change has already made transcending sex-related differences seem easier to conceive than once was the case. Recognizing that categorization is a historically recent phenomenon will also help further change.

What sex-related differences remain should be the result of individual choices. This suggests some degree of pluralism, but exactly what would be involved is not yet clear. The biosocial complexity of all aspects of sexuality must not be ignored either by assuming that elements of culture can be quickly changed or that what is "natural" can be easily identified and readily isolated. Still, it must be recognized that individuals are far too complex sexually for a few generalized labels to have any real validity. Such complexity can be encouraged by an increased awareness of a multiplicity of culturally sanctioned possibilities open to each person regardless of sex or sexual object choice.

Liberationists tend to be more concerned with individual consciousness and reformulating cultural symbols than with actual institutional changes. Thus it is possible to strive for personal liberation and autonomy in a world as yet unliberated. Gertrude Stein is one example of an individual who stressed in her own life the importance of equality and personhood. In so doing she embodied the meaning of the American experience in her sense of self. If each of us cannot be totally self-determining, we nevertheless can affirm for ourselves the right to come to terms with sexuality in our own personal ways.

CONCLUSION

The centrality of individualism in American life is a reminder of the fact that ours was really the first modern society. America came into being as the organic world of pre-modern Europe was beginning to disintegrate, leaving the individual without a fixed place in society or the universe and thus, in terms of what had existed earlier, increasingly alone. Many people over the centuries have lamented this process and particularly in Europe since the early nineteenth century have conceived of individualism in negative terms. Here it has generally had a more positive meaning, and yet Americans have often harbored a certain wistful fondness for pre-modern society as a place of security, order and community.

In fact elements of the older world disappeared slowly in many respects, and nowhere more than in the area of sex-related forms of behavior. Traditionalism remained important especially in the nineteenth century in buttressing a degree of patriarchal authority over wives and children. As Nancy Cott has shown, woman's sphere preserved much of the old order, and so women became the custodians of values that men increasingly rejected in their own lives and honored vicariously in their wives. Female role expectations still retain a greater degree of traditionalism than do male role expectations. The former are more clearly ascriptive, learned in apprentice-like ways, tend to be less internalized and are enforced more by outward social pressures. Marriage as an institution continues to seem more fitting for women than men. Among gay women there has been an emphasis upon fixed roles until very recently. Many men have engaged in role-appropriate homosexual acts that in their own minds have nothing to do with being a homosexual.

For a variety of reasons a traditional world view persisted in America throughout the colonial period even though elements of modernity can be discerned in certain Puritan beliefs and attitudes and in the lives of success-oriented men like Benjamin Franklin. The late eighteenth and early nineteenth centuries marked a time of fundamental cultural transition. This was most evidenced in the premium that came to be placed on the primacy of the individual. American identity itself was defined in individualistic terms, and we remain committed still to the proposition that anyone can become an American by an act of personal choice.

In the open and success-oriented society of the nineteenth century each person was presumably free to determine his place in a context in which status was no longer fixed but was still hierarchically ordered to reflect individual achievement. Power, which had been the key element in determining people's relationships with one another, now became one element of a polarity in which individual freedom and self-determination were the other. What linked the two poles was successful self-aggrandizement. All of these elements became the fundamental constituents of masculinity in a society based on male ascendancy. Not everyone of course shared equally in the power and privileges supposedly available to all, but each person was presumed to have his fate in his own hands and thus to deserve his lot in life. If one could stop the world at any given moment, it would in theory resemble the fixed and structured world of the past. Yet because American males also valued change, they had structured relatedness without absolute fixity of status. Nothing validated their masculinity more than demonstrable economic advancement. While they honored independence and self-reliance, they also saw themselves as linked with all other males by bonds based upon a common gender identity.

Sex therefore had become one of the grand organizing principles of American life. The transitional period of the late eighteenth century involved the emergence of the disposition to view all men and women in categorical terms. The appeal of such a distinction was that it seemed "natural" rather than artificial in contrast to distinctions based on class and status. Men and women were inherently different rather than unequal, and within their separate spheres were assumed to function as individuals. Women remained under the control of men in many respects though in others they had a good deal of latitude in determining the content of their daily lives. Men came to expect a willing supportiveness from their wives rather than outward obedience, and the home became a valued refuge from the turbulence of the outside world. Women who fulfilled men's needs were left relatively free to cultivate friendships with other women and to engage in activities outside the home that accorded with categorically defined expectations. Men and women, therefore, were neither wholly separate nor equal, but in many specific ways they led lives which validated the logic of categorizing and dichotomizing everyone along sexual lines.

Since the early nineteenth century cultural categories and their social embodiments have complemented the world of ambitious striving. Society has been divided into recognizable though abstractly defined groupings of people differing in privileges and status. The result has been a much more flexible form of social organization than classes within a traditional context, and yet it has offered many of the advantages of fixed orders and gradations. Individualistic values have applied to members of all categorically defined groupings, but in different ways presumably dictated by inherent factors rather than arbitrary custom. Thus individualism has been acknowledged and yet also kept within bounds. People have been called upon to behave only in ways appropriate to their collective identities and thus to cooperate in maintaining distinctions that society has considered too important to ignore. At the same time because groupings are vague and fluid in many ways, they can change to reflect new cultural perceptions and individualistic strivings. Also they allow each person the freedom to take advantage of the fact that he or she belongs simultaneously to a great many social groupings.

Mainstream American culture remains committed to a belief that all men are self-interested, and yet of necessity they must work with and for one another if they are to be successful. Social structures do not cease to be important, but they are seen as intrinsically or at least potentially inauthentic. Masculinity is linked with the ability of the individual to control or at least to deal effectively with the external structures that surround him without being bound by them. Yet as the institutional structure of American life has become increasingly complex and increasingly inauthentic at the same time, men have been steadily robbed of their ability to remain self-determining and thus to preserve their manhood. Since the incorporation of America--to borrow again Alan Trachtenberg's term--began in the late nineteenth century, men have felt themselves on the defensive in many respects and looked longingly back at a simpler time. They have been obliged to function in ways which some social critics have seen as a repudiation of individualism. However, it is more correct to argue that masculinity has been modified to take into account the necessity of dealing with large organizations without rejecting a basically individualistic orientation. The social barriers between the sexes have increasingly broken down as women have entered the workforce and men and women have turned to one another almost exclusively for intimate companionship.

Still, the commitment to categorically based distinctions has remained. The second major turning point in the history of sex-related differences in America is thus marked by the emergence of homosexual categorization. While homosexual acts had been previously stigmatized, it was not until the late nineteenth century that homosexuality became a cultural category and homosexuals came to be seen as members of a wholly distinctive social grouping. The long-term significance of this change has been two-fold. The development of a series of gay communities in most American cities of any size has followed as people attracted to members of their own sex have come to identify themselves in terms of sexual object choice and join together with like-minded others. In a second respect, the impact has been more widespread, for homosexuality became a central element of the MSRI paradigm. It has thus operated as the categorical opposite of male heterosexuality, thereby shoring up conventional masculinity without relying exclusively on the masculine-feminine dichotomy. The continued dependence on external pressure to insure acceptably feminine behavior has meant that the fear

of being thought lesbian has been much less significant in women's lives. The emphasis upon heterosexuality underscores the
premium placed upon intimate relationships which link men and
women together in mostly unequal ways that buttress weakening
traditional expectations. Homophobia thus functions to dramatize the importance of the family and of the need for women to
subordinate their individuality to its claims.

Despite the changing reality of men's and women's lives in
the twentieth century, on a very basic level men have continued
to want women to be essentially invisibly supportive non-compe-
titors. The result is a complex and at least in the long-term
sense an unstable situation which depends finally upon society's
ability to keep women from making truly individualistic claims
for themselves. This has generally worked in the past, and one
might argue that there is no reason why it cannot continue to
work. The instability, however, derives from the fact that individualism logically applies to everyone in the same ways.
Categorization denies this, but once people come to see themselves as potentially separate from the social status that had
previously defined them, there is no fixed line that can be
drawn between those to whom individuality fully applies and
those to whom it does not. Thus individualism threatens to
undercut the ability of American society to manage differences
even as it makes people more sensitive to them.

In our own day there have been many challenges to the limitations imposed by categorization. In some respects women and
gay people can be seen as minority groups faced with the opposing alternatives of assimilation and pluralism. Because cultural categories are much broader than subcultures, however, it
makes more sense to think of a great many individual responses
to a growing desire for greater sex-role flexibility on the part
of American men as well as women and gay people. Since sex-related categories are not being rejected or identities really
challenged, these changes remain within the primary tradition of
American individualism. Whether what is happening is likely to
be extensive enough or radical enough to say we are in the midst
of another fundamental cultural transition is impossible to tell
at this time.

In terms of our culture's operating assumptions the contrasting ideals of basic equality, freedom and individuality
long embodied in the secondary tradition represent an impossible
hope for a world without all the tensions and contradictions
that are part of the human condition. To take them really seriously is to call into question the very essence of the mainstream value system. It is easier, therefore, to dream of an
alternative that we never seriously expect to be realized--to
identify with Shane and the Leatherstocking and yet to return to
our everyday realities as they go off into the sunset. The

dream is not only impossible but ultimately frightening as long as human beings are considered basically selfish and antisocial. The dark side of the hope of liberation can be seen not just in contemporary works like The Women's Room but in the lives of all the hypermasculine heroes who seek to depend solely on themselves in a world without categories where no one--and especially women--can be trusted. Like it or not, we all know that we have no choice but to accept the burden of our own individuality or selfhood. If we feel that our sense of self is threatened by ties with others, we are obliged to reject the dream of the good society and to settle for one based on impersonal and categorically defined forms of interaction. The alternative is very different if one believes that it is possible to harmonize a sense of human relatedness with a sense of one's own individuality. Only then are real involvements natural rather than ego-threatening.

More than a decade ago Vivian Gornick and Barbara Moran described women's liberation as "in some sense the end point of the individualist ethic--freedom and self-determination for the last group of adults to whom it has been denied." Many are frightened because this suggests "the disappearance of the last ascribed rather than earned position, the demise of the family, and the destruction of the last haven from competitiveness-- indeed, the last reservoir of amity--in the society." The virtues with which women have long been entrusted--virtues which are not part of the dominant ethic--must now be found by each of us within ourselves.[1] Particularly in the nineteenth century but to some degree still women have been the custodians of traditional values. These have been symbolically preserved and socially perpetuated within the framework of categorization by limiting the applicability of individualism to women's lives. If they enter fully into the modern world, the link with the past will be severed and we will all be responsible for redefining its meaning in our lives today.

A world of snowflakes would be very different from our present world of snowdrifts. It would be a place where familiar distinctions of sex and sexuality would have little if any cultural significance--a world indeed of individuals, but not of isolated and wholly self-centered individuals. We cannot fully enter that world without leaving the present one behind, and our reluctance to do so is why we cling to familiar sex-related categories and conventional (though increasingly instrumentally defined) sex roles. These not only reconcile us to our mainstream culture, but also offer the last familiar glimpse of the orderly, hierarchical world we began to leave behind so long ago. In terms of the contemporary effort to balance the vestigial values of that world against those of individualism, the impossible dream is a society based on freedom, equality and unthreatening involvements. In terms of the logic of individualism and of modernity, one might argue, the impossible dream is to believe that elements of that long-lost world can be indefinitely preserved.

NOTES

Introduction--
1. Clifford Geertz, The Interpretation of Cultures (New York: Basic Books, 1973), pp. 361, 144.
2   Richard D. Brown, Modernization: The Transformation of American Life, 1600-1865 (New York: Hill and Wang, 1976), p. 8.

Chapter One--
1   Alexis de Tocqueville, Democracy in America, eds. J. P. Mayer and Max Lerner, trans. George Lawrence (New York: Harper and Row, 1966), p. 477.
2. Ibid., pp. 487, 542.
3. Ibid., pp. 478, 564.
4. The American Man, eds. Elizabeth H. Pleck and Joseph H. Pleck (Englewood Cliffs., N. J.: Prentice-Hall, 1980), p. 12.
5. John Cawelti, Apostles of the Self-Made Man (Chicago: The University of Chicago Press, 1965), p. 36.
6. Ibid., p. 12.
7. Richard D. Brown, Modernization: The Transformation of American Life, 1600-1865 (New York: Hill and Wang, 1976), pp. 15, 95.
8. David Hackett Fischer, Growing Old in America, The Bland-Lee Lectures Delivered at Clark University, expanded ed. (New York: Oxford University Press, 1978), pp. 109-110.
9. Dictionary of the History of Ideas: Studies of Selected Pivotal Ideas, ed. Philip P. Wiener (New York: Charles Scribner's Sons, 1973), II, 594.
10. Yehoshua Arieli, Individualism and Nationalism in American Ideology (Cambridge, Mass.: Harvard University Press, 1964), pp. 193, 345, 323.
11. Cawelti, pp. 43, 172.
12. William Graham Sumner, What Social Classes Owe to Each Other (New York: Harper & Brothers, 1883), reprinted (Caldwell, Idaho: The Caxton Printers, 1963), p. 24.
13. Frederick Jackson Turner, The Frontier in American History (New York: Henry Holt & Co., 1920), p. 32.
14. The American Gospel of Success: Individualism and Beyond, ed. Moses Rischin (Chicago: Quadrangle Books, 1965), p. 4.
15. Quoted in Arthur A. Ekirch, "Individuality in American History," in Essays on Individuality, ed. Felix Morley (Philadelphia: University of Pennsylvania Press, 1958), p. 216.
16. Ibid., p. 212.
17. Essays on Individuality, p. 5.
18. David M. Potter, "American Individualism in the Twentieth Century," in History and American Society: Essays of David M. Potter, ed. Don E. Fehrenbacher (New York: Oxford University Press, 1973), p. 264.

19. Arieli, p. 340.
20. Dictionary of the History of Ideas, II, 594.
21. John Dewey, Individualism Old and New (New York: Minton, Balch & Co., 1930), pp. 74, 18, 50, 167, 170.
22. David Riesman, Individualism Reconsidered and Other Essays (Glencoe, Ill.: The Free Press, 1954), pp. 27, 28, 32, 38.
23. John Kenneth Galbraith, The New Industrial State, 2nd. ed. revised (Boston: Houghton Mifflin, 1971), pp. 219, 383.
24. Cawelti, p. 204.
25. Peter N. Stearns, Be a Man! Males in Modern Society (New York: Holmes & Meier, 1979), p. 130.
26. Boris Emmet and John E. Jeuck, "New Patterns of Organization," in American Gospel of Success, pp. 339, 341.
27. American Gospel of Success, p. 19.
28. W. Lloyd Warner, "The Corporation Man," in American Gospel of Success, p. 162.
29. John W. Gardner, "Organizing for Renewal," in American Gospel of Success, pp. 352, 357.
30. Dictionary of the History of Ideas, II, 594, 597.
31. John Stuart Mill, The Subjection of Women, intro. Wendell Robert Carr (Cambridge, Mass.: The MIT Press, 1970), p. 96.
32. Potter, p. 275.
33. Felix Morley, "Individuality and the General Will," in Essays on Individuality, pp. 83, 98.
34. Fischer, p. 110.
35. Cawelti, pp. 226, 209.
36. Charles Royster, A Revolutionary People at War: The Continental Army and American Character, 1775-1783 (Chapel Hill: University of North Carolina Press, 1979), esp. pp. 18-21.
37. Garry Wills, Inventing America: Jefferson's Declaration of Independence (New York: Random House, 1978), pp. 202, 236.
38. Richard M. Weaver, "Individuality and Modernity," in Essays on Individuality, pp. 78-79.
39. Quoted in Cawelti, p. 240.
40. Philip Gleason, "American Identity and Americanization," in Harvard Encyclopedia of American Ethnic Groups, eds. Stephan Thernstrom et al (Cambridge, Mass.: Harvard University Press, 1980), pp. 32, 56.
41. J. Hector St. John de Crevecoeur, Letters from an American Farmer and Sketches of Eighteenth-Century America, ed. Albert E. Stone (New York: Penguin Books, 1981), pp. 70, 84.
42. Arieli, p. 26.
43. Wills, pp. 289-290, 304.
44. George M. Fredrickson, White Supremacy: A Comparative Study of American and South African History (New York: Oxford University Press, 1981), pp. 250, 252, 250.

Chapter Two--
1. The Forty-Nine Percent Majority: The Male Sex Role, eds. Deborah S. David and Robert Brannon (Reading, Mass.:

Addison-Wesley Publishing Co., 1976), p. 19.

2. Ibid., p. 25.

3. W. D. Howells, The Rise of Silas Lapham, intro. and notes by Walter S. Meserve, A Selected Edition of W. D. Howells (Bloomington: Indiana University Press, 1971), XII, 58, 67.

4. Thomas Bailey Aldrich, The Story of a Bad Boy (Boston: Houghton Mifflin Co., 1869, 1951), p. 58.

5. April Smith, James at 15, adapted from a screenplay by Dan Wakefield (New York: Dell Publishing Co., 1977), pp. 135, 149, 181, 187, 191.

6. Jeffrey P. Hantover, "The Social Construction of Masculine Anxiety," in Men in Difficult Times: Masculinity Today and Tomorrow, ed. Robert A. Lewis (Englewood Cliffs, N. J.: Prentice-Hall, 1981), p. 89.

7. Robert Sklar, Movie-Made America: A Cultural History of American Movies (New York: Random House, 1975), p. 99.

8. Hantover, p. 91.

9. Mark Gerzon, A Choice of Heroes: The Changing Faces of American Manhood (Boston: Houghton Mifflin, 1982), p. 179.

10. James A. Doyle, The Male Experience (Dubuque, Ia: W. C. Brown Co., 1983), p. 149.

11. Forty-Nine Percent Majority, p. 33.

12. Burt Avendon, Ah, Men! What Do Men Want? A Panorama of the Male in Crisis--His Past Problems, Present Uncertainties, Future Goals (New York: A & W Publishers, 1980), p. 100.

13. G. J. Barker-Benfield, The Horrors of the Half-Known Life: Male Attitudes Towards Women and Sexuality in Nineteenth-Century America (New York: Harper & Row, 1976), p. 30.

14. Saul Bellow, Seize the Day (New York: The Viking Press, 1961), pp. 55, 25.

15. Forty-Nine Percent Majority, p. 50.

16. Smith, p. 96.

17. Avedon, p. 88.

18. Sinclair Lewis, Babbitt (New York: Harcourt, Brace & Co., 1922), pp. 58, 151.

19. Quoted in Joe L. Dubbert, A Man's Place: Masculinity in Transition (Englewood Cliffs, N. J.: Prentice-Hall, 1979), p. 232.

20. Gerzon, p. 54.

21. Clyde W. Franklin II, The Changing Definition of Masculinity (New York and London: Plenum Press, 1984), p. 49.

22. John Knowles, Indian Summer (New York: Random House, 1966), pp. 105-106.

23. C. Wright Mills, The Power Elite (New York: Oxford University Press, 1959), p. 9.

24. Quoted in Doyle, p. 261.

25. John Stuart Mill, The Subjection of Women, intro. Wendell Robert Carr (Cambridge, Mass.: The MIT Press, 1970), p. 97.

26. Horatio Alger, Julius or The Street Boy Out West, in Strive and Succeed: Two Novels by Horatio Alger, intro. S.

257

N. Behrman (New York: Holt, Rinehart & Winston, 1967), p. 3.

27. Evan S. Connell, Jr., Mr. Bridge (New York: Alfred A. Knopf, 1969), pp. 319-320.
28. F. Rief, "The Competitive World of the Pure Scientist," in Forty-Nine Percent Majority, pp. 149, 152.
29. The American Gospel of Success: Individualism and Beyond, ed. Moses Rischin (Chicago: Quadrangle Books, 1965), p. 208.
30. Robert H. Wiebe, The Search for Order: 1877-1920 (New York: Hill & Wang, 1967), pp. 222, 223.
31. Charles Horton Cooley, Social Organization: A Study of the Larger Mind (New York: Charles Scribner's Sons, 1909), pp. 3, 81, 119, 319, 324, 322, 342.
32. Roy R. Grinker and John P. Spiegel, Men under Stress (Philadelphia: Blakiston, 1945), pp. 445-448.
33. Ibid., pp. 452, 456-458.
34. Joseph H. Pleck, The Myth of Masculinity (Cambridge, Mass.: The MIT Press, 1981), pp. 159, 158.
35. David Riesman with Nathan Glazer and Reuel Denney, The Lonely Crowd (New Haven: Yale University Press, 1950), p. 56.
36. Michael Korda, Male Chauvinism! How It Works (New York: Random House, 1973), p. 10.
37. Ibid., p. 18.
38. Franklin, p. 39.
39. Peter N. Stearns, Be a Man! Males in Modern Society (New York: Holmes & Meier, 1979), pp. 83, 16.
40. Lionel Tiger, Men in Groups (New York: Random House, 1969), pp. 60, 160, 191.
41. Pleck, p. 142.
42. Stephen Crane, The Red Badge of Courage: An Episode of the American Civil War, ed. Fredson Bowers, intro. J. C. Levenson, The University of Virginia Edition of the Works of Stephen Crane (Charlottesville: The University Press of Virginia, 1975), II, 34, 35, 106, 115, 133, 135.
43. Tennessee Williams, A Streetcar Named Desire, in The Theatre of Tennessee Williams (New York: New Directions, 1971), I, 403, 374.
44. Mario Puzo, The Godfather (New York: G. P. Putnam's Sons, 1969), pp. 18, 38, 49.
45. Ibid., pp. 442, 364, 293.
46. Franklin, p. 119.

Chapter Three--
1. Carl N. Degler, At Odds: Women and the Family in America from the Revolution to the Present (New York: Oxford University Press, 1980), p. 9.
2. Helmut Schoeck, "Individuality vs. Equality," in Essays on Individuality, ed. Felix Morley (Philadelphia: University of Pennsylvania Press, 1958), p. 118.

3.   "Father, Consider Your Ways: A Message from the Church of Jesus Christ of Latter-day Saints" (Salt Lake City, Utah: Corporation of the President of the Church of Jesus Christ of Latter-day Saints, 1973), pp. 4, 5.

4.   Mary P. Ryan, _Womanhood in America: From Colonial Times to the Present_ (New York: New Viewpoints, 1975), pp. 44, 64.

5.   Laurel Thatcher Ulrich, "Vertuous Women Found: New England Ministerial Literature, 1668-1735," in _A Heritage of Her Own: Toward a New Social History of American Women_, eds. Nancy F. Cott and Elizabeth H. Pleck (New York: Simon & Schuster, 1979), pp. 76, 68.

6.   Alexis de Tocqueville, _Democracy in America_, eds. J. P. Mayer and Max Lerner, trans. George Lawrence (New York: Harper & Row, 1966), p. 577.

7.   Nancy F. Cott, _The Bonds of Womanhood: "Woman's Sphere" in New England, 1780-1835_ (New Haven: Yale University Press, 1977), pp. 61, 98, 197.

8.   Johnny Faragher and Christine Stansell, "Women and Their Families on the Overland Trail to California and Oregon, 1842-1867," in _Heritage_, pp. 250, 255.

9.   Aubrey P. Andelin, _Man of Steel and Velvet_ (Santa Barbara, Calif.: Pacific Press, 1972), pp. 78, 31, 46, 34, 147.

10.   Hilary M. Lips and Nina Lee Colwill, _The Psychology of Sex Differences_ (Englewood Cliffs, N. J.: Prentice-Hall, 1978), p. 127.

11.   Andelin, pp. 152, 153.

12.   C. A. Tripp, _The Homosexual Matrix_ (New York: McGraw-Hill Book Co., 1975), p. 55.

13.   Peter N. Stearns, _Be a Man! Males in Modern Society_ (New York: Holmes & Meier, 1979), p. 86.

14.   Ann Douglas, _The Feminization of American Culture_ (New York: Knopf, 1977), p. 60.

15.   Degler, pp. 28, 38, 301, 306.

16.   Quoted in Joe L. Dubbert, _A Man's Place: Masculinity in Transition_ (Englewood Cliffs, N. J.: Prentice-Hall, 1979), p. 89.

17.   Nancy F. Cott, "Passionlessness: An Interpretation of Victorian Sexual Ideology, 1790-1850," in _Heritage_, pp. 168, 175.

18.   Henry Adams, _The Education of Henry Adams_, ed. Ernest Samuels (Boston: Houghton Mifflin, 1974), pp. 12, 451.

19.   Elizabeth Janeway, _Man's World, Woman's Place: A Study in Social Mythology_ (New York: Dell, 1971), p. 184.

20.   Michael Korda, _Male Chauvinism! How It Works_ (New York: Random House, 1973), pp. 72, 222-223.

21.   _Ibid._, pp. 180-181.

22.   Ryan, pp. 145, 155, 287.

23.   Joseph H. Pleck, _The Myth of Masculinity_ (Cambridge, Mass.: The MIT Press, 1981), p. 141.

24.   Philip Slater, _Footholds: Understanding the Shifting Family and Sexual Tensions in Our Culture_, ed. Wendy Slater

Palmer (Boston: Beacon Press, 1977), p. 31.

25. Nathaniel Hawthorne, The Marble Fawn: Or, The Romance of Monte Beni, eds. Roy Harvey Pearce et al, The Centenary Edition of the Works of Nathaniel Hawthorne (Columbus: Ohio State University Press, 1968), IV, 285.

26. Helen B. Andelin, Fascinating Womanhood, new enlarged ed. (New York: Bantam, 1975), pp. 48, 107, 123.

27. Marie N. Robinson, The Power of Sexual Surrender (New York: Doubleday & Co., 1959), reprinted (New York: New American Library, 1962), pp. 129, 33, 34.

28. Marabel Morgan, The Total Woman (Old Tappan, N. J.: Fleming H. Revell Co., 1973), pp. 60, 55, 123-124.

29. Ibid., pp. 68, 69-70.

30. Clyde W. Franklin II, The Changing Definition of Masculinity (New York and London: Plenum Press, 1984), p. 150.

31. Stearns, p. 160.

32. Ibid., p. 165.

33. Alexis de Tocqueville, "Fortnight in the Wilderness," in George Wilson Pierson, Tocqueville and Beaumont in America (New York: Oxford University Press, 1938), pp. 243-244.

34. W. D. Howells, A Modern Instance, intro. and notes by George N. Bennett, A Selected Edition of W. D. Howells (Bloomington: Indiana University Press, 1977), X, 341.

35. Evan S. Connell, Jr., Mr. Bridge (New York: Knopf, 1969), pp. 4, 56.

36. H. Andelin, p. 66.

37. Ibid., p. 243.

38. Ibid., pp. 265, 152.

39. Ibid., p. 271.

40. Morgan, p. 17.

41. W. D. Howells, A Chance Acquaintance, intro. and notes by Jonathan Thomas and David J. Nordloh, A Selected Edition of W. D. Howells (Bloomington: Indiana University Press, 1971), VI, 36, 37, 106, 123, 160.

42. Tocqueville, pp. 568, 577; see also G. J. Barker-Benfield, The Horrors of the Half-Known Life: Male Attitudes Towards Women and Sexuality in Nineteenth-Century America (New York: Harper & Row, 1976), p. 43.

43. Charles Horton Cooley, Social Organization: A Study of the Larger Mind (New York: Charles Scribner's Sons, 1909), p. 365.

44. David M. Potter, "American Women and the American Character," in History and American Society: Essays of David M. Potter, ed. Don E. Fehrenbacher (New York: Oxford University Press, 1973), p. 302.

45. Janeway, pp. 98, 99.

46. Degler, pp. 191, 189, 348, 351, 343, 472.

47. Sheila M. Rothman, Woman's Proper Place: A History of Changing Ideals and Practices, 1870 to the Present (New York: Basic Books, 1978), ch. 5.

48. Janet Saltzman Chafetz, Masculine, Feminine or Human? An

Overview of the Sociology of the Gender Roles, 2nd ed. (Itasca, Ill.: F. E. Peacock Publishers, 1978), p. 135.
49. Shulamith Firestone, The Dialectic of Sex: The Case for Feminist Revolution (New York: William Morrow & Co., 1970), pp. 148, 170-171, 146.
50. John Stuart Mill, The Subjection of Women, intro. Wendell Robert Carr (Cambridge, Mass.: The MIT Press, 1970), p. 50.
51. Korda, p. 153.
52. James Fenimore Cooper, The Sea Lions, Or The Lost Sealers, The Works of James Fenimore Cooper, Mohawk Edition (New York: G. P. Putnam's Sons, 1896), XII, 223.
53. George F. Gilder, Sexual Suicide (New York: Quadrangle/The New York Times Book Co., 1973), pp. 14, 23, 84, 58.
54. Ibid., pp. 245, 246.
55. Janeway, p. 56.

Chapter Four--
1. Philip Roth, Portnoy's Complaint (New York: Random House, 1967), pp. 41, 8, 11, 145, 235, 37.
2. Willaim Reynolds, The American Father: A New Approach to Understanding Himself, His Woman, His Child (New York and London: Paddington Press, 1978), pp. 138, 56, 112.
3. Jack Kerouac, On the Road (New York: The Viking Press, 1957), pp. 7, 190, 303.
4. Ibid., pp. 254, 125, 186.
5. Ibid., pp. 193-194.
6. James Fenimore Cooper, The Water-Witch: Or, The Skimmer of the Seas, The Works of James Fenimore Cooper, Mohawk Edition (New York: G. P. Putnam's Sons, 1896), X, 410.
7. James Fenimore Cooper, The Red Rover, The Works of James Fenimore Cooper, Mohawk Edition (New York: G. P. Putnam's Sons, 1896), VIII, 299.
8. Ken Kesey, One Flew Over the Cuckoo's Nest (New York: The Viking Press, 1962), pp. 19, 89.
9. John Knowles, The Paragon (New York: Random House, 1971), p. 21.
10. Jack London, Burning Daylight (New York: The Macmillan Co., 1910), pp. 61, 118.
11. Richard Hofstadter, The American Political Tradition and the Men Who Made It (New York: Knopf, 1948), p. 208.
12. Kesey, p. 58.
13. Knowles, pp. 98, 35, 37.
14. London, pp. 156, 180, 204.
15. Ibid., pp. 340, 346.
16. Ibid., p. 10.
17. Ibid., pp. 225, 236-237, 242, 247, 350.
18. Knowles, pp. 57, 59, 184.
19. See, for instance, Norman Mailer, The Prisoner of Sex (Boston: Little, Brown & Co., 1971), esp. Ch. II.
20. Norman Mailer, An American Dream (New York: The Dial Press, 1964), pp. 20, 30, 100, 119.

21. G. J. Barker-Benfield, The Horrors of the Half-Known Life: Male Attitudes Towards Women and Sexuality in Nineteenth-Century America (New York: Harper & Row, 1976), p. 17.
22. Joe L. Dubbert, A Man's Place: Masculinity in Transition (Englewood Cliffs, N. J.: Prentice-Hall, 1979), p. 156.
23. Ibid., p. 186.
24. Ibid., pp. 187, 179.
25. Arnold Beisser, "The American Seasonal Masculinity Rites," in Jock: Sports and Male Identity., eds. Donald F. Sabo, Jr. and Ross Runfola (Englewood Cliffs, N. J.: Prentice-Hall, 1980), p. 177.
26. Peter Gabriel Filene, Him/Her/Self: Sex Roles in Modern America (New York: Harcourt, Brace, Jovanovich, 1975), p. 196.
27. Robert P. Odenwald, The Disappearing Sexes (New York: Random House, 1965), pp. 19, 168, 56, 100-101.
28. Jack Nichols, Men's Liberation: A New Definition of Masculinity (New York: Penguin Books, 1975), p. 138.
29. Barker-Benfield, pp. 23, 27, 48, 190.
30. Ibid., pp. 96, 120, 249, 148, 215.
31. Bernard Malamud, The Natural (New York: Farrar, Straus & Giroux, 1952), pp. 114, 103, 74, 126, 157, 185, 166, 180.
32. Ernest Hemingway, "In Another Country," in Men without Women (New York: Charles Scribner's Sons, 1927), p. 66.
33. "Now I Lay Me," ibid., p. 232.
34. Elia Kazan, The Understudy (New York: Stein & Day, 1975), pp. 93, 123, 87, 118, 186.
35. Louis L'Amour, Shalako (New York: Bantam Books, 1962), pp. 1, 5, 65, 81, 16.
36. John Steinbeck, East of Eden (New York: The Viking Press, 1952), pp. 133, 562, 20, 349, 497.
37. F. Scott Fitzgerald, The Great Gatsby (New York: Charles Scribner's Sons, 1953), pp. 99, 155, 148.
38. Quoted in Willa Cather, My Mortal Enemy, intro. Marcus Klein (New York: Vintage, n. d.), p. xvi.
39. Willa Cather, My Mortal Enemy (New York: Knopf, 1926), pp. 54, 38, 98-99, 104, 121.
40. Philip Greven, The Protestant Temperament: Patterns of Child-Rearing, Religious Experience, and the Self in Early America (New York: Knopf, 1977), pp. 99, 42, 26, 50, 34.
41. Ibid., pp. 147, 76, 124, 125.
42. Ibid., pp. 156, 178, 194, 234.
43. Ibid., pp. 310, 322, 331.

Chapter Five--
1. Herb Goldberg, The Hazards of Being Male: Surviving the Myth of Male Privilege (New York: Nash Publishing Co., 1976), pp. 145, 146.
2. Tony Silvestre, "Becoming Brothers and Unbecoming Barriers," in Men in Difficult Times: Masculinity Today and Tommorow, ed. Robert A. Lewis (Englewood Cliffs, N. J.:

Prentice-Hall, 1981), pp. 218-219.

3. Jack Schaefer, <u>Shane</u>, in <u>The Short Novels of Jack Schaefer</u>, intro. Dorothy M. Johnson (Boston: Houghton Mifflin, 1967), pp. 89, 46, 86, 16.
4. <u>Ibid.</u>, pp. 37, 39, 40, 76-77.
5. <u>Ibid.</u>, pp. 106, 9, 12, 15.
6. John Knowles, <u>A Separate Peace</u> (New York: Macmillan, 1959), pp. 10, 14, 25, 34, 36.
7. <u>Ibid.</u>, pp. 38, 43, 44, 47, 49.
8. <u>Ibid.</u>, pp. 72, 162, 173, 184.
9. James Fenimore Cooper, <u>The Pathfinder, or The Inland Sea</u>, <u>The Works of James Fenimore Cooper.</u>, Mohawk Edition (New York: G. P. Putnam's Sons, 1897), III, 46, 97, 139.
10. <u>Ibid.</u>, p. 77.
11. <u>Ibid.</u>, pp. 258, 295, 455.
12. <u>Ibid.</u>, pp. 461, 478, 490.
13. <u>Ibid.</u>, pp. 498-499, 501, 494.
14. Leslie A. Fiedler, <u>Love and Death in the American Novel</u> (New York: Criterion Books, 1960), pp. xx-xxi.
15. J. D. Salinger, <u>The Catcher in the Rye</u> (Boston: Little, Brown & Co., 1951), pp. 34, 36, 64, 92.
16. <u>Ibid.</u>, pp. 99, 120-121, 125, 191.
17. <u>Ibid.</u>, pp. 59, 117.
18. John Knowles, <u>Indian Summer</u> (New York: Random House, 1966), p. 112.
19. James Leo Herlihy, <u>Midnight Cowboy</u> (New York: Simon & Schuster, 1965), pp. 19, 40, 28.
20. Knowles, <u>Indian Summer</u>, p. 17.
21. James Jones, <u>From Here to Eternity</u> (New York: Charles Scribner's Sons, 1951), pp. 791, 89, 67, 95, 272, 93.
22. <u>Ibid.</u>, pp. 39, 46, 105, 208, 210.
23. Knowles, <u>Indian Summer</u>, pp. 12, 74, 56, 57-58, 120, 243.
24. <u>Ibid.</u>, p. 93.
25. Herlihy, pp. 21-22, 24, 164, 241, 248, 253.
26. Jack London, "The Heathen," in <u>South Sea Tales</u> (New York: Macmillan, 1911, 1967), pp. 168, 174, 179, 196.
27. Herman Melville, <u>Israel Potter: His Fifty Years of Exile</u>, ed. Harrison Hayford <u>et al</u>, <u>The Writings of Herman Melville</u> (Evanston and Chicago: Northwestern University Press and the Newberry Library, 1982), VIII, 8, 162.
28. <u>Ibid.</u>, p. 56.
29. Edith Wharton, <u>Summer</u>, intro. Marilyn French (New York: Berkeley Books, 1981), pp. xxxv-xxxvi, xxx.
30. Edith Wharton, <u>Summer: A Novel</u> (New York: D. Appleton & Co., 1917), pp. 106, 76, 234.
31. Jane Kramer, <u>The Last Cowboy</u> (New York: Pocket Books, 1977), pp. 9, 51, 63.
32. <u>Ibid.</u>, pp. 109, 35, 111, 113.
33. <u>Ibid.</u>, pp. 70, 143, 15.

Chapter Six--

1. John D'Emilio, <u>Sexual Politics, Sexual Communities: The Making of a Homosexual Minority in the United States, 1940-1970</u> (Chicago: The University of Chicago Press, 1983), p. 10.
2. Wainwright Churchill, <u>Homosexual Behavior among Males: A Cross-Cultural and Cross-Species Investigation</u> (New York: Hawthorn Books, 1967), p. 38.
3. Carol Warren, "Homosexuality and Stigma," in <u>Homosexual Behavior: A Modern Reappraisal</u>, ed. Judd Marmor (New York: Basic Books, 1980), p. 124.
4. D'Emilio, p. 4.
5. John Boswell, <u>Christianity, Social Tolerance, and Homosexuality: Gay People in Western Europe from the Beginning of the Christian Era to the Fourteenth Century</u> (Chicago: The University of Chicago Press, 1980), p. 73.
6. Dennis Altman, <u>The Homosexualization of America, The Americanization of the Homosexual</u> (New York: St. Martin's Press, 1982), p. 52.
7. Lionel Tiger, <u>Men in Groups</u> (New York: Random House, 1969), p. 146.
8. Boswell, pp. 74, 184.
9. Tennessee Williams, <u>Cat on a Hot Tin Roof</u>, in <u>The Theatre of Tennessee Williams</u> (New York: New Directions, 1971), III, 57, 120, 125.
10. Peter and Barbara Wyden, <u>Growing Up Straight: What Every Thoughtful Parent Should Know about Homosexuality</u> (New York: Stein & Day, 1968), pp. 104, 63, 237, 238-239.
11. Joseph H. Pleck, <u>The Myth of Masculinity</u> (Cambridge, Mass.: The MIT Press, 1981), pp. 36, 73.
12. <u>The Forty-Nine Percent Majority: The Male Sex Role</u>, eds. Deborah S. David and Robert Brannon (Reading, Mass.: Addison-Wesley Publishing Co., 1976), p. 18.
13. Gregory K. Lehne, "Homophobia among Men," in <u>ibid.</u>, p. 77.
14. Jack Nichols, <u>Men's Liberation: A New Definition of Masculinity</u> (New York: Penguin Books, 1975), p. 279.
15. <u>Forty-Nine Percent Majority</u>, p. 18.
16. Blanche Wiesen Cook, "Female Support Networks and Political Activism: Lillian Wald, Crystal Eastman, Emma Goldman," in <u>A Heritage of Her Own: Toward a New Social History of American Women</u>, eds. Nancy F. Cott and Elizabeth H. Pleck (New York: Simon & Schuster, 1979), p. 420.
17. Caroll Smith-Rosenberg, "The Female World of Love and Ritual: Relations between Women in Nineteenth-Century America," in <u>ibid.</u>, p. 316.
18. Churchill, p. 58.
19. Ibid., p. 45.
20. C. A. Tripp, <u>The Homosexual Matrix</u> (New York: McGraw Hill, 1975), p. 171.
21. Ruth E. Hartley, "Sex-Role Pressures and the Socialization of the Male Child," in <u>Forty-Nine Percent Majority</u>, p. 241.
22. George Gilder, <u>Sexual Suicide</u> (New York: Quadrangle/The

New York Times Book Co., 1973), p. 227.

23. Jock: Sports and Male Identity, eds. Donald F. Sabo, Jr. and Ross Runfola (Englewood Cliffs, N. J.: Prentice-Hall, 1980), p. 42.

24. Donald H. Bell, Being a Man: The Paradox of Masculinity (Lexington, Mass.: The Lewis Publishing Co., 1982), p. 35.

25. Del Martin and Phyllis Lyon, Lesbian/Woman (San Francisco: Glide Publications, 1972), p. 17.

26. Jack Kerouac, On the Road (New York: Viking Press, 1957), p. 206.

27. Howard Brown, Familiar Faces, Hidden Lives: The Story of Homosexual Men in America Today (New York: Harcourt, Brace, Jovanovich, 1976), p. 122.

28. J. D. Salinger, The Catcher in the Rye (Boston: Little, Brown & Co., 1951), pp. 251, 186.

29. Mickey Spillane, Vengeance Is Mine (New York: New American Library, 1950), pp. 34, 69, 176.

30. Norman Mailer, Why Are We in Viet Nam? (New York: G. P. Putnam's Sons, 1967), pp. 202, 203-204, 161, 179.

31. Forty-Nine Percent Majority, p. 18.

32. Tripp, pp. 74, 81.

Chapter Seven--

1. Del Martin and Phyllis Lyon, Lesbian/Woman (San Francisco: Glide Publications, 1972), p. 15.

2. James Spada, The Spada Report: The Newest Survey of Gay Male Sexuality (New York: New American Library, 1979), p. 24.

3. Sasha Gregory Lewis, Sunday's Women: A Report on Lesbian Life Today, updated ed. (Boston: Beacon Press, 1979), p. 87.

4. C. A. Tripp, The Homosexual Matrix (New York: McGraw Hill, 1975), p. 142.

5. Ibid., p. 127.

6. Paul C. Larson, "Gay Male Relationships," in Homosexuality: Social, Psychological, and Biological Issues, eds. William Paul et al (Beverly Hills, Calif.: Sage Publications, 1982), p. 221.

7. Carol Warren, "Homosexuality and Stigma," in Homosexual Behavior: A Modern Reappraisal, ed. Judd Marmor (New York: Basic Books, 1980), p. 134.

8. Martin Hoffman, The Gay World: Male Homosexuality and the Social Creation of Evil (New York: Basic Books, 1968).

9. Evelyn Hooker, "The Homosexual Community," in Sexual Deviance, eds. John H. Gagnon and William Simon (New York: Harper & Row, 1967), p. 171.

10. John D'Emilio, Sexual Politics, Sexual Communities: The Making of a Homosexual Minority in the United States, 1940-1970 (Chicago: The University of Chicago Press, 1983), pp. 11, 12.

11. Laud Humphreys, Tearoom Trade: Impersonal Sex in Public

Places, enlarged ed. (Chicago: Aldine Publishing Co., 1975), pp. 13, 60, 67, 52.

12. John Rechy, The Sexual Outlaw, A Documentary: A Non-Fiction Account, with Commentaries, of Three Days and Nights in the Sexual Underground (New York: Grove Press, 1977), p. 34.
13. Martin S. Weinberg and Colin J. Williams, "Gay Baths and the Social Organization of Impersonal Sex," in Gay Men: The Sociology of Male Homosexuality, ed. Martin P. Levine (New York: Harper & Row, 1979), p. 175.
14. Hooker, p. 175.
15. Lewis, pp. 55, 46.
16. Rechy, pp. 254, 253.
17. Spada, p. 91.
18. Rechy, pp. 68, 75, 114.
19. Seymour Kleinberg, Alienated Affections: Being Gay in America (New York: St. Martin's Press, 1980), pp. 43, 150, 155.
20. Howard Brown, Familiar Faces, Hidden Lives: The Story of Homosexual Men in America Today (New York: Harcourt, Brace, Jovanovich, 1976), p. 66.
21. Spada, pp. 94, 79.
22. Deborah Goleman Wolf, The Lesbian Community, with an Afterword 1980 (Berkeley: University of California Press, 1980), p. 43.
23. D'Emilio, pp. 106, 99.
24. Martin and Lyon, p. 78.
25. Letitia Anne Peplau and Hortensia Amaro, "Understanding Lesbian Relationships," in Homosexuality, p. 237.
26. Dennis Altman, The Homosexualization of America, The Americanization of the Homosexual (New York: St. Martin's Press, 1982), p. 179.
27. Spada, p. 68.
28. Larson, p. 231.
29. Altman, p. 187.
30. Tripp, p. 168.
31. Spada, pp. 167, 231, 233.
32. Tripp, p. 163.
33. Altman, p. 187.
34. Larson, pp. 224-225.
35. James A. Doyle, The Male Experience (Dubuque, Ia: W. C. Brown Co., 1983), p. 251.
36. Bruce Voeller, "Society and the Gay Movement," in Homosexual Behavior, p. 240.
37. Lewis, pp. 83, 14.
38. Wolf, p. 94.
39. Kate Millett, Sita (New York: Farrar, Straus & Giroux, 1977), pp. 71, 229, 167.
40. Rechy, pp. 188, 189.
41. John Malone, Straight Women/Gay Men: A Special Relationship (New York: The Dial Press, 1980), pp. 34, 56, 186,

106.

42. Spada, pp. 228, 219.
43. Martin and Lyon, p. 84.
44. James Baldwin, Giovanni's Room (New York: The Dial Press, 1956), pp. 152, 6, 92, 12, 208.
45. Patricia Nell Warren, The Front Runner (New York: William Morrow & Co., 1974), reprinted (New York: Bantam, 1975), pp. 11, 311, 23.
46. Ibid., pp. 61, 64, 65, 253, 82, 56.
47. Ibid., pp. 109, 146, 198.
48. Ibid., p. 303.
49. Patricia Nell Warren, The Fancy Dancer (New York: William Morrow & Co., 1976), reprinted (New York: Bantam, 1977), p. 191.
50. I owe my comparison with Irish-Americans to Andrew McCullough, whose ideas both in conversation and in his unpubl. diss. (University of Hawaii, 1981), "Shades of Green: A Comparison of Literary and Sociological Images of Irish-Americans," were most helpful to me.
51. Tripp, p. 273.

Chapter Eight--
1. Helen Mayer Hacker, "Women as a Minority Group," in Female Psychology: The Emerging Self, ed. Sue Cox (Chicago: Science Research Associates, 1976), pp. 156, 157. See Also William Paul, "Minority Status for Gay People: Majority Reaction and Social Context," in Homosexuality: Social, Psychological, and Biological Issues, eds. William Paul et al (Beverly Hills, Calif.: Sage Publications, 1982), p. 358.
2. Nancy F. Cott, The Bonds of Womanhood: "Woman's Sphere" in New England, 1780-1835 (New Haven: Yale University Press, 1977), pp. 168, 187, 190, 194, 206.
3. Philip Gleason, "American Identity and Americanization," in Harvard Encyclopedia of American Ethnic Groups, eds. Stephen Thernstrom et al (Cambridge, Mass.: Harvard University Press, 1980), p. 38.
4. June Singer, Androgyny: Toward a New Theory of Sexuality (Garden City, N. Y.: Anchor Press, 1976), p. 24.
5. Quoted in Carol Ehrlich, "Evolutionism and the Place of Women in the United States 1885-1900," in Woman Cross-Culturally: Change and Challenge, ed. Ruby Rohrlich-Leavitt (The Hague: Mouton, 1975), p. 323.
6. Victoria Billings, The Womansbook (Los Angeles: Wollstonecraft, Inc., 1974), pp. 23, 30, 110, 42, 134, 137.
7. Betty Friedan, The Feminine Mystique (New York: W. W. Norton & Co., 1963), pp. 248, 312, 373, 276, 375.
8. Stephen Steinberg, The Ethnic Myth: Race, Ethnicity, and Class in America (New York: Atheneum, 1981), p. 47.
9. Wainwright Churchill, Homosexual Behavior among Males: A Cross-Cultural and Cross-Species Investigation (New York:

Hawthorn Books, 1967), pp. 187, 274.

10. Morton Hunt, Gay: What You Should Know about Homosexuality (New York: Farrar, Straus & Giroux, 1977), pp. 175-176, 161, 187.

11. Richard Zoglin, "The Homosexual Executive: What It's Like to be Gay in a Pin-Striped World," in Gay Men: The Sociology of Male Homosexuality, ed. Martin P. Levine (New York: Harper & Row, 1979), p. 76.

12. John D'Emilio, Sexual Politics, Sexual Communities: The Making of a Homosexual Minority in the United States, 1940-1970 (Chicago: The University of Chicago Press, 1983), p. 84.

13. Barry D. Adam, "A Social History of Gay Politics," in Gay Men, pp. 296-297.

14. Jack Nichols, "Butcher Than Thou: Beyond Machismo," in ibid., pp. 328ff.

15. Wayne Sage, "Inside the Colossal Closet," in ibid., pp. 156, 154.

16. Milton Friedman, "Capitalism and Freedom," in Essays on Individuality, ed. Felix Morley (Philadelphia: University of Pennsylvania Press, 1958), p. 175.

17. Chester I. Barnard, "The Economy of Incentives," in The American Gospel of Success: Individualism and Beyond, ed. Moses Rischin (Chicago: Quadrangle Books, 1965), pp. 294, 295.

18. Betty Lehan Harragan, Games Mother Never Taught You: Corporate Gamesmanship for Women (New York: Rawson Associates, 1977), pp. 254, 24, 84, 98, 290.

19. Thomas Berger, Regiment of Women (New York: Simon & Schuster, 1973), pp. 48, 249.

20. Natalie Gittelson, Dominus: A Woman Looks at Men's Lives (New York: Farrar, Straus & Giroux, 1978), pp. 7, 13, 20, 25, 161.

21. Gleason, pp. 43-45, 50.

22. Laud Humphreys and Brian Miller, "Identities in the Emerging Gay Culture," in Homosexual Behavior: A Modern Reappraisal, ed. Judd Marmor (New York: Basic Books, 1980), p. 143.

23. D'Emilio, pp. 39, 139, 148, 248.

24. Humphreys and Miller, p. 154.

25. Laud Humphreys, "Exodus and Identity: The Emerging Gay Culture," in Gay Men, p. 143.

26. Dennis Altman, The Homosexualization of America, The Americanization of the Homosexual (New York: St. Martin's Press, 1982), p. 8.

27. Toby Marotta, The Politics of Homosexuality (Boston: Houghton Mifflin, 1981), pp. 110, 144, 163.

28. Ibid., pp. 326, 328.

29. Deborah Goleman Wolf, The Lesbian Community, with an Afterword 1980 (Berkeley: University of California Press, 1980), pp. 67, 171.

30. A Heritage of Her Own: Toward a New Social History of American Women, eds. Nancy F. Cott and Elizabeth H. Pleck (New York: Simon & Schuster, 1979), p. 16.
31. William Petersen, "Concepts of Ethnicity," in Harvard Encyclopedia, p. 241.
32. Martin P. Levine, "Gay Ghetto," in Gay Men, p. 201.
33. Jill Johnston, Lesbian Nation: The Feminist Solution (New York: Simon & Schuster, 1973), pp. 153, 175, 154, 167, 278.
34. Sasha Gregory Lewis, Sunday's Women: A Report on Lesbian Life Today, updated ed. (Boston: Beacon Press, 1979), p. 174.
35. John Rechy, The Sexual Outlaw, A Documentary: A Non-Fiction Account, with Commentaries, of Three Days and Nights in the Sexual Underground (New York: Grove Press, 1977), pp. 31, 126, 233, 301.
36. Quoted in Roger Austen, Playing the Game: The Homosexual Novel in America (Indianapolis: Bobbs-Merrill, 1977), p. 217.
37. Marotta, see for example pp. 149-150, 163, 171, 188.
38. Altman, pp. x, 54, 210.
39. Gleason, p. 55.
40. Steinberg, p. 6.
41. Singer, p. 24.
42. James Spada, The Spada Report: The Newest Survey of Gay Male Sexuality (New York: New American Library, 1979), p. 306.
43. Billings, p. 13.
44. Michael Walzer, "Pluralism: A Political Perspective," in Harvard Encyclopedia, p. 784.
45. Steinberg, pp. 258, 256.

Chapter Nine--
1. C. Wright Mills, The Power Elite (New York: Oxford University Press, 1959), pp. 31, 53, 281.
2. Ann Douglas, The Feminization of American Culture (New York: Knopf, 1977), p. 300.
3. George M. Fredrickson and Dale T. Knobel, "History of Prejudice and Discrimination," in Harvard Encyclopedia of American Ethnic Groups, eds. Stephen Thernstrom et al (Cambridge, Mass.: Harvard University Press, 1980), p. 847.
4. David Riesman with Nathan Glazer and Reuel Denney, The Lonely Crowd (New Haven: Yale University Press, 1950), pp. 331, 328, 335.
5. Margaret Hennig and Anne Jardim, The Managerial Woman (Garden City, N. Y.: Anchor Press/Doubleday, 1977), pp. 184, 177, 157, 158.
6. Ibid., pp. 200-201.
7. Mirra Komarovsky, Dilemmas of Masculinity: A Study of College Youth (New York: W. W. Norton, 1976), pp. 255, 256.
8. Betty Friedan, The Second Stage (New York: Summit Books, 1981), pp. 239, 86, 95, 219, 329, 321-322.

269

9.   Carol Andreas, <u>Sex and Caste in America</u> (Englewood Cliffs, N. J.: Prentice-Hall, 1971), pp. 48, 65.
10.   Leonore Fleischer, <u>Making Love</u>, from the screenplay by Barry Sandler, story by A. Scott Berg (New York: Ballantine, 1982), pp. 74, 177, 172, 173.
11.   <u>Ibid.</u>, p. 173.
12.   Rebecca Nahas and Myra Turley, <u>The New Couple: Women and Gay Men</u> (New York: Seaview Books, 1979), pp. 282, 264.
13.   Toby Marotta, <u>The Politics of Homosexuality</u> (Boston: Houghton Mifflin, 1981), pp. 310, 323.
14.   Toby Marotta, <u>Sons of Harvard: Gay Men from the Class of 1967</u> (New York: William Morrow & Co., 1982), pp. 56, 261, 286.
15.   Dennis Altman, <u>The Homosexualization of America, The Americanization of the Homosexual</u> (New York: St. Martin's Press, 1982), pp. 211, 223, 224.
16.   <u>The American Man</u>, eds. Elizabeth H. Pleck and Joseph H. Pleck (Englewood Cliffs, N. J.: Prentice-Hall, 1980), p. 35.
17.   Komarovsky, p. 160.
18.   Anthony Pietropinto and Jacqueline Simenauer, <u>Beyond the Male Myth: What Women Want to Know about Men's Sexuality</u> (New York: New York Times Books, 1977), p. 36.
19.   Komarovsky, p. 34.
20.   Pietropinto and Simenauer, pp. 4, 8, 105, 140.
21.   Quoted in Herb Goldberg, <u>The New Male: From Self-Destruction to Self-Care</u> (New York: William Morrow & Co., 1979), p. 146.
22.   Pietropinto and Simenauer, pp. 327, 328.
23.   Donald H. Bell, <u>Being a Man: The Paradox of Masculinity</u> (Lexington, Mass.: The Lewis Publishing Co., 1982), p. 66.
24.   Pietropinto and Simenauer, pp. 119, 113.
25.   Komarovsky, pp. 37, 154, 22.
26.   Pietropinto and Simenauer, p. 38.
27.   Goldberg, p. 275.
28.   Anne Steinmann and David J. Fox, <u>The Male Dilemma: How to Survive the Sexual Revolution</u> (New York: Jason Aronson, 1974), pp. 70, 52.
29.   <u>Ibid.</u>, pp. 213, 242, 249-250, 255.
30.   <u>Ibid.</u>, pp. 212, 285.
31.   Stuart Carter, "Male Chauvinism: A Developmental Process," in <u>Men in Difficult Times: Masculinity Today and Tomorrow</u>, ed. Robert A. Lewis (Englewood Cliffs, N. J.: Prentice-Hall, 1981), p. 106.
32.   George B. Leonard, "Winning Isn't Everything, It's Nothing," in <u>Jock: Sports and Male Identity</u>, eds. Donald F. Sabo, Jr. and Ross Runfola (Englewood Cliffs, N. J.: Prentice-Hall, 1980), p. 262.
33.   <u>Jock</u>, pp. 335, 332.
34.   Burt Avedon, <u>Ah, Men! What Do Men Want? A Panorama of the Male in Crisis--His Past Problems, Present Uncertain-</u>

ties, Future Goals (New York: A & W Publishers, 1980), pp. 11, 205, 206, 10.

35. Harold C. Lyon, Jr., Tenderness Is Strength: From Machismo to Manhood (New York: Harper & Row, 1977), pp. 12, 50, 185, 209.

36. Unbecoming Men: A Men's Consciousness-Raising Group Writes on Oppression and Themselves (New York: Times Change Press, 1971), pp. 7, 10, 60.

37. Clayton Barbeau, Delivering the Male: Out of the Tough-Guy Trap into a Better Marriage (Minneapolis: Winston Press, 1982), pp. 96, 104, 126.

38. King David Boyer, Jr., "Changing Male Sex Roles and Identities," in Men in Difficult Times, p. 160.

39. Joseph H. Pleck, The Myth of Masculinity (Cambridge, Mass.: The MIT Press, 1981), pp. 4, 160, 134, 137.

40. Ibid., p. 143.

41. Bell, pp. 154, 153-154.

42. Riesman, p. 285.

43. Komarovsky, p. 23.

44. Philip Gleason, "American Identity and Americanization," in Harvard Encyclopedia, p. 36.

45. Ibid., p. 33.

46. Michael Walzer, "Pluralism: A Political Perspective," in ibid., p. 786.

47. Michele Wallace, Black Macho and the Myth of the Super-Woman (New York: The Dial Press, 1979), pp. 42, 81.

48. Stephen Steinberg, The Ethnic Myth: Race, Ethnicity, and Class in America (New York: Atheneum, 1981), pp. 208-209.

49. Fredrickson and Knobel, p. 837.

50. Mary E. Hotvedt, editorial comment, in Homosexuality: Social, Psychological, and Biological Issues, eds. William Paul et al (Beverly Hills, Calif.: Sage Publications, 1982), pp. 289, 291.

51. William Paul, "Minority Status for Gay People," in ibid., pp. 366, 367.

52. Clyde W. Franklin II, The Changing Definition of Masculinity (New York and London: Plenum Press, 1984), p. 212.

Chapter Ten--

1. Myron Brenton, The American Male (New York: Coward-McCann, 1966), pp. 53, 211, 220, 230, 233.

2. Warren Farrell, The Liberated Man: Beyond Masculinity: Freeing Men and Their Relationships with Women (New York: Random House, 1974), pp. 8, 174.

3. Mark Gerzon, A Choice of Heroes: The Changing Faces of American Manhood (Boston: Houghton Mifflin, 1982), pp. 229, 237, 255, 262.

4. Peter Fisher, The Gay Mystique: The Myth and Reality of Male Homosexuality (New York: Stein & Day, 1972), pp. 88, 217, 229-230.

5. Toby Marotta, The Politics of Homosexuality (Boston:

Houghton Mifflin, 1981), pp. 105, 107, 121.
6.   Quoted in William H. Chafe, <u>Women and Equality: Changing</u>
      <u>Patterns in American Culture</u> (New York: Oxford University
      Press, 1977), p. 151.
7.   Quoted in Burt Avedon, <u>Ah, Men! What Do Men Want? A</u>
      <u>Panorama of the Male in Crisis--His Past Problems, Present</u>
      <u>Uncertainties, Future Goals</u> (New York: A & W Publishers,
      1980), p. 107.
8.   Mary Ryan, <u>Womanhood in America: From Colonial Times to</u>
      <u>the Present</u> (New York: New Viewpoints, 1975), pp. 8, 16.
9.   Janet Saltzman Chafetz, <u>Masculine, Feminine or Human? An</u>
      <u>Overview of the Sociology of the Gender Roles</u>, 2nd ed.
      (Itasca, Ill.: F. E. Peacock Publishers, 1978), pp. 223,
      252, 3, 61, xiii, 258, 12.
10.   Carolyn Heilbrun, <u>Toward a Recognition of Androgyny</u> (New
      York: Knopf, 1973), pp. ix-x, xi.
11.   June Singer, <u>Androgyny: Toward a New Theory of Sexuality</u>
      (Garden City, N. Y.: Anchor Press/Doubleday, 1976), p. 275.
12.   Jack Nichols, <u>Men's Liberation: A New Definition of Mascu-</u>
      <u>linity</u> (New York: Penguin Books, 1975), pp. 39, 93.
13.   Jack Sawyer, "On Male Liberation," in <u>The Forty-Nine Per-</u>
      <u>cent Majority: The Male Sex Role</u>, eds. Deborah S. David
      and Robert Brannon (Reading, Mass.: Addison-Wesley Pub-
      lishing Co., 1976), pp. 290, 288.
14.   Marc Feigen Fasteau, <u>The Male Machine</u> (New York: McGraw
      Hill, 1974), p. 202.
15.   Quoted in Avedon, p. 204.
16.   Andrea S. Hayman, "Legal Challenges to Discrimination
      against Men," in <u>Forty-Nine Percent Majority</u>, p. 298.
17.   Hilary M. Lips and Nina Lee Colwill, <u>The Psychology of Sex</u>
      <u>Differences</u> (Englewood Cliffs, N. J.: Prentice-Hall,
      1978), p. 144.
18.   Singer, pp. 278, 286, 294.
19.   Fasteau, pp. 205, 204.
20.   Linda E. Olds, <u>Fully Human: How Everyone Can Integrate the</u>
      <u>Benefits of Masculine and Feminine Sex Roles</u> (Englewood
      Cliffs, N. J.: Prentice-Hall, 1981), pp. 17, 24, 46, xiii.
21.   <u>Ibid.</u>, pp. 170, 13, 173.
22.   Suzanne J. Kessler and Wendy McKenna, <u>Gender: An Ethno-</u>
      <u>methodological Approach</u> (New York: John Wiley & Sons,
      1978), pp. 12, 38, 27, 38, 162, 83.
23.   <u>Ibid.</u>, pp. 164, 166.
24.   Philip Slater, <u>Footholds: Understanding the Shifting Fam-</u>
      <u>ily and Sexual Tensions in Our Culture</u>, ed. Wendy Slater
      Palmer (Boston: Beacon Press, 1977), p. 38.
25.   Chafe, pp. 168, 167, 178.
26.   Singer, pp. 334, 29.
27.   Nichols, pp. 213, 218, 248-249, 250, 261.
28.   Fasteau, pp. 205, 206, 207.
29.   Charlotte Perkins Gilman, <u>Women and Economics: A Study of</u>
      <u>the Economic Relation Between Men and Women as a Factor in</u>

<u>Social Evolution</u> (1899), ed. Carl N. Degler (New York: Harper & Row, 1966), pp. 100, 107, 138-139, 220, 325.

30. Herbert Marcuse, <u>Eros and Civilization: A Philosophical Inquiry into Freud</u> (Boston: Beacon Press, 1955, 1966), pp. 143, 224, 227, 201.

31. Shulamith Firestone, <u>The Dialectic of Sex: The Case for Feminist Revolution</u> (New York: William Morrow & Co., 1970), pp. 233, 234, 236, 264, 274.

32. Jean Baker Miller, <u>Toward a New Psychology of Women</u> (Boston: Beacon Press, 1976), pp. 79, 69, 41, 83, 119, 115, 116, 124.

33. Nancy Chodorow, <u>The Reproduction of Mothering: Psycho-analysis and the Sociology of Gender</u> (Berkeley: University of California Press, 1978), pp. 169, 67, 176, 181.

34. <u>Ibid.</u>, p. 218.

35. Olds, pp. 204, 244, 208, 248.

36. Dorothy Dinnerstein, <u>The Mermaid and the Minotaur: Sexual Arrangements and Human Malaise</u> (New York: Harper & Row, 1976), pp. 5, 112, 161, 202.

37. <u>Ibid.</u>, pp. 189, 249, 244, 11.

38. Sacvan Bercovitch, <u>The Puritan Origins of the American Self</u> (New Haven: Yale University Press, 1975), pp. 18-19.

39. Marilyn French, <u>The Women's Room</u> (New York: Summit Books, 1977), pp. 11, 32, 162, 146, 60.

40. <u>Ibid.</u>, pp. 374, 318, 323, 459.

41. <u>Ibid.</u>, pp. 443, 453.

Chapter Eleven--

1. Michael Levin, "The Feminist Mystique," <u>Commentary</u>, December, 1980, pp. 27, 28.

2. Steven Goldberg, <u>The Inevitability of Patriarchy</u> (New York: William Morrow, 1973), pp. 93, 105-106, 117, 191, 224.

3. Hilary M. Lips and Nina Lee Colwill, <u>The Psychology of Sex Differences</u> (Englewood Cliffs, N. J.: Prentice-Hall, 1978), p. 5.

4. Thomas F. Pettigrew, "Prejudice," in <u>Harvard Encyclopedia of American Ethnic Groups</u>, eds. Stephen Thernstrom <u>et al</u> (Cambridge, Mass.: Harvard University Press, 1980), p. 822.

5. Sandra L. Bem and Daryl J. Bem, "Training the Woman to Know Her Place: The Power of a Non-conscious Ideology," in <u>Female Psychology: The Emerging Self</u>, ed. Sue Cox (Chicago: Science Research Associates, 1976), pp. 184-185.

6. Goldberg, p. 147.

7. <u>Ibid.</u>, pp. 228-229.

8. Phyllis Schlafly, <u>The Power of the Positive Woman</u> (New Rochelle, N. Y.: Arlington House, 1977), pp. 41, 15, 17.

9. <u>Ibid.</u>, pp. 47, 76, 45, 35.

10. <u>Ibid.</u>, pp. 139, 174, 29.

11. Midge Decter, <u>The New Chastity and Other Arguments against Women's Liberation</u> (New York: Coward, McCann & Geohegan,

1972), pp. 43, 98.
12. Ibid., pp. 55, 56.
13. Ibid., pp. 178, 180.
14. John Stuart Mill, The Subjection of Women, intro. Wendell Robert Carr (Cambridge, Mass.: The MIT Press, 1970), p. 27.
15. Peter N. Stearns, Be a Man! Males in Modern Society (New York: Holmes & Meier, 1979), pp. 2, 3, 4.
16. Ibid., pp. 154-155, 169, 181.
17. Ibid., pp. 195, 194.
18. Peter Gabriel Filene, Him/Her/Self: Sex Roles in Modern America (New York: Harcourt, Brace, Jovanovich, 1975), pp. xiii-xiv, 235, 239, 240.
19. Mary Daly, Gyn/Ecology: The Metaethics of Radical Feminism (Boston: Beacon Press, 1978), pp. 387, 68, 26, 341, 379, 382.
20. Alexandra G. Kaplan and Mary Anne Sedney, Psychology and Sex Roles: An Androgynous Perspective (Boston: Little, Brown, 1980), pp. 6, 7, 8, 9.
21. Ibid., pp. 340, 341, 358, 359.
22. Christopher Lasch, The Culture of Narcissism: American Life in an Age of Diminishing Expectations (New York. W. W. Norton & Co., 1978), pp. xv, 190, 206.
23. Marvin Harris, America Now: The Anthropology of a Changing Culture (New York: Simon & Schuster, 1981), pp. 183, 112, 15-16.
24. Carolyn Heilbrun, Reinventing Womanhood (New York, W. W. Norton & Co., 1979), pp. 29, 38, 72, 95, 140, 204.
25. Caroline Bird, The Two-Paycheck Marriage: How Women at Work Are Changing Life in America, an In-Depth Report on the Great Revolution of Our Times (New York: Rawson, Wade Publishers, 1979), pp. 45, 83, 252, 244.
26. Ibid., pp. 235, 236, 264.
27. Elizabeth Nickles with Laura Ashcraft, The Coming Matriarchy: How Women Will Gain the Balance of Power (New York: Seaview Books, 1981), pp. 106, 197, 206, xiii, 213, 222.
28. Mill, p. 91.
29. American Association of University Professors Bulletin, June 1979, p. 9.
30. David Hackett Fischer, Growing Old in America, The Bland-Lee Lectures Delivered at Clark University, expanded ed. (New York: Oxford University Press, 1977), pp. 199, 210, 215.
31. John Boswell, Christianity, Social Tolerance, and Homosexuality: Gay People in Western Europe from the Beginning of the Christian Era to the Fourteenth Century (Chicago: The University of Chicago Press, 1980), pp. 135, 35.
32. Quoted in Betty Friedan, The Second Stage (New York: Summit Books, 1981), p. 109.
33. Michael Novak, "Pluralism: A Humanistic Perspective," in Harvard Encyclopedia, pp. 776, 778.
34. Roger J. Williams, "Individuality and Its Significance in

Human Life," in <u>Essays on Individuality</u>, ed. Felix Morley (Philadelphia: University of Pennsylvania Press, 1958), p. 143.

35. Herb Goldberg, <u>The New Male: From Self-Destruction to Self-Care</u> (New York: William Morrow, 1979), pp. 77, 213, 220, 289.
36. <u>The Other Persuasion</u>, ed. Seymour Kleinberg (New York: Random House/Vintage, 1977), p. xiii.
37. Rita Mae Brown, <u>Rubyfruit Jungle</u> (Plainfield, Vt.: Daughters, Inc., 1973), pp. 53, 78, 62, 95.
38. <u>Ibid</u>., pp. 88, 111, 152, 130.
39. Rita Mae Brown <u>Six of One</u> (New York: Harper & Row, 1978), pp. 296, 17, 138.
40. <u>Ibid</u>., pp. 99, 100, 210, 93.
41. [Gertrude Stein], <u>The Autobiography of Alice B. Toklas</u> (New York: Harcourt Brace & Co., 1933), pp. 19, 86, 187.
42. <u>Ibid</u>., pp. 263, 215.
43. Sacvan Bercovitch, <u>The Puritan Origins of the American Self</u> (New Haven: Yale University Press, 1975), p. 186.

Conclusion--

1. <u>Woman in a Sexist Society: Studies in Power and Powerlessness</u>, eds. Vivian Gornick and Barbara K. Moran (New York: Basic Books, 1971), p. xx.

INDEX

Rechy, John, 138, 140, 141,
   149, 174-175
Reynolds, William, 75
Rief, F., 37
Riesman, David, 13, 42, 183,
   197-198
Rischin, Moses, 11, 37
Robinson, Marie, 60, 63
Rockefeller, John D., 11
Roosevelt, Theodore, 78
Roth, Philip, 75
Runfola, Ross, 124, 194
Ryan, Mary, 59, 207

Sabo, Donald, 124, 194
Sage, Wayne, 165
Salinger, J. D., 102, 127
Sawyer, Jack, 209
Schaefer, Jack, 96-97, 99
Schlafly, Phyllis, 229-230
Schoeck, Helmut, 50
Sedney, Mary Anne, 234
Sex Roles, among men, 27-29,
   30, 31; among women, 52,
   63; among gay people,
   143, 144; sex-role free-
   dom, 184, 186, 190, 193,
   196-197, 202, 209
Shane, 96-97, 108, 242, 252
Simenauer, Jacqueline, 190,
   191, 192
Sims, J. Marion, 85
Singer, June, 161, 208, 210-
   211, 214
Sklar, Robert, 29
Slater, Philip, 59-60, 213-214
Smith-Rosenberg, Caroll, 121
Social Class, 27, 37, 46, 181-
   182, 202
South Africa, 22
Spada Report, 140, 143-144,
   145, 149, 177
Spiegel, John P., 39-40
Spillane, Mickey, 127
SRS paradigm, 196-197
Stansell, Christine, 53
Stearns, Peter, 14, 42, 57,
   61-62, 231-232
Stein, Gertrude, 245-246, 248
Steinbeck, John, 88
Steinberg, Stephen, 162-163,

   176, 177-178, 201
Steinmann, Anne, 192-193
Stereotyping, 21, 83, 228
Subcultures and subsocieties,
   169, 171-172, 177, 179
Success, for men, 34f; for women, 162, 185-186; and
   assimilation, 165f; re-
   jections of, 198, 208-
   209, 223
Sumner, William Graham, 10

The Great Gatsby, 88
Tiger, Lionel, 42-43, 115
Title VII, 1964 Civil Rights
   Act, 239
Tocqueville, Alexis de, 7, 53,
   62, 65
Todd, John, 85
Trachtenberg, Alan, 67, 251
Traditional Cultures and Socie-
   ties, 2, 8, 15, 20, 210
Traditional Values, 237, 249;
   and the male role, 31,
   40, 43; and masculine/
   feminine relationships,
   49-50, 54, 61, 69, 115-
   116; and women's role,
   51-52; and power, 36; and
   gay women, 150
Tripp, C. A., 56, 123, 131, 135-
   136, 145, 146
Turley, Myra, 188
Turner, Frederick Jackson, 10

Ulrich, Laurel Thatcher, 52
Unbecoming Men, 195
Unisex, 186, 193, 209

Valentino, Rudolph, 29
Voeller, Bruce, 147
Voluntarism, 8, 16, 18, 39-40,
   46, 61, 139, 177, 200, 241

Wadsworth, Benjamin, 52
Wallace, Michele, 200-201
Walzer, Michael, 177, 200
Warner, W. Lloyd, 14
Warren, Patricia Nell, The Front
   Runner, 151-152; The
   Fancy Dancer, 153

281

Weaver, Richard M., 18
Weinberg, Martin S., 139
West, the, 10, 11, 53, 56, 82, 92
Wharton, Edith, 110
Wiebe, Robert, 38
Williams, Colin J., 139
Williams, Roger, J., 242
Williams, Tennessee, _A Street-Car Named Desire_, 44; _Cat on a Hot Tin Roof_, 116-117
Wills, Garry, 17, 20
Wirth, Louis, 159

Wolf, Deborah Goleman, 144, 171-172
Women, and role expectations, 51, 59, 203; and work, 58, 166; as a minority, 159-160; women's subculture, 172; and liberation, 217-218, 224, 235; see also Femininity, Lesbians
Wyden, Peter and Barbara, 119

Zoglin, Richard, 164